GINGER

DATE DUE

Ginger

The Life and Death of Albert Goodwin

SUSAN MAYSE

HARBOUR PUBLISHING

HARBOUR PUBLISHING
P.O. Box 219
Madeira Park, BC Canada V0N 2H0

Cover design by Roger Handling
Cover painting by Gordon Halloran
Printed and bound in Canada

CANADIAN CATALOGUING IN PUBLICATION DATA

Mayse, Susan, 1948–
    Ginger

    Includes bibliographical references.
    ISBN 1-66017-018-X

    1. Goodwin, Ginger.   2. Trade unions — Coal miners —
British Columbia — Officials and employees — Biography.
3. Coal mines and mining — British Columbia — Vancouver
Island — History.   I. Title.
HD6525.G66M39 1990   331.88′12234′092   C90-091294-4

Contents

Acknowledgments

Many people made this book possible through their encouragement and ongoing help of all kinds. I especially thank all the people who allowed me and other researchers to interview them over the last twenty years (see appendices and works consulted) for sharing their knowledge and life experiences. Their memories make up the heart not only of this book but of history.

Others made special contributions. Dale Reeves, former Curator of the Cumberland Museum, selflessly applied his many skills in service to Cumberland and the historical record. Linda Reeves shared her medical expertise and an unforgettable tour of Cumberland. George Brandak, Special Collections Librarian at the University of British Columbia, offered professional guidance with unfailing accuracy and tact. Buddy de Vito provided an important taped interview and his confidence that this book was worth writing. Roy Genge, President of the Cumberland and District Historical Society, like a mine muleskinner, always knew when to wait patiently and when to suggest a little haste. Barbara Lemky, Curator of the Cumberland Museum, kept me endlessly informed and laughing—who said history has to be serious? Barney McGuire kept the faith with his Mine-Mill predecessor Ginger Goodwin and worked tirelessly to prevent his name from being forgotten. John Stanton's legal knowledge rescued me from factual blunders and turned up theoretically nonexistent documents. Christina Nichol provided stimulating conversation and insights. Dr. Maier B. Fox, Research Coordinator of the United Mine Workers of America, allowed access to union documents and his own research notes. T. Dennis Devitt went to much trouble to make available his father's unpublished correspondence and field notes. Archivists and other staff members of the British Columbia Archives and Records Service notably Derek Reimer, Indiana Matters and Frances Gundry saved me much time and trouble by pointing out useful directions for research. Many others helped in diverse ways; all have my gratitude.

Ruth Masters — outdoorswoman, mountaineer, environmentalist, local historian — deserves special recognition. Her oral histories and documentary research on Ginger Goodwin prevented the loss of an entire body of information. I thank her for this, for her open-handed sharing of research and for her spirited encouragement.

A former police reporter with an instinct for uncovering half-truths makes the best accomplice in writing history. Stephen Hume's sleuthing in Ottawa and Victoria produced military and police information that made possible a more complete understanding of Ginger Goodwin's death. In coal towns and closed stacks and dark-age hillforts, he has been my peerless companion.

S.M.

Armed and dangerous

Brutal heat, heavy and close as a fever blanket, was one thing people remembered about July 1918.

On Vancouver Island the fire hazard rose to extreme danger. A single spark could ignite hundreds of square miles, levelling virgin forest and Indian settlements and raw new towns without prejudice. It was no time to be in the woods anyway; mosquitoes, bad that summer, added to the misery of hot, restless nights. People in the town of Cumberland retreated to beach shacks or tents at nearby Comox Lake. It was only a three-mile walk, unless they rode the Canadian Collieries train carrying workers up to Number Four pit at the lake and coal from Number Four down to tidewater at Union Bay. Cumberland was a coal mining town.

Only the police worked hard in the sultry weather. Posses of British Columbia Provincial Police had been searching for fugitives since May in the mountainous wilderness around the far end of Comox Lake. The police considered the handful of men they hunted armed and dangerous, but the Cumberland people in lake tents or shacks were untroubled for their own safety. These fugitives were not murderers. In a black year when even Quakers and Mennonites were denied exemption from military service as conscientious objectors, the young men were socialist and pacifist draft evaders.

Cumberland people had distrusted the police since the bitter coal strike four years earlier. Now the posses were an incessant irritation, as bad as the mosquitoes. Cumberlanders instructed their children to answer police questions, "I don't know." By July, they had organized supply lines to keep the draft evaders provided with food.

The police, aware of this illegal aid, intensified the search. Cruising the bush, searching the long lake in a small motor launch, several times they came close enough to recognize the fugitives—one had a bushy black beard, another had red hair. A party of British Columbia Provincial Police even made the arduous hike from Port Alberni on the west coast over the central mountains and glaciers of Vancouver Island. They returned empty-handed. By the dog days at the end of July, provincial constables like ex-miner Robert Rushford of Cumberland were back to their town foot patrols and petty theft cases, leaving enforcement of the Military Service Act to others. Draft evasion and desertion in 1918 were serious offences which drew sentences of a year or more at hard labour. The men now combing the bush around Comox Lake belonged to the Dominion Police, a military force responsible in part for security and counter-subversion.

Survey Point lay at the top of the lake, roughly twelve miles southwest of the tenters and about fifteen miles from Cumberland. The distances were deceptive. Mature second-growth timber grew on slopes as steep as forty-five degrees, tangled in almost impenetrable undergrowth, rocky underfoot, broken by creeks and gullies, blocked by fallen logs. The hillsides were studded with tall notched stumps, signs of first-cut logging in earlier whipsaw and ox-team days. The terrain was so punishing that a good woodsman, to travel one mile as the crow flies, sometimes had to hike three miles up mountainsides and around streams or pothole lakes. It was mostly too rough for saddle horses or pack mules. There were no roads or real trails. Only half-imagined game trails indented the dense bush, marked by the solitary passages of cougar, black bear and small island deer.

The police sweated at their strenuous work this scorching Saturday. Inspector William Devitt, forty-nine, had recently joined the military police after nearly two decades as city clerk, tax assessor and police chief in the BC interior towns of Trail, Rossland and Nelson. Corporal George Rowe was a former customs collector. Special Constable Daniel Campbell, forty-five, an experienced hunter and woodsman, had until recently managed a hotel and saloon near Victoria. Campbell took off his jacket and pinned his glittering badge to his vest. His smart white-striped black shirt would not be too conspicuous in the dim light filtering between tall trees. It was early afternoon. This morning near Survey Bay, guided by local trappers Tommy Anderson and Dad Janes, they had made the first real breakthrough in the long pursuit.

About a mile in from the lake the three policemen located one of the fugitives' caches near a large boulder. There they found a rifle, cooking utensils, clothing, a pair of miner's boots and other supplies which they recached nearby. The trappers reported a faint trail leading toward the south fork of Cruikshank Creek — a good trout stream even in high summer when smaller streams produced wormy fish with a muddy taste — and then onward up the steep timbered flank of Alone Mountain. But had the draft evaders fled up the mountain or were they hiding near the creek?

Janes and Anderson took the mountain trail. Campbell led Devitt and Rowe along a small blazed path nearer to the creek below. When Campbell saw fresh footprints on an even fainter trail, Devitt took Rowe to investigate.

Campbell continued alone on a path blocked by fallen logs and heavy underbrush. After a few minutes, shockingly, he almost collided with a stranger. The slight red-haired man in a faded blue shirt carried a rifle which he quickly pointed at the special constable. Campbell had no time to aim, but pulled the trigger even as he raised his own weapon, a custom-made .30 Marlin hunting rifle. His soft-nosed bullet ricocheted off the fugitive's wrist and struck him in the throat, severed the spinal cord and blasted a hole through the back right side of his neck. The man fell, clutching his rifle in both hands, and quickly died.

Campbell stood paralyzed by fear and dismay. As soon as he gathered his wits he yelled for the others. "Come!"

A few minutes later they crashed through the undergrowth to find the special constable standing dumbstruck on a fallen log on the steep hillside, still holding his rifle. They had heard a single shot, but still did not know what had happened. Devitt approached, asking for an explanation, and saw a man lying face-down on the mossy ground.

Private Goodwin, serial number 270432, was the name on his unclaimed order to report for military service; this was one of the draft evaders identified in a military police description. Albert Goodwin was the name on his union card. He was Brother Goodwin to fellow executives of the British Columbia Federation of Labour, and to other Marxian socialists he was Comrade Goodwin. He signed his letters "Yours in Revolt," and later "Fraternally Yours for Socialism." Casual acquaintances called him Al or Sandy or Sam or Red. His friends called him Ginger.

"Arrest military defaulters" was the posse's order, not "shoot on sight." Yet inadvertently or otherwise the government was rid of a vociferous critic of key policies, and a troublesome source of wartime dissent and socialist subversion. In Dan Campbell's preliminary investigation for manslaughter in Victoria a week and a half later, his lawyer said, "Why put this man to the expense of a trial when it is a foregone conclusion that no reasonable, fair-minded jury would convict him? As to the use of a soft-nosed bullet, Campbell would have been justified in using a bomb in self-defence."

"I am sorry for Mr. Campbell," said one of the two presiding judges. "We will commit him to the higher court."

On October 1, 1918, the grand jury of the Victoria fall assizes heard witnesses for several hours in the afternoon. The next morning, after less than forty-five minutes in court, the grand jury judges decided not to send the matter to trial. Dan Campbell walked away a free man.

This official account of Albert "Ginger" Goodwin's shooting resides in transcripts of the Cumberland coroner's inquiry and the Victoria preliminary investigation, and newspaper accounts inoffensive enough to escape stringent wartime censorship.

The case would go no further in court. Troubling discrepancies and difficulties, however, have to this day kept it unofficially active. Any one of these discrepancies would seriously discredit the legitimacy of Dan Campbell's hearings, let alone the legitimacy of his shooting of Albert Goodwin. Many discrepancies taken together suggest a serious miscarriage of justice.

The official story reconstructed above derives entirely from public records. If these provided the only available information, Goodwin's story would remain an insignificant case of a criminal who died violently resisting arrest. But we have more. No information ban, no "exoneration of guilt by the province's highest court," as one newspaper called it, could fully suppress the other side of the story, the unofficial side.

At the coroner's inquiry Joseph Naylor, speaking for Goodwin's family and friends, was first to challenge the approved version. In two weeks he was behind bars on a charge of aiding draft evaders, a charge dismissed months later for lack of evidence. In the three-quarters of a century since, many have spoken up to counter and fill gaps in the police claims. Some are on the record in considerable detail, unofficially and uncensored. Many of these voices of dissent have now fallen silent in death.

At first the people who spoke up were Goodwin's friends and labour movement associates like Joe Naylor. Then they were friends of his friends—like my father Arthur Mayse, who first heard the story from Dick James and Waddy Williams in 1934—and their children. Later still they were people who stumbled across an enigmatic story between the lines of fragmentary texts, or discovered an extraordinary headstone in a Cumberland cemetery. All have raised the same challenge, the same question.

Why, and how, did Albert Goodwin die? Violently resisting arrest, or trying to surrender, or walking into an ambush? What had he done, what was he planning to do, that would bring military police after him shooting to kill?

Our deaths often define our lives. Goodwin's death has overlaid his life with both the official story's base residue and a radiant patina of legend that obscures the truth just as surely. Ginger Goodwin would love every gleaming word; for a man committed to commonality, he clearly prized his own singularity. But as this story is too consequential for repressive falsehoods, it is likewise too consequential for flattering iconography. Instead it demands the difficult task of going back to uncover — beneath the passions and confusions and lies — something like the truth. Let us ask again, and until we have an answer: Why, and how, did Ginger Goodwin die?

1

A portrait

In the sunlit photo a young man pauses on the porch step. On his way to work, he's clean for a coal miner. His freckles show clearly, and his hair shines so its bright red is lost to the brighter blaze of morning sun. Earlier sometime he's pulled on dungarees and laced up his hobnail boots. At his neck his sweat rag is crossed in front with ends tucked to the sides, as miners wore them in Yorkshire, to keep the coal dust out. His waistcoat, buttoned all the way down, traps the ends of the sweat rag. The left pocket of his dark jacket bulges with his dinner, and an enamelled oval pin shines on his left lapel. A wet comb through his hair, and out the door to the photographer.

Smile. Don't look at the camera. Not knowing what to do with his hands, he folds them in front of his waistcoat. He looks about sixteen. He's twenty-four, and has already worked nine years deep underground in the dark. The light is in his eyes, turning his half-smile into a perplexed half-frown as he looks west, where sunshine is striking the glacier on Mount Albert Edward and the wooded flanks of the Forbidden Plateau. Here at the furthest shore of the British Empire, north of the railroad and north of almost everything else on Vancouver Island, raw stumps stand at the town limits. Beyond them waits a dark wall of fir and cedar, then wilderness. *All right, mate. Got it.* And on a sunny 1911 day, he steps down into a red-dirt Cumberland street, out of the photograph and into the morning.

"Hi, kid." Many years later, in the smoky office of Cumberland's

14

new museum, John Marocchi admired the likeness. "Oh, that's a good one. That's Ginger!"

The Cumberland photo remains in Cumberland, like much of the scant information about Goodwin. Other pictures are illuminated by the same fitful British Columbia sunlight. A few show him a little older, a little wearier. This one seems to capture his youth, even innocence. Karl Coe of Cumberland told an interviewer, looking at the photo, "You see, he looks a timid lad."

"He was a little bit of a guy with red hair. He wasn't healthy," Donetta Rallison remembered. "There was nothing to him when you saw him. He seemed to be very meek and quiet."

Quiet and timid he might have been, but Goodwin already showed promise as a tough, smart political and union organizer. The labour movement's success rate in those years for direct action, including strikes, was low. In his nearly twelve years in Canada, as rank-and-file striker or union official, Goodwin would in a sense lose every battle and win every war. Every strike he took part in failed to achieve its short-term goals, yet had long-term effects on local working conditions. But the sunlit 1911 photo reveals none of this, only an oblique blue-eyed gaze westward, upward to the hills. *Whence cometh my help* would not readily occur to Goodwin, a strong socialist and immune to religious cant. Events proved the psalm untrue in this case, anyway. In July 1918 those hills would bring not help but destruction.

Looking more closely at the snapshot one sees that his jacket, worn around the hem and grey with coal dust, has been made for someone inches taller. The narrow-legged cotton dungarees hang loose. His legs are bandy, perhaps from crouching to heft shovel and pick in coal seams so low that men occasionally have to be pulled by their feet from their working places. The trousers are creased; underground, he wears them rolled above his boot tops to keep them dry. Alternating dust and damp are bad enough without courting lung diseases like the dreaded tuberculosis, widespread among coal miners. Only the hobnail boots, well-made and well-kept on his small feet, show quality. Scots miners call them "tak-ye-ta-bits," as useful in back-alley brawls as in mine work. But Goodwin also owns more elegant clothes. He wears the light grey suit with a white shirt—its detachable collar rounded in the fashion of the day—and a pale silk tie. The worker in hand-me-down pit clothes on a Cumberland porch is also the debonair young man in a convention group photo taken earlier that year.

Albert Goodwin stood a slight five feet six and a half inches, short even by the standards of malnourished European immigrants. Two team photos taken around the same time show him as a soccer player: well-proportioned and athletic, but not robust.

The photo reveals nothing of Goodwin's health. "They say he had consumption, very poor teeth, very poor health all the time," Karl Coe said. "He wasn't a very strong man, you know. He was quite frail, actually."

"I don't know how he ever worked, he was such a frail fellow, even as a kid I remember that. I don't know how he got along and done as much as he did."

Poor teeth among working-class English immigrants usually resulted from a starchy, sugary diet and ignorance of dental hygiene. An acquaintance later described Goodwin's teeth as rusty-looking stubs; they must have given him constant pain. He also reportedly had ulcers. But most serious by far of Goodwin's complaints was lung disease.

Tuberculosis or consumption was—in Cumberland still is—mentioned in whispers. Nearly always fatal, it was a leading cause of death in Canada at the time. The disease results from poverty, overcrowded and unsanitary living conditions, poor nutrition, stress, air pollution: all the industrial revolution's assaults on the human body. Rest, nutritious food and good hygiene were the main treatment for "the white plague" before the development of a vaccine in the 1920s. In the early twentieth century, TB patients from privileged families might recover at private sanatoria. TB patients without means died a lingering death, consumed by their disease. An industrial lung disease, pneumoconiosis, was equally common among miners working in dusty conditions without adequate ventilation. Blacklung or miner's TB, the coal miner's equivalent of the silicosis found among hardrock miners, is a common form. Like tuberculosis, blacklung causes lung lesions, progressive breathing difficulty, pain, weakness and—if untreated—death.

Goodwin's lung disease, later described loosely in non-medical terms by lay people, may have been tuberculosis or pneumoconiosis. No one can now be certain. In 1911 he was healthy enough to play soccer, swim and carry out a coal mine job. Yet a 1918 newspaper account said that his ailment was obvious even to those not informed of it; he probably suffered conspicuous shortness of breath and coughing attacks. By 1918, after sixteen years of mine work, he may have been too weak for heavy labour. All this was to be critical in the last year of his life.

None of this was apparent, perhaps least of all to Ginger Goodwin, on that 1911 day when he directed his ambivalent smile toward the island's mountain spine, where one hillside probably carried more trees than the whole South Riding of Yorkshire, his birthplace.

Albert Goodwin was born 10 May 1887 to Mary Ann Goodwin, formerly Brown, and Walter Goodwin, a coal miner, in the small town of Treeton near Rotherham just northeast of Sheffield. Albert was a popular name at the time. It derived from the Old English Athelbeorht, which meant "noble and shining." Anglian kings ruling the area that was later Yorkshire bore the name as early as the late sixth century. The name Goodwin was equally ancient, and equally Anglian. Pre-Christian English interpreted Godewine as "good friend" or "friend of goodness;" later Christians interpreted it as "God's friend." Walter and Mary Ann Goodwin probably knew little history. Like thousands of other English parents, they were naming their son after the beloved husband of Queen Victoria.

Goodwin had at least two brothers, a newspaper later claimed. Elsie Marocchi of Cumberland recalled seventy years later that he arrived with a brother who died young of tuberculosis. When a friend provided the details for Goodwin's death certificate in 1918, he knew of no living relatives. Friends later agreed that Ginger never spoke to them of his family or childhood. Pansy (Jimmy) Ellis said, "I never knew him as anything but Ginger, and I knew him pretty near all the time he was in the country. Never, never heard him mention about when he was a young fellow in the old country or anything." He wouldn't be the only young man to emigrate alone, unwilling to talk of his past. England, the family, the grey stinking skies, the poverty and sickness, the hateful class system — all fell behind in the wake of sailing ships and steamships bound west, always west.

Karl Coe, who remembered Ginger as a "big brother," had only a vague idea about his origins. "I always figured he'd come from Yorkshire, because him and Joe were such pally friends." Joe Naylor was from Lancashire. Canadians confused the broad midlands and north-country English accents; their different intonations carried similar social and economic messages. Goodwin was later identified as having a Cockney accent, perhaps because of this confusion about old-country dialects and his largely unknown past.

In August 1906 Goodwin boarded the SS *Pretoria* as a steerage passenger in England, bound for Boston and Halifax. The passenger list recorded a minimum of information on the young immigrant: Albert Goodwin, nineteen, single, miner, English, from Yorkshire, destination New Aberdeen, able to both read and write. He was one of 110 steerage passengers, many of them bound for New Aberdeen, Glace Bay and other Cape Breton Island mining communities. Most had jobs arranged. Upstairs in second class was Lily Goodwin, twenty-six, miner's wife, with her two small children Olive and Watts, from Chesterfield, Derbyshire, about twenty kilometres south-west of Treeton. Lily was the wife of Watts Goodwin, whose entire family eventually settled in Alberta. She may have been a distant relative by marriage, but Goodwin was a common name in the English midlands. The *Pretoria* steamed into Halifax at 9:45 p.m. on Sunday, September 2, the day before Labour Day.

In 1907 and 1908 Albert Goodwin lived at 471 New Aberdeen in Glace Bay (George Goodwin from Chesterfield lived nearby at 362 New Aberdeen). By 1910 he was boarding at Caledonia. His move from company housing to a boardinghouse probably resulted from an event that turned the Nova Scotia labour movement inside out for two years. In July 1909 the American-based United Mine Workers of America (UMWA), having by their count organized ninety-five per-cent of the Cape Breton miners, called their first Canadian strike.

The violence and distress that followed are remembered even today. Sydney's annual police report for 1910 includes—in addition to the usual drunkenness and bawdy house offences—a sizeable list of assaults, refusals to move after the Riot Act was invoked, fighting, obstructing police officers, unlawful assembly, obstructing a man going to work, and calling men "scab."

"These [UMWA] papers kept urging the men to strike and remain on strike," thundered the *Sydney Record*, no friend of organized labour, six months into the strike. "They kept on repeating the falsehood that ample provision in the way of food, clothing and shelter would be made for all. Many of the workmen, unfortunately, took these representatives of the UMW at their word. The result we have witnessed during the past few weeks. A more pitiful one we have never been called to witness in this province. And all because of the deception practised by the UMW, its press, and paid agents and solicitors. . ."

Soldiers were called in to control strikers and protect strikebreak-ers, as often happened during early Canadian strikes. To governments of the day, employers were allies and workers were enemies. Glace Bay council bickered over who should foot the bill, but the soldiers stayed on duty. Meanwhile an editorial in the *Record* claimed that the strike was a ploy by the UMWA to put control of Canadian workers in American hands, and ultimately to raise and stabilize American mine workers' wages. Just when Montreal was bidding on a major coal supply contract, the strike forced Nova Scotia mine operators to discuss their pricing structure openly, the *Record* said, "The very secrets our American competitors are paying money to get in order to underbid our Canadian business just sufficiently to get the contracts."

Wilfred Gribble analyzed the strike in the *Western Clarion*, the Socialist Party of Canada's newspaper, as a party organizer in Vancouver in 1912. "This was a wage dispute. It was an argument between buyers and sellers over a just price for labour power . . .

"I might remark here that any dispute between employer and labour is always a wage struggle. Whether the men are asking for higher wages, shorter hours, or better conditions, it is always asking more material advantages for the same work, and these material advantages always mean money.

"The miners thought the trouble was with wages. They did not know that the wages were fixed by laws of supply and demand, and, therefore, beyond control either by labourers or owners.

"They said, 'If you will not pay us more for our labour power we will take it out of your mines,' and they did so. Now, if every man in Canada had had a job they would have won their cause. Then they would have been stronger and would have had the right to higher wages."

Instead, Gribble wrote, the owners imported labour and broke the strike. "They had the power, therefore they had the right.

"These 5,000 able-bodied men were beaten by a mere handful of men, inferior to them in nearly every way, because they fought on the wrong field. Dollars were the weapons, and the capitalist has the most dollars. Votes should be the weapons and labour has the most votes."

Goodwin probably left Nova Scotia in 1910, like other union miners, blacklisted and penniless. Some of his Cape Breton Island friends—the Boothman and Weir and Patterson and Walker families among them—had the same notion of heading west.

"They all grouped together. The Walkers were there, and Arthur Boothman, and my uncle Tom. They all seemed to move away together, up into the Crowsnest to work, and then they moved from the Crowsnest up to here," Jim Weir said, though he couldn't remember hearing Ginger Goodwin travelled with them. "The others just seemed to be a tight group. When one moved, they all moved."

"We knew him east, too, in Glace Bay, Nova Scotia. My brother knew him but I didn't know him," Gert Somerville told me. Her brother Arthur Boothman, when the Cape Breton crowd had settled again, would become a coal digger and star soccer player for another coal town, another island.

Alberta was a disappointment to some Cape Breton miners, although coal mines pocked the face of the new province—carved from the Northwest Territories only five years earlier—from Edmonton south to the American border. Nova Scotia and British Columbia produced mainly steam coal, hard and clean-burning anthracite, for industrial use; Alberta produced mainly foul-burning soft bituminous or lignite for domestic use. Large mines in the Crowsnest Pass and Drumheller operated year-round, but most workings were small and seasonal. Mine owners expected miners to work underground in the winter, then hire on as farm hands or labourers during the prairie summers when householders bought no coal. The prosperous mines scattered through a score of towns and hamlets of "The Pass" attracted blacklisted Nova Scotia miners, but just as quickly sent many on their way. UMWA District 18 struck in 1911 for better wages and union recognition. Union miners, faced with a choice between scabbing and starving, pushed on. Some pushed west, still further west, to Vancouver Island.

Ginger Goodwin reached Cumberland in time to play for the town's championship soccer team in September 1910 and to appear on the 1911 voters' list as *Albert Goodwin, miner*. He was the only Goodwin on the list, but others would turn up over the next few years. The Marocchi bakery's cash book listed among its credit customers *Robert Goodwin, somil*. The Italian-speaking accountant, with his typically phonetic interpretation of names and descriptions, possibly wrote Robert for Albert as he wrote "somil" for sawmill. A July 1910 *Cumberland Islander* story lists men and women who chipped in to help a recent Courtenay widow. An H. Goodwin, at Fraser River Mills Logging Camp near Cumberland, contributed fifty cents, roughly a quarter of his day's wages. Neither H. nor Robert Goodwin appears elsewhere in Cumberland records, which were notoriously inaccurate and variable for names. Ginger Goodwin may have worked in a sawmill or logging operation near Cumberland when he first arrived. Securing a mine job, no matter how experienced the worker, was often a matter of crossing the right palm with silver.

Albert Goodwin worked in Cumberland's Number Five pit. The company and union records are long gone—"Goodwin's name was all over them," said one of the crew that destroyed them with the miner's recreation centre in 1969—but he left other traces. A few years later in another coal town Ginger Goodwin gave his occupation as miner and hired on as a mule driver.

By his own account, Goodwin first went down the pit in 1902 when he was fifteen. He was literate, and that was no mean accomplishment for a coal miner's son. He probably had several years of education, either free or paid for by his parents. The Goodwin family must have been more solvent than others who sent their boys to work younger still. Boys had to be twelve or fourteen to work full-time, depending on local labour laws. When a family needed another wage-earner, however, boys would pad their ages. Foremen, often in return for gifts or outright bribes, would wink at their lies. Ginger Goodwin worked four years in the Yorkshire mines in some capacity. It was long enough to get a grasp of the coal miner's skills, long enough to learn to cross the neck rag tight, keeping out some — not enough — of the pervasive and fatal coal dust.

Cumberland's Number Five pit lay scarcely a mile from the sunlit porch, with its kerosene lamp bracket beside the plank door. After the shutter's snap, after he clattered down the steps into the dusty street, Ginger Goodwin was only a few minutes' walk from work in probably the world's most dangerous coalfield. In 1902, *World Mining Statistics* (quoted in William Bennett's book, *Builders of British Columbia*) listed deaths per one thousand persons employed in coal mining: 1.29 for the British Empire, 2.38 for foreign countries, 3.38 for Nova Scotia and 4.15 for British Columbia. Vancouver Island, The Pass, Cape Breton, South Wales and Pennsylvania all had their explosions and fires and deadly vapours: blackdamp, whitedamp, firedamp, afterdamp. Some debated which mines were most lethal, but it was an abstract argument, since each field killed hundreds or thousands during a scant century of coal extraction. Island miners went underground all the same. In 1911 they had little choice.

Coal miners called British Columbia's first strike over working conditions in 1855, just a few years after mining began on Vancouver Island. For another century the island coalfield produced handsome profits at the cost of grisly mine disasters which crushed, drowned, suffocated or dismembered workers. Strikes were endemic. Miners were clannish, proud and quick to help each other on or off the job; even so, they needed more than personal self-help networks. As individuals they were helpless against wage rollbacks, discrimination, arbitrary dismissal, unsafe practices, job-buying, all the injustices of the nineteenth-century workplace.

In December 1911 Vancouver Island became District 28 of the United Mine Workers of America. Cumberland Local 2299 organized energetically with meetings, lively dances, concerts, moving picture shows, smokers and other entertainments. About 150 men signed up. One member was Joseph Naylor, a coal digger in Number Four pit and a former organizer for the militant Western Federation of Miners. Another 250 union miners — many of them blacklisted elsewhere in Canada and the United States — had recently arrived in town. One of them was probably Ginger Goodwin.

Older, seasoned miners formed the executive of Local 2299, but Goodwin may have assisted in the membership drive. Johnny Marocchi remembered him as a union organizer. Cumberland knew him before Vancouver and Trail knew him, before he was a strong public speaker. He used to go into the woods alone to work on his technique. Standing on a high-cut stump left by pioneer loggers, he would address an unresponsive audience of other stumps. His self-taught public speaking skill repaid his efforts. People later said that he spoke forcefully about the wrongs he'd suffered and seen as a worker. Even the military police in 1918 noted "speaks volubly and assertively" on his search description.

"He used to go out and practise speaking all by himself out in the bush," Cumberland's retired barber Peter Cameron said. "Just so he could get up in a crowd, I guess."

Passionate intensity and a highly-coloured style distinguish his few surviving letters. He used graphic examples, and deployed a dark humour that must have been especially biting at first hand. His rhetoric was industrial-strength socialist doctrine about slaves of the system and capitalist imperialism. Complex, sometimes shaky, his grammar revealed the extensive vocabulary of someone with little formal education but a voracious appetite for knowledge and ideas. Clearly he put words on paper just as he spoke them, in a rush toward meaning and effect. A labour newspaper later described Ginger Goodwin as an informed and well-spoken socialist, a gentleman in the best sense, whose language was inoffensive even to an unsympathetic audience.

Socialism flourished in Cumberland as early as 1903, when the town sent delegates to a gathering of twenty-one diverse groups in British Columbia which planned to form a national party. The convention resolved to stand firm on "the one issue of the abolition of the present system of wage slavery as the basis for all political propaganda." A year later the British Columbia groups founded the Socialist Party of Canada, with Vancouver organizing Local 1.

Ginger Goodwin, like Joe Naylor, was a charter member of Local 70 of the Socialist Party of Canada in Cumberland, another party member recalled years later.

"Oh, he was a socialist," Gert Somerville said. "A real good one."

British Columbia socialists and trade unionists would fall into bitter schism within a few years, but in 1912 they shared common goals. The executive officers of the new UMWA local, despite the international union's relative conservatism, were all socialists.

Local 70 met at least once a week to discuss "the principles and programmes of the revolutionary working class." Their book list included *Class Struggle in America*, *Ethics and the Materialist Concept of History* and Karl Marx's *Capital*—weighty off-shift reading.

"Labour produces all wealth, and to the producers it should belong," the party platform stated. "The present economic system is based upon capitalist ownership of the means of production, consequently all the products of labour belong to the capitalist class. The capitalist is therefore master; the worker is slave."

About a hundred men and women joined, though not all attended every meeting. Three members pooled their funds to buy an old store opposite the post office on Dunsmuir Avenue, which they turned into a meeting place. This drew the mockery of local newspaper editor E.W. Bickle, a former miner who had profited as notary and city clerk. In his weekly *Cumberland Islander* he suggested, when someone painted "socialist hall" on the meeting place door, that an E in the second word would be more appropriate than an A. The socialists fired their own verbal barrages in return, though not on the pages of the *Islander*.

"Bickle run it. He was never much as far as the men were concerned," Peter Cameron explained. The *Islander* usually supported the company and attacked the union and its organizers.

Children of the Cumberland socialists remembered waiting impatiently for interminable meetings to end. Elsie Marocchi told interviewers, "[Ginger] used to come down there with all the other radicals, as we used to call them, and they used to have meetings there. All us kids used to be locked in the bedrooms. We weren't allowed out, so we started to say, Oh, if only they would go home. Well, eventually they would start to sing. . . ."

> The workers' flag is deepest red,
> it shrouded oft our martyred dead.
> And ere their limbs grew stiff and cold
> their life blood dyed its very fold.

The Workers' Flag signalled adjournment and, for the children, escape.

"They used to hold socialist meetings. One time Tim [Walker] asked me. . . . I went, but I wasn't interested in socialism. Oh boy, they were going at it," Johnny Marocchi told me. He knew Ginger well. "At nighttime we'd meet in Shorty's poolroom and talk. And then of course he was a union organizer, he worked for them. I was in business, I was at the Big Shop in the grocery store. But we'd meet there and we'd talk."

Like other Cumberlanders, Johnny listened with interest to touring speakers such as American UMWA organizer Mother Jones and later Canadian communist Tim Buck. He never joined the socialist party. "You see, I was a capitalist. I'd sit on the fence."

His friend Ginger stood firm on the revolutionary socialist side of the fence. His activism separated him not only from the social mainstream but apparently from his own family. No one survives who can explain how and when this happened—arguably before he reached Cumberland.

Goodwin's 1911 photo is faded and speckled with age. Even so, grey gradations in the black-and-white print show his neck rag was a lighter shade and a different hue from his coat and dungarees. Clean, carefully wrapped, it seems as deliberate a statement as the oval pin on his left lapel. We can safely guess it was, like his hair and his politics, blazing socialist red.

A less serious-minded Ginger Goodwin—ruffled, breathless, warily regarding the camera—looks out from the soccer team photo. In the grey island mid-day the Number Five Thistles are grouped before Cumberland's usual backdrop of evergreens stunted by coal dust. One player is darkly handsome, another is a jug-eared teenager, several are smiling. They are sweaty, but scrubbed pale: coal diggers, mule drivers, rope riders, they spend their waking hours down the shaft at Number Five mine. Even in their twenties, already a few have the sloped shoulders of men who spend their days at heavy labour.

The goaltender and fullbacks stand with arms folded across their black jerseys, moustachio'd bruisers who gleefully shut out haughty Nanaimo and trounce effete Victoria. At their knees crouch the three glowering midfielders. The five forwards pose artfully in front, two wingers leaning languidly against the inside forwards, the centre sitting up straight behind the scuffed ball.

Inside left forward and inside right forward, those are the goal scorers. Today they'd be called the strikers, the lads who drive the ball into the net once midfielders or halfbacks and wingers have set up the shot.

Agility is more important than size in soccer, which is nominally not a contact sport. The two smallest men on this team, neatly matched for size, are the inside forwards. The inside left, dark and lean, is still remembered by a few old-timers as one of Cumberland's finest players. Arthur Boothman's mine nickname was Duffy; his nimbleness earned him his soccer nickname of The Spider. The inside right looks chunky by comparison, clasping his shins with square hands. He's been out on the playing field or riverbank enough to tan between his freckles. His knee socks are slipping and his high soccer boots look the worse for wear. Unlike the others he hasn't combed his hair, as though he's decided soccer is no place for the bourgeois cult of personality. For his flaming hair or his spirited nature, on or off the field, he's called Ginger.

Soccer, *fitba* to Cumberland's Scots miners, was clean, fast and elegant as played by near-professional island mine teams in 1911. Coal companies always somehow found work for good footballers as a matter of corporate and civic pride. Soccer was important. Ben Horbury said, "When Nanaimo came to Cumberland to play football half of Nanaimo come up. They had special trains."

"We played to win. We trained hard. We practised hard," Chuna (Charles) Tobacco told a Cumberland student who interviewed him for a 1975 school project. He was speaking of basketball; his words apply equally to soccer. "We wanted to be the best."

Goodwin still occupies a place in Cumberland memories as an exceptionally good player. This may just reflect the town's lasting affection. Johnny Marocchi and a handful of other people told me Arthur Boothman was a dazzling player. Ginger played soccer as he played pool, Johnny said, well but not brilliantly. It was a pastime. "He wasn't what you'd call a top-notch player. You see, Canadian Collieries used to bring in players, semi-pros."

Though Johnny thought otherwise, Goodwin and Arthur Boothman may have been among these star imports. A September 1911 *Islander* story lists among recently signed Number Five Thistles players "C. Walker, A. Goodwin, and A. Boothman from Tottenham Hot Spurs, Runners up of the English League." The "Spurs" for years ran circles around other soccer sides. There was professional English football and, in a class apart, there were the Tottenham Hotspurs. Even today they hold their own in North London, less magnificent perhaps than eighty years ago, but still trailing wisps of glory. If the three young arrivals from Cape Breton Island (or even just Boothman) had indeed played for Tottenham, they would be great assets to the Thistles. The *Islander* story promises "This team with good support will show first class football to the people of Cumberland during this coming season."

A gold soccer medal is one of Goodwin's meagre possessions that found its way into the collection of Cumberland Museum. Its complex florette gleams with red, white and blue enamel spelling out CNP. Engraved script on the back spells out Albert Goodwin, Soccer, Crow's Nest Pass. He won it either on his way west to the Island in 1910 or during a four-month stay a few years later.

Ginger always asked Arthur's sister Gert Somerville about her children. "'Are they playing football yet?' That's all he talked was football. And I said, 'Not bad.' He said, 'Tell Arthur to get after them, make them play football.'"

Nine feet of split cane, a long true cast, days dappled with river light, the silver arc of a fighting fish: this other off-hours pleasure of Ginger Goodwin's offered a contemplative and solitary counterpoint to football's noisy camaraderie. With Joe Naylor he fished the island lakes and rivers freely, unchallenged, as he could never have fished England's gentry-owned waters.

Barber's Hole and Meeker's Hole on the Puntledge River, which slides tawny and talkative down to tidewater; glacier-fed Trent River, frothing through alpine meadows; wild green Cruikshank River and Rees Creek; Tsolum River, Tsable River, Little Oyster River, Comox Lake, Willemar Lakes: today the waters draining the Beaufort Range lie beautiful and remote at the unsettled heart of Vancouver Island. Seventy years ago they were almost unimaginably lovely to poor folk from the black English midlands, the desolate Scots and Welsh coal valleys, and industrial Northern Italy. Birds sang. Panthers sunned on rock outcrops. Bears combed the blackberry patches. Rivers seethed with game fish. If Cumberland's coal mines tunnelled near the boundaries of hell, solace lay south of Jerusalem on the Perseverance Trail and north along Paradise Creek to Paradise Meadows.

"We used to walk to Courtenay and stay four or five days on that little sandy beach in the park." Karl Coe remembered his fishing trips with Ginger Goodwin and Joe Naylor when he was a young boy. "There used to be a nice beach in there, at the top end of it. We used to go down there and camp right there, put our tents up there and start fishing from there."

"If we knew it was going to be good weather we wouldn't take the tent. We'd just sleep right on the beach. Of course that was wild, in those days."

Goodwin's fishing rod is now in the Cumberland Museum; he left it to Karl, who still kept it in his house when we talked not long before he died. Its nearly ten-foot length is phenomenal by modern standards; a strong wrist and good co-ordination are needed to drop a trout fly where you want it. Its solid brass lock-screw ferrules prevent the tip from shooting off on a powerful cast. The work of a renowned English rod maker, Henry J. Wilkes, it probably cost Ginger Goodwin a month's pay. Karl said, "He prized it very well. He was a true sportsman when it came to fishing."

Ginger and Joe were both strictly trout fishermen, though Joe sometimes stooped to fishing with a worm instead of a fly on his fine Hardy fly rod. Other equipment was more rudimentary, like Ginger's simple wood and brass reel. Rubber hip-waders and multi-pocketed

fishing vests were for well-heeled swells; the miners waded from pool
to pool in their trousers and hobnailed mine boots.

Karl was only seven or eight years old on the earliest of these trips
to the Puntledge River near Courtenay, and used to stay in camp while
his "big brothers" fished. "It was too far for me to walk, and they'd
be in and out of the river, wading across the river, back across to the
other side. Joe he'd go up the river all the time toward the power
house, Ginger he'd go down toward the Tsolum River, he'd always
fish that part. And I would stay in camp playing around on that beach
there all the time. Joe would say, Don't worry about him, he'll be all
right," Karl said. "Ginger used to worry. What are you going to do,
are you going to be there?"

Joe knew the boy's self-reliance. On an earlier grouse-poaching
trip, Joe and Karl's father Richard Coe were lost for two days and a
night in the wild mountain country between Cumberland and Alberni. Karl sat in their camp, playing with a friendly mink, yelling for his
dad once in a while but unafraid.

The friends were always trying to best each other in fishing. "I can
remember one time when both of them were coming back to camp.
Joe had a pretty nice catch, he caught several like this [in the timeless
fisherman's gesture, Karl spread his hands to demonstrate trout of two
or three pounds] and he was bragging away there. Pretty soon Ginger
walked into the camp, and Joe said, 'Christ!' He had several nice ones,
and besides, they were big steelhead. Joe said, 'Hey, I'm not going to
try to fish upriver again, the hell with them.' They was always trying
to beat each other, you know. And Joe said, 'Oh, I quit. I'm not going
to try to beat you no more.'"

Ginger, having perhaps lost one brother and left the rest of his
family in Yorkshire, seems to have found another brother in Karl. In
Joe, fifteen years his elder, he may have found another father. An
anonymous letter to the UMWA *Journal*, if not written by Goodwin,
at least expressed his feelings that Joe "had practically come to be
looked upon as a father for his wisdom and judgment in all matters
was asked and worked upon." Karl said that whenever they were both
in town on organizing trips, Ginger and Joe were almost inseparable.
Union and political organizing, mine work, soccer and dances were
an adult world; Karl knew Ginger mostly from the child's world of
fishing. "But when I was with him he seemed to be a very jolly man,
easy to get along with, that's why he always treated me so good. Just
like a big brother."

"He always seemed to be happy and talkative when we were fishing
down there, when he come back in—what have you been doing, and
how are you feeling, and what did you do today? All that kind of stuff.

Just simple stuff, nothing serious about any politics or unions or anything like that."

Karl Coe told often and eloquently of those long-ago summer days by the Puntledge: camping under the stars, Ginger's strong swimming as a young man, Joe's jokes and friendly teasing. Karl's memories endured most of a century and still survive in others' telling, still illuminated with a great poignancy.

"They used to kid me quite a bit down there in the pool when they were fishing. And one time when Ginger used to swim across that river, he'd take me on his back and swim across the river." Once when they were halfway to the far shore, as a joke Joe shouted out to let Karl go in mid-stream. "I damn near choked Ginger to death before we got to the shore." Karl laughed. "He said, Let go, Karl! Let go, I can't breathe! By heck, I'll never forget that."

Ginger Goodwin's workmates and comrades in Cumberland had names he'd never have heard in Yorkshire, and accents to match. There were Austro-Hungarians like Johnny Marocchi, Welsh like Dai Davis, Norwegians like Ole Oleson, Americans like Richard Coe, a Finn who changed his name after a dockside incident he'd rather forget, Chinese, Japanese, blacks and Slavs. Many had old-country English voices like Joe Naylor and Arthur Boothman. In a virulently racist era, across language and ethnic distinctions, a startling assortment of people proudly called themselves Ginger's friends. They would remember him all their lives.

Sam Robertson: "He was my chum, we were good friends. My wife and Ginger were good friends, too."

Pansy Ellis: "He was a well-liked fellow, not only through his union activities, he had a great personality with him."

Jack Horbury: "Dad always said that Goodwin practised what he preached."

A former Cape Breton miner who knew Ginger as a greenhorn immigrant saw in him a carefully engineered reputation and a towering ambition. Chas Walker was secretary of the Socialist Party of Canada local for years, a soccer club official and a fellow mine worker, yet he didn't know his friend had lung disease. He thought Goodwin was swell-headed and wanted the limelight as a labour leader. Walker's observations are exceptional in the flood of unconditional praise. Overreaching pride, the Greeks' *hubris*, since time out of mind has brought down the mighty. Did Goodwin fall of his own weight, having overestimated his self-created importance? He was described as quiet and meek, even furtive, yet he thought well enough of himself to endure hostility to his radical activities. It seems an unworthy view of a man loved by friends and often respected by opponents, but

Walker's criticism was not the only hint of this, as events were to unfold.

"He was very popular with the girls," labour organizer Bill Pritchard of Vancouver said.

"He loved to dance. He liked to have a good time, all right," said Karl, whose big sister Mabel used to dance with Ginger at Cumberland's Saturday night gatherings. A local orchestra played the popular music of the day: sentimental waltzes, spirited ragtime. It was all above-board, even innocent. Cumberland was too close-knit a town for young men to get away with much licentious behaviour, at least overtly. Karl said, "They all had good words for Ginger."

"He was a nice dancer, and he attended all the dances," Sam Robertson said.

"He was a willing sort of a person. If you were going to the show, he'd pay your way into the picture show. He was a generous sort of a man. If you'd got a book he'd ask you what kind you had. He said, 'Do you mind if I have a lend of it?'" — Gert Somerville recalled. The socialists sometimes held informal meetings in her house when she was a young wife with small children; her brothers Arthur and Bill boarded there. She would make tea and excuse herself; she'd heard enough discussion around her parents' dinner table about the rights and wrongs of socialism and the labour movement.

"He was a wonderful young man. I don't know if he was ever married or not, I couldn't say. I don't think he was."

Gert said she never looked closely enough to notice the colour of his eyes. "But I always remembered his hair. You could see the stars just shine . . . I said to him one time, You've got hair something like some of our kids have got . . . shiny red hair. He said, I don't have red hair! And you could see the red sparks every once in a while all over his head. And he couldn't see it . . . He wouldn't even look in the mirror."

Ginger Goodwin looked in the mirror before he stepped onto the porch for his 1911 snapshot, at least long enough to slick down his hair. Such sparse information survives about his life that the photograph itself is a remarkable document. Perhaps its most remarkable feature is that it exists. What event, what circumstances, led to this photo?

Another early photo in the Cumberland Museum shows the Number Five miners and mule drivers and bosses standing and kneeling in grimy rows, squinting into the camera's gaze. All look weary: Chinese and Japanese workers ranked behind polyglot white Europeans and one black worker. The hastily daubed placard says they've broken a pit record for tons of coal loaded, 524 tons in eight hours. Such an event called for a photo of mine workers still in their coal dust.

But for most occasions—sending a portrait home as proof of prosperity in the new land, an engagement, a marriage, a birth— working-class people donned their best, or borrowed clothes to venture among the potted palms and painted backdrops of a photographic studio. They didn't want to be recorded for eternity in the coal miner's hobnails and dungarees, the factory girl's apron and clogs. Even once Kodak box cameras were commonplace, they would at least scrub themselves shiny and pose on the sidewalk in Sunday finery.

Albert Goodwin was different. He was proud to be a worker, and he was proud of a thumbnail-sized enamelled metal oval on his left lapel. On his way to drive a mule or load coal in Number Five pit, a friend—they were all friends then—photographed him with his new United Mine Workers of America membership pin. It was so bright its details burned themselves to overexposure on a lost negative, brighter than his hair, brighter than the sun.

Cumberland and Union

Cumberland delighted or dismayed new arrivals, even before they stepped down from the mine train, depending on their outlook.

Delight, or at least determination, accompanied the battered trunk holding an entire family's motley treasures; dismay attended the matched leather valises and equally fastidious backgrounds and expectations. Cumberland, days by steamship from Vancouver, stood alone at the end of the tracks. Nearby Courtenay was a crossroads; Comox was a farming enclave among Indian lands. It was a far cry from sophisticated London or dynamic San Francisco or pretentious Victoria. Cumberland wasn't even a settled coal mining town like Nanaimo, sixty miles south, though its small mercantile elite optimistically incorporated as a city of three thousand residents in 1897. From Brown's upstairs brothel and the fancy houses in Minto district to the Bucket of Blood saloon, despite the earnest endeavours of the righteous in "church street" and "Little Jerusalem," Cumberland was less a coal town than a coal camp.

A few newcomers, standing amidst their baggage on the plank station platform, probably decided to climb aboard again and head straight back to civilization via Union Bay steamship wharf. It was too late. The train had already steamed off toward Comox Lake hauling a load of miners, equipment and empty coal cars to Number Four mine. The newcomer's view of Cumberland was of raw red earth, bristling stumps, rivers of mud politely called streets, board sidewalks, mine whistles, coal smoke and rain. The contradictions were dizzying: prosperous merchants on a hustling main thorough-fare, squalid Matthewson Square shanties with privies flowing into the gutters, coal mine tipples and headworks, the spacious park and roofs of the mine supervisor's Beaufort House, neat rows of company miners' cottages, and not too far in any direction, ranks of cedars and firs sickening under the murky effluvium from Number Four, Number Five and Number Six. To the west, eagles spiralled over the Beaufort Range's snow fields, shining above the reach of coal dust.

Dunsmuir Avenue rose from "down camp" in the original settle-ment of Union to the new city of Cumberland, then fell again in a slow decline to the sea at Roy's Beach four miles east. The main street was an expanse of dust in summer and in every other season an expanse of mud. Mostly people remembered the mud. Apparently bottomless and limitless, the mud mired horse teams, tracked into bars and poolrooms and houses, and swallowed gumboots whole. An expedition across the street demanded more fortitude than finesse. Board sidewalks and a few clumps of grass bordered this wallow, which teemed with the constant traffic of delivery wagons from the general merchants and bakery and grocer, hired saddle horses and carriages from the two livery stables, the two-horse stagecoach from Comox harbour by way of Courtenay village. Horses, cows and dogs regularly escaped backyard confinement and wandered around town. Runaway pigs rooted under the windows of merchants offering Paris millinery and grand pianos. But people didn't come to Cumberland and Union for urbane refinements or genteel company. They came to work in the mines, or by second choice, at the logging camps and farms and sawmills.

Canadian Collieries (Dunsmuir) Limited owned Cumberland, though the Victoria coal magnates no longer owned the company Robert Dunsmuir hewed from island anthracite. In 1910 James Dunsmuir sold to the railway interest of Mackenzie and Mann, which was then laying elaborate plans — but scant trackage — for the Canadian North-ern Railway. CNR's bond-issue bubble would burst a few years later, damping Cumberland's economy among others. Meanwhile, the new city offered apparently unlimited opportunity. The pages of the *Cumberland News* and later the *Cumberland Islander* gave off an electric excitement. Anything could happen.

"I have heard lots of the old-timers speak of it, saying you could nearly walk on the heads of the people in Cumberland in 1912 when everybody was working and everybody had money," retired grocer Tom Mumford told an interviewer not long before he died at a vigorous 105 years. "It was pretty nearly a wild west town in those days."

Union was the heartland, the original 1887 settlement east of Coal Creek, where Robert Dunsmuir's Union Colliery Company built its first fifty "cottages" for its mine workers at the raw frontier. Photos of old Union Camp show new railway tracks running below three rows of plain just-finished houses on a southward slope. In a morass of red island mud, cedar stumps with twelve-foot girths tower eaves-tall among the houses. Most of the houses down camp (including my own) are still family homes, still recognizable from the 1889 photos despite their new porches and garages and second stories. Small, simple, anything but luxurious, they were nonetheless built to last; they outlasted all nine of Cumberland's coal mines. Robert Dunsmuir, though later miners rightly condemned his labour practices, was a progressive if paternalistic employer by 1887 standards. He provided not only houses for miners but schools for their children. For better ot worse, he also established a company store; in other one-industry towns, such closed economies kept some workers in debt their entire working lives. Soon it was clear that high-quality "Comox No. 4" coal was in plentiful supply and strong demand. Other merchants carved out retail territory in Union, until they ran out of space on the steep south-facing hillside. Since Chinese workers and merchants occupied the swampy bottomland to the west, there was only one direction to expand. Just east of Union, on colliery land, developed the orderly grid-plan community of Cumberland.

Cumberland blossomed in a few short years into Canada's western-most, and possibly smallest, city. Brick and granite and elegant wood-frame blocks lined Dunsmuir Avenue, where anyone who had the leisure to window shop could ogle garments fit for garden party or pit work, sides of pork, pianos, seed packets and pilsner. Cumberland's mines often worked two or three shifts around the clock to keep abreast of orders, and money poured through the Royal Bank and city coffers to underwrite the latest technological advances: a telephone exchange, electrical street lamps, cement sidewalks to replace the old boardwalks, motor cars for retail deliveries and motor stages for the bumpy stump-dodging drive to Courtenay or Comox. The Esquimalt and Nanaimo railway, until recently a Dunsmuir holding, soon made the grade to Union Bay where a colliery spur continued to Cumberland. Cumberland, at the raw edge of a vast wilderness, became instant civilization.

Men found life in the mines gruelling, often dangerous, sometimes fatal. Yet their off-shift recreations — hours at the brass rail of the Cumberland or Union or Bucket of Blood saloon, lodge meetings, sports, gambling, union and political organizing, whoring, hunting, fishing — provided distraction or at least a change of scenery. Most of these activities were closed to girls and women. Girls were soon women in any case; coal miners' daughters had little leisure to enjoy the protracted childhood of more privileged classes. Donetta Rallison was twelve when her mother died, and she had to leave school to keep house for her father. He showed her how to do her tasks and even helped when he wasn't too exhausted after his shift. But her girlhood was behind her forever. "I saw kids outside playing, and I was inside doing housework."

Many girls married as young as they could to escape drudging in their parents' homes. Though she loved her husband, Gert Somerville soon regretted marrying in her teens. "I was too young. I wanted to get away from home. I was getting tired of it."

Men's work lasted a long shift, theoretically eight hours but often as long as sixteen hours. Women's work lasted from first light to lamp light, and much of it was strenuous labour: handwashing a mountain of clothes permeated with coal dust, scrubbing floors on hands and knees, thumping bread dough, beating carpets, hauling coal, chopping wood. Hospital records list many women's cases of general debility, abortion (more likely miscarriage than induced abortion) and hysteria. Childbirth generally called for a two-week stay in hospital. Somehow women found energy to enjoy dances and socials and their own lodge gatherings, and somehow they kept a sense of humour.

"We didn't have a bathroom either," Doll Williams told an interviewer. "We had a little tub, as the saying goes you wash down as far as possible, and up as far as possible, and the question is when does possible get washed? I've seen those days, soaking dirty and all this stuff to wash, and you had to wash it by hand, no washers in them days."

People soon settled out into their chosen districts. Most of the families in Cumberland were of British, Eastern Canadian or American origin. Presbyterian Scots clustered not far from their church, in the southwest corner of Cumberland which lively wits dubbed Little Jerusalem. The eastern reaches would eventually be called the Townsite. But Cumberland's population was really scattered into a handful of towns and hamlets, most divided along ethnic lines. The Italians clustered in Union Camp, sometimes called West Cumberland. The English-speaking immigrants crudely dubbed other outlying enclaves Japtown and Chinatown and Coontown.

Chinatown sprawled around two main thoroughfares, Shan gai (upper street) and Ha gai (lower street), both crooked doglegs. Here European eyes saw a distressingly chaotic sprawl, but Chinese eyes saw a wisely contrived confusion to keep demons at bay. This didn't always work; non-Chinese sometimes descended to Chinatown to sample strong Chinese whisky and gamble a few rounds of *fan tan* or *pai gow.* This was one of the largest Chinese communities of the Gold Mountain, as the Chinese called North America, with a population of three thousand reported for 1900. Among the slapdash houses on haphazard streets, Chinese trade and culture flourished. There were butchers, laundries, herbalists, restaurants, drygoods shops and other merchants. Opera companies, entertainers, Buddhist and Christian ministers, and teachers arrived regularly from China. Dr. Sun Yat-sen visited Cumberland for four days in 1911 with a four-man armed bodyguard. The Wo-Yick Theatre was packed with six hundred people who eagerly provided money for his fall 1911 revolution in China.

From the 1880s, Chinese companies organized the emigration of labourers, especially from poverty-stricken Guangdong province. In Canada the workers were underpaid, overworked and shamefully mistreated — they paid a discriminatory "head tax" to enter the country, their families were excluded, they were denied full citizenship until 1947 — and tradition has it that a Chinese labourer died for every mile of trackage laid on the Canadian Pacific Railway. These early Chinese arrivals were not settlers but sojourners who sent money home and hoped themselves to return one day.

Chinese generally gave non-Chinese better treatment than they received, from mixed humanitarianism and self-preservation. Cumberlanders today remember the open invitations to Chinese New Year in Chinatown, with apparently unlimited food and drink and fireworks. Forcibly separated from their own families, Chinese men missed children's laughter and women's graces. Their kindness was repaid with lurid "yellow peril" newspaper stories about kidnapped children, and repressive laws forbidding them to hire white women.

Bitterness over this mistreatment still seethes to the surface of Canadian society, especially in British Columbia. Individual men and women steadfastly rose above the discrimination, however. Retired railwayman Piggy (Jimmy) Brown told me about Sam, a Chinese miner his father and uncle contracted for pit work. Unusually big and strong, Sam could carry heavy mine timbers over his shoulder like so many tentpoles, and earned two men's wages each shift. In one of Cumberland's many mine explosions Sam, without breathing equipment, somehow made his way from the mine portal down into the dust-filled black maze of the drifts, found his boss and carried him out to safety before collapsing outside the headworks. Thanks to Sam — who recovered and worked many more years underground — Piggy Brown's uncle lost only one finger. Twenty-three other miners and mine workers lost their lives.

Some Cumberland Chinese did return home to Asia with their earnings. Others who died on the Gold Mountain instead were buried facing the sunrise in the Chinese cemetery, a slope of grass and wildflowers. After several years their bones were exhumed, crated and sent to distant Guangdung. The small wooden crates were a familiar sight, awaiting their long journey home on Station Cumberland platform under the soft rain and the ravens' cries.

Japanese communities of small, neat wooden houses grew up near the area's coal mines, logging camps and other industries. Number One Japtown near Comox Lake and Number Five Japtown just north of Cumberland were the largest sites, with stores and halls and churches. The Japanese, eligible for citizenship unlike the Chinese, could bring their families to Canada. They planned to stay, and soon assimilated into the business community. A Japanese tailor shop, photographic studio, hardware and jeweller all operated on Dunsmuir Avenue. In 1899, about eight years after the first Japanese arrived in Cumberland, visiting Japanese consul Shizaburo Shimizu said, "...I am very favourably impressed with the general appearance of the town. I am quite struck with the progressive spirit of the citizens, and have no doubt that a few years will see a large city here."

Black workers, many from families that fled the United States for British Columbia as early as the 1850s, formed their own community. Coontown was a cluster of houses and small businesses near Number One Japtown. White Cumberland regarded its inhabitants with suspicion and, if mine jobs were scarce, with outright hostility. Police blotters show repeated complaints of Negro women practising prostitution, though investigation found some complaints to be malicious and unfounded. One of Cumberland's respected black residents, however, did run a brothel above his store.

John Brown was a summer gold prospector and winter coal miner, general merchant and no-holds-barred entrepreneur. Nigger Brown's Creek north of Cumberland is said to commemorate him, though the provincial government has recently tried unsuccessfully to sanitize the name as Brown's Creek (nearby Sheba's Tits Mountain and Mount Ginger Goodwin also offend the government's decorum and political proprieties). Brown prospected—packing his supplies over his shoulder in a potato sack—into his late eighties, when a broken kneecap restricted his expeditions, and was over ninety when he died in the 1960s. Islanders remember his long loping stride, slow deliberate diction, quick temper and aristocratic manner. Once he met another prospecting party high in the Little Oyster River watershed, Piggy Brown recalled. The prospectors invited him to have a drink. John eyed their whisky bottle and portable radio, and nodded slowly. "My, you boys do travel in style. I do believe I will."

Italians made up one of Cumberland's biggest ethnic groups, and were soon a major presence in the mines and the business community. A few came from Southern Italy, many more from Northern Italy and Italian-speaking parts of the Austro-Hungarian Empire. Joe Franceschini's family arrived in stages; his uncle came to work on the Fraser River road in 1901 and later returned to Lombardy, his father arrived in 1920 and stayed, joined by his mother in 1930. Other families arrived en masse, all the men and boys seeking work in the mines. The community was close-knit, like most immigrant communities, for self-help and support in a new land. At the turn of the century they formed the Mutual Relief Society Felice Cavallotti. Members had to be of Italian ancestry. Their dollar-a-month in dues paid them a dollar a day in benefits—the going rate for a day's room and board—for sickness or injury. In the early years, Italians clustered in the far western end of Union Camp, nearly as far down as Chinatown. The Felice Cavallotti hall was there, too, surrounded by its members. Two of its first-generation members were still active when the dwindling society disbanded in 1974, having served its purpose for seventy years.

Italian musicians quickly formed into a popular concert and marching band. The West Cumberland Band played at picnics, parties, parades and other gatherings. They played at the train station for Lance-Corporal Robert Rushford's 1915 war-hero homecoming, and they led the 1918 parade for Ginger Goodwin's funeral. Miners said only two kinds of men got a good deal from the company, fine musicians and star soccer players. Not everyone applauded this system.

"My dad worked in the timber yard at Number Four with two others," Jim Weir told me. "They loaded all the timber that went down the mine. They had about four football players added who were supposed to help them, but in weather like this they would be out at the lake—it wasn't too far from Number Four out to the lake, and they'd be out at the lake laying around in the sunshine. My dad and the other two did all the work."

The Italian bandsmen, like the soccer players, were company favourites as long as they didn't rock the boat. Knowing the Italians' importance to the union's success, in 1911 the UMWA sent an Italian-speaking organizer to make matters clear to all. Italian mine workers, despite company threats of deportation, became some of Cumberland's staunchest supporters of the union.

Other immigrants passed through Cumberland and the mines—
Slavs, Finns, Russians, Germans—but most were working-class British. Their regional dialects bespoke poverty and disadvantage: broad
Yorkshire and Lancashire, lilting southern "valleys" Welsh, Scots
lowland burr. But they spoke some approximation of the King's
English, which made it easier to climb to shiftboss or pitboss. Some
climbed out of the mines altogether to wrestle with a merchant's
starched white collar every morning instead of gritty pit clothes.

In the early years the ethnic communities mixed little, but also
experienced little friction. There were occasional outbursts. In one
case European discrimination provoked a scuffle between Japanese
and Chinese workers. Hostility to blacks peaked when some stayed
on the job during the Big Strike. And a Chinese man's temper finally
snapped at rock-throwing and name-calling white youths in 1911. He
shot and fatally wounded a boy, then rode the Chinese community's
"underground railway" to Port Alberni and Vancouver, never to be
found or charged.

Photos showing a single ethnic group, perhaps carefully posed and
smiling at a picnic, give a falsely benign impression. Any mixed-race
photo—Japanese and Chinese workers standing in the background,
always, European workers sitting in the foreground—sharply points
out the discrimination. In 1910 Cumberland people sought to keep
children from outside Cumberland city limits—mainly Chinese, Japanese, Italian, and other non-English speaking children—out of their
school, ostensibly to lower their school taxes. Their attempt at
segregation failed. For the next half-century, students from these
ethnic groups often led their classmates in sport and academic prowess. Cumberland was a small and blinkered society, but it was no more
racist than other places. In fact, its exuberant ethnic mix worked like
yeast, leavening the age-old weight of bigotry. Scots learned Italians
were industrious and family-loving; Slavs learned the English admira-
tion for fair play; Irish learned the intricacies of Chinese gambling.
Chinese and Japanese and blacks, however, mainly relearned the
timeworn lessons of discrimination and survival.

Men and women could sometimes reach across the barriers of race,
religion and class when they found common cause. Sports, annual
miners' picnics and Christmas socials brought people together in a
convivial atmosphere. Mine disasters, fires and other community
crises evoked extraordinary outpourings of generosity and co-operation. So did strikes.

"Cumberland was always a great-hearted town," said retired dairy
farmer Roy Genge. Born in 1921, he grew up in the farming district

of Minto or Happy Valley, halfway between Royston and Cumberland, but learned the town inside-out by delivering milk twice a day.

His onetime teacher at Minto School, Margaret Eggar, agreed. "They were a very well organized and generous, kind-hearted community. They liked to pull their weight and feel that as a city they were doing what a city should do."

"As they always say, once you've got a friend in Cumberland, you've always got a friend," Piggy Brown reminded me of the local proverb.

A fierce clannishness that survives today, like so many early Cumberland ways, was the flip side of this community spirit. Margaret Eggar, a Minto farm girl, discovered this in her teens. "At one time Courtenay and Cumberland were rivals, who had the better football team—they hated one another, even the schools. I know when I moved to Cumberland High School from Courtenay, I wasn't accepted there for about two years."

This Cumberland exclusivity could embrace outlying communities on occasion. A few people still know the words to *Are You From Bevan?*, a song which carries memories of the island's bitter 1912–14 coal strike:

> If you're from Union Bay or Courtenay or Cumberland,
> Anywhere below that Bevan second dam,
> If you're from Bevan, I said from Bevan,
> Well, I'm from Bevan, too!

Minto wasn't on the list, maybe because it wouldn't rhyme with much besides pinto. But it had its own eccentrics and a well-developed tradition of practical jokes. Silos sprouted red flags and milk cans, outhouses tipped with or without occupants, and livestock wandered, especially on Halloween.

"One farmer had left his wagon on the road outside his barn with a load of hay in it," Mrs. Eggar remembers. "Ted and Harry . . . decided to be horses and they pulled this wagon about a quarter of a mile down the road. By the time they got it down to the next farm they were tired, and they stopped to rest. Then all of a sudden something popped up from the middle of the hay, and it was the old gentleman that owned the wagon. He said, 'Now boys, you've run it this far, now run and take it back again.' He had a big whip in his hand. He had hidden in the hay, you see, anticipating something like this."

Character and characters made early Cumberland. Nicknames are a longstanding local tradition. No one knows quite why; it could be a legacy of coal miners from South Wales, where nicknames are a pastime and a passion. Cumberland nicknames could even be passed from generation to generation, and they have formidable staying power. Jimmy Brown said he gave up introducing himself by name at reunions; old acquaintances didn't know him until he used his nickname of Piggy. Mayor William Moncrief has said even his mother called him Bronco.

"Everybody goes by nicknames in this town," Karl Coe told me. "You hardly hear anybody's right name around here. They take it to the grave with them, when they get one."

Even the merchants, far from being stuffy and dull, were a gallery of nicknamed rogues and saints. Shorty Perodi—his given name was soon forgotten—was the tough little Southern Italian who ran one of the poolrooms. The town constable turned a blind eye to his back room gambling and unofficial trade in alcoholic beverages as long as things stayed quiet.

The Campbells of Campbell Brothers store—brothers Red (Alex), Black (William) and Dan, and their shy sister Mary—were said to be Quakers, although the Victoria and Vancouver meetings of the Religious Society of Friends made no mention of them in early records. Perhaps their way of life created the rumour. Their thoughtfulness was legendary. "Whenever anybody said there was somebody hungry, they always sent an order down," Piggy Brown said. "My dad brought a monkey home one day, and God, [Red] was sending coconuts down every week. They were so kind."

Strong socialists, during the Big Strike they gave strikers credit and shelter almost to their own ruin. The Campbells were also to demonstrate conscience and compassion worthy of the Quakers when they aided young men evading military service in July 1918.

Edward W. Bickle, the miner who became a notary and city clerk, in 1912 joined the weekly *Cumberland Islander* and eventually bought it. The paper still publishes today as the *Comox District Free Press*, though the Bickle family sold to a newspaper chain in 1989. The opposition *Cumberland News* reported on 13 December 1911 that one Edward Bickle (whether E.W. or his son Edward is not clear) was charged with drunk and disorderly behaviour and breaking windows, and was under prohibition from being served liquor. E.W. Bickle, undaunted, less than a month later ran for school trustee. Stories about Bickle and his brother Tom—a bossy-man or contractor of Chinese workers to the mines—are plentiful, possibly apocryphal and usually outrageous. Miners long resented the *Islander* as a pro-company, anti-union paper, and thoroughly begrudged Bickle his financial opportunism and success. Their attitude embodied an irony, since early trade unionists generally believed workers should own the means of producing wealth. This was exactly Bickle's self-help strategy, after all, perhaps with rather more emphasis on self than on help.

But most of Cumberland's character and characters were inextricably linked with the coal mines. Miners, mine work, mine accidents, mine unions, miners' nicknames, miners' picnics — Cumberland and Union from the earliest days to the present have revolved around mining. The coal dust still hasn't quite settled.

Down pit

"I heard a Blue Funnel captain saying down at Union Bay once that he would steam halfway around the world to fill his bunkers with Comox coal," said Tom Mumford. "That was the reputation that coal had, it was supposed to be the best steam coal."

Coal was not only Cumberland's reason for existing but Vancouver Island's first major industry. Retired newspaperman Torchy (H.H.C.) Anderson of Saltspring Island told me that Kwagiut Indians showed coal to one of his ancestors, a Hudsons Bay Company factor, at Fort Rupert near Port Hardy during the 1820s. The HBC began mining the area in 1847, but soon abandoned it for a richer opportunity. In 1849 Chewechikan, a S'nenymos Indian, led Hudsons Bay Company officers to accessible, high quality coal deposits near Nanaimo. This act gave Chewechikan the title of Coal Tyee (chief), arguably the only benefit to him or his people; settlers and industry steadily encroached on S'nenymos tribal lands. Nanaimo mining began in 1852 with miners brought from England and Scotland, and continued for more than a century. By 1910 Nanaimo was a prosperous — and relatively stable and orderly — city with a population of predominantly British origin. Outlying communities such as Wellington, Ladysmith and Extension went through a roistering coal-camp phase en route to a staid maturity. Miners there had their sights fixed on a security and dignity which often eluded working people in the "old country." Such stability lay far in the future for Cumberland.

Cumberland's mines governed the town's life. Number Six pithead stood at the centre of town a block from the fire station and city hall, Number Five lay only about a mile's walk northwest, and the mine train took only minutes to reach Number Four at Comox Lake. Number Seven operated at Bevan about three miles away. The small Number One, Two and Three mines were defunct, and short-lived Number Eight was still on the drawing board.

When the whistle blew, mine workers streamed toward the Cumberland pits. Married men, sons at home and lucky boarders carried galvanized dinner pails. Men who batched in shanties or rented rooms shoved their dinners in their pockets, twisted in oiled paper if they were too fastidious to accept pocket lint in their cheese butties. No one carried smokes; taking matches into a mine was a firing offence. Some favoured chewing tobacco, which didn't call for a match. Tobacco gobs were far from the worst thing encountered underfoot in a coal mine. Smokers ditched their makings somewhere outside the portal, to be reclaimed after shift.

Boys usually started colliery work on the surface, picking or sorting coal as it travelled past them on a screen conveyor belt, and injured or older men ended their working days there. Coal was graded and sold by lump size, and the pickers separated lump coal from nut coal from pea coal. Compared to hewing coal all day in a low seam, it was easy work. Compared to today's largely mechanized labour jobs, it was gruelling. Tending the pit ponies or mules was often the next job for young mine workers.

Trapper, rope rider, tunneller, timberman, mule driver and coal digger were some of the specialized jobs in a mine (detailed descriptions of mine work enliven Lynne Bowen's books *Three Dollar Dreams* and *Boss Whistle,* and retired miner Bill Johnstone's book *Coal Dust In My Blood*). Coal digging—Joe Naylor's and Arthur Boothman's livelihood in Cumberland—was the most highly skilled work, wielding pick and shovel to load cars at the coal face. In many mines coal diggers worked on contract, paid by the ton for the coal they loaded. Only a strong, deft and tireless man could make a living this way. A lad whose father or brother was a coal miner might go backhand for him, working as his assistant and student. Not every mine worker aspired to be a miner. Some were content working on day wages as labourers or timbermen or mule drivers. Many spent their working lives in an environment they hated and feared.

"It wasn't a thrill to me, because every little squeak of a timber, they were caving in on me," Jim Weir said. "I always say it was the conditions that formed the union. The men wouldn't have so anxious to join a union if the conditions had been better."

"Mining? Today I would never walk into a mine if I . . . but in them days there was nothing else to do," Chuna Tobacco told an interviewer. "If you had friends that started work in the mines and when you met them downtown they all had money in their pocket, and you had ten cents, what would you do? You would go to where the money was, and there was nothing else but the mines or the logging camps."

Wink English told me, "It was a rotten system, boy. I got fired for no reason at all. I got fired dead off a job I wasn't even on it. Yeah, and then those others guys were walking around the mine . . . them guys walking around doing nothing . . . the buggers never did five minutes' work in a day. They were cousins and uncles and all kinds of relations."

Women never worked in the early Vancouver Island mines. In Britain until the 1840s women crawled through the dark on hands and knees, harnessed to haul coal cars, while their small children worked as trappers, opening and closing the canvas doors between mine sections. Their tendency to fall asleep in ditches after sixteen-hour shifts, their frequent illness or death, their malnourishment and alcoholism, irritated the coal masters. Humanitarians were pleased to see women and children finally banished from coal workings, although some mine workers regretted the resulting loss of family income. Miners, deeply conservative in many ways, had long memories. When a guest party including a woman went down pit in the Nanaimo mines, my grandfather said, the warning would echo down the shaft and along the drifts: "Woman in the mine!"

Some men liked the work and got ahead in life, especially if the bosses took a liking to them.

One mine manager "switched me around with a lot of different men," Ben Horbury said. "I was backhanding. If you were willing to learn, and able to learn, you got all the experiences from all these different miners. That way I was a little bit ahead, and I was younger. There was only about four or five young fellows that actually went to the face when they were young. I got my miner's certificate through [Charlie] Parnham. He sent me in for it."

Mules, ponies and a few horses — even years after mine locomotives were available — hauled coal cars along trackage in many mines. Mules were smart and sturdy, and ponies were small enough to enter low workings. Some miners claimed mules fared better than humans. Mine owners found mules harder to train and costlier to replace than men.

Only a few old-timers now recall the pleasures and purgatories of mule-driving, Ginger Goodwin's occupation in at least one pit.

Bill Marshall first worked in Number Five switching empty cars.

"Then I got a job doing what they call skinning mules, and that's the worst job that ever was invented, I think. Some of those mules would try to kick your head off."

The top levels of Number Four suffered constant seepage from nearby Comox Lake. Jim Weir drove a mule there, putting coal cars into three or four working places. Sections of the travelling roads were so low the spaces between ties had to be dug out so the mules could get through, and these holes filled with water. When the mules' hooves slipped off the ties, a great shower of water would drench the driver.

"If you got an ornery mule, you were in trouble. I never saw any biting, but kick! And kick they would, too," Weir said. Some mules refused to stop; others would get into a tight spot and refuse to start, like one mare he drove. "I couldn't get past the car. There was no room, it was too tight. There she was standing there, and me cursing and swearing trying to get her going. She'd take time, she'd stop for a little while, then she'd make up her mind and away she'd go. She knew I couldn't get at her."

"Sometimes it was nice, if you got a good mule. Most of the mules knew as much as the driver did, once they got onto the system of how they changed the cars. They'd run the load down and then they'd pull the empty up," Weir said. "You'd block the empty and unhook the mule from the front, and he'd climb back down past the car. Then you'd push the car up close to the face where the miner could work on it," loading it with coal.

Pithead photos of mule drivers often show them with formidable whips coiled several times over one shoulder and under the other arm. But Weir said stories about whips were exaggerated. Good drivers didn't need whips. "There was one or two that had whips, but very few. You didn't need a whip. The mule knew what to do, and they went and did it. Sure."

Several people told me mine haulage animals were well treated, even pampered, on shift and in their underground stables. No doubt many were well treated. Others were less fortunate.

"Things I could tell you about animals you would never believe," Chuna Tobacco said. "Horses with broken legs, and the scars, and no skin on them. They would be working in places and they would be maybe six foot high, and then the roof would keep squeezing, coming down, coming down, and then the first thing you know their hind and backs and heads was rubbing, all the skin coming off. They never stopped them horses from working."

"Today I would never do what I did in them days to hang onto a job," Tobacco said. "I would never treat an animal like I did in them days. We had no option. We had to do it or we didn't work. That animal you'd got down there had to pull that coal out of the mine. If you couldn't make him pull somebody else would."

Danger was never far away in the mines. Sometimes haulage ropes would break, sending fifteen or twenty cars hurtling back down a slope. "They'd pile up and they'd cause a cave-in that would take maybe a day, maybe four hours, maybe twenty hours to get cleaned up. It would be just the same when the wall caved in, men would be hurt or trapped underneath a fall of rock—not timbered, not done right, not done properly—their timber wasn't big enough or not strong enough. It would collapse and the whole thing would come down and fall on top of them and kill them or maim them."

"It was more carelessness than anything else that would cause a mine disaster," said Jim Weir, who tried every mine job before joining management. "You knew there was gas there so you didn't take any chances."

He did survive one explosion when he was installing machinery in wet, gassy Number Five. The fireboss was on a lower level firing shots (controlled detonations to loosen coal from the working face) so miners on the next shift could start loading. Smoke started to rise through the ventilation system. "Usually it came up and went, until he fired another shot. This time it came, and it started to keep coming. We looked down the wall and we could see this gas exploding from underneath the coal, shooting out in a flame. So it was time we got out of there, and we got out of there."

And he saw the aftermath of other explosions. "I saw the results of it, the men bringing the dead men, the bodies, out. One of the bodies they brought out was a Chinaman, all he had on was a pair of shoes. It just blew the clothes right off him."

Ben Horbury's father quit one mine because of the hazard. "It was so bad in Number Six with firedamp and blackdamp—they were working with open lamps, the old teapot [a lamp mounted on a soft cap] and fish oil—he had to go into his place packing his lamp halfway. If you put it down, it went out in the blackdamp, and if you put it up, well, you had a fire going. Flash fires."

An uncle who was "cross-shifting," working a different shift in the same mine, decided he couldn't take any more. "His brother says, I'm finished. I'm not going down there again. The tools are down there. If you want them, you can go down and get them. You know, they bought their own tools then. My father went down and got them. Of course he was finished. They went to Number Four. About two weeks after, she blew."

"Years ago I don't think human life meant very much. I can remember my dad coming home and saying that he wondered who was going to get it, because the ceiling was so low, and it was tough. I think all miners were [worried] when they worked in the mine," Mary Fedichin told me. "Naturally, when the town depends on the mines, all the men worked in the mines. So it was, 'We were lucky this time, will we be lucky next time?'"

British Columbia's department of mines knew of the perils. Local historian and retired schoolteacher Margaret Eggar researched in the provincial archives, often rising before dawn for a four-hour bus trip to Victoria, an afternoon's study of musty documents, and another four-hour ride home. Her findings were disturbing. "The inspector of mines would recommend that certain things should be done, but they weren't always done. And then sometimes the inspector was only allowed to see a certain part of the mines when he came to inspect."

Another more insidious hazard was getting and keeping a job under bosses who could fire without notice or cause. Piggy Brown said men evolved their own solutions: gifts of liquor, cigarettes or cold cash. "In those days there was lots of hanky panky. When pay day come, some of the bosses — they'd hire a guy and give him a job — well, he'd leave money in hidey places, you know, kickbacks."

A 1912 letter from Cumberland illuminates the workers' frustrations and fears. The eloquence is unpolished but impassioned. Perhaps Ginger Goodwin, who drove a mule in at least one mine, or a friend wrote to the *United Mine Workers Journal* under the pseudonym "A Driver in the Mud Hole":

> I just send you a few of the facts regarding the conditions in this, one of the camps which is a part of Vancouver Island. Well, I might as well say that the conditions of the mines are rotten. There are four mines and one they are sinking will be five someday. The first one which I will write about is No. 4, a slope over one and a half miles down. This mine is very poorly ventilated, according to the gas that accumulates. The return airways in some parts is unfit to travel in on account of standing water, which it is impossible to get through without gumboots. The company, on several occasions, has been notified concerning the ventilation, but could not see their way clear to improve it in any way for fear of the expense, although they may have been told by the inspector of mines that if there was no improvement made soon and a certain amount of air travelling that

it would have to be closed down. It can easily be understood what is the condition of this mine when it had to be stopped for over a week till safety lamps were put in.

Another thing you never hear about or seen in this particular mine, although there is an accumulation of dust all over it, is the sprinkling of the roads. The only time that there is any water put on it is when there is a fire, which, I might say, has happened lately in this particular mine. The next is No. 6 mine, which is connected with No. 5, both being shafts. This mine in itself is a little better than the last, with the same failing regarding the sprinkling, and I am very much in doubt whether there is a sufficient number of man-holes or not or travelling roads along the different inclines. No. 5 in itself is what you would call a mud hole from leaving the cage until you land at your working place.

This mine I may say is the training quarters for drivers. Without fear of being contradicted, there have been more drivers in this mine since it was a mine, or mud hole, than all the mines on this island put together. This is the condition the drivers have to work under from month end to month end for the paltry sum of $2.85 a day the price for the use of his power. The next mine, No. 7, is a slope which is about as bad as No. 5 for water, and I see that the report of the chief inspector of mines was that it was in a very unsanitary condition. I think all miners know what that means.

These are a few of the conditions the miners have to work under. In the first place, you receive 60 cents per ton for coal, only have to produce about 2,700 pounds of coal before you receive your 60 cents for 1 ton of coal. To produce this coal it is all got through shooting off the solid and in turn you have to pay 15 cents for every stick of powder to shoot it with, where the company only pays six cents. It's a regular thing for a miner to have $50 or $60 for powder alone in one month. In all these mines a miner is troubled with a certain quantity of rock, which you have to shoot with your coal, varying from one foot to three feet, and some parts more. You get a little remuneration for picking this rock in the way or yardage which in turn varies from $1.50 to $3, and then at all times, unless the miner is a sucker, is liable to be cut at the month end say 25 or 50 cents per yard. Unless it is a good shooting place, where you don't use much powder, you don't get as much for your yardage as will pay your expenses.

When a miner starts in these mines to dig coal he has to work till measuring day before he knows what he is going to get as yardage; that is, after he starts to work, the rock in his place gets thicker and might continue to do so for three weeks out of the month before it becomes better. You think or have an idea that the bosses might be a little generous and give you a little more yardage according to the thickness of this rock which you have worked through for the preceding three weeks. But no, nothing doing. You get as much as your fellow workman in the next place, who, I might say, has loaded two or three cars a shift more, as he had not the same amount of rock to handle. If your place is wet and the other fellow's is dry, it is just the same. If your place is bad to shoot and you use twice the powder as the other fellow, it is just the same. You get what you make, which in lots of cases comes to about $2 to $2.50 a day. There is a minimum wage of $3.30 for a few who get a stand in with the bosses, or a man that comes from the face to drive, but without there is nothing doing.

Here is the way they have robbed us for years: At No. 7 mine they were using a car on which the men were getting from 14 to 17 hundredweight. The same cars were sent to No. 5 and the men got from 20 to 25 hundredweight and some as much as 29 hundredweight on the cars, and the cars that they were using in No. 5 then went to No. 6. Where the men were getting from 16 to 18 hundredweight in No. 5 for these cars, they got from 14 to 16 hundredweight in No. 6 mine, a matter of 2 hundredweight difference in the cars. In No. 4 and No. 7 they have put in new cars, which are bigger in height, length and breadth, and still the men are not getting as much weight as they did before. The machines they have for weighing coal are, I think, one of the latest patents that were put on the market 100 years ago.

These are a few of the conditions which drivers and miners are working under here. There is lots more I will write about at some future date. Taking all these things into consideration, I think you will agree with me in saying that we should in the near future go in for recognition as we have no agreement of any kind. I think if the men were putting their heads together and studying the powder ques-

tion they would find the company reaping the benefit of
$10,000 profit per month.

They are also selling their coal in San Francisco at $12.50
per ton, and I also see where Mr. Clapp, the geological
surveyor for British Columbia, says that the coal in Comox
district can easily be mined at $3.50 per ton, leaving a
balance of $9 per ton, for which the miner receives 60 cents
for 2,700 pounds.

That there be no misunderstanding in any way, I would
like to say that the coal in Nos. 5 and 6 mines is practically
the same and that the men have no checkweighman. So you
will see what some of the good company weighmen that
were never in a coal mine in their lives, don't even know the
weight of a shovel or a pick, would not even know how to
make a charge of powder up, and these are the nincompoops, good looking idiots and know nothings that we
have to buck against and be barefacedly robbed by . . .

The *Journal*'s editor noted that he'd run the letter under a nom de
plume to allow the writer, working in a non-union mine, to "spread
the healthy discontent that will lead to organization."

Cumberland lacked union recognition, but unions were much on
men's minds.

Vancouver Island miners — as an inevitable response to dangerous
and oppressive working conditions, and a natural evolution from
informal mutual aid societies — began organizing workers' associations such as the 1890 Miners' and Mine Labourers' Protective Association. Mine owners like coal baron Robert Dunsmuir opposed
every move by the infant organizations with threats, firings, evictions
and blacklists. When these tactics failed, owners hired private police
forces or called on the new province's obliging government for artillery and troops. But if government and capital attempted a colonial
version of feudalism, workers countered with the revolutionary ideas
that had reshaped mid-nineteenth-century Europe.

British Columbia, with many organized workers arriving direct
from Britain and the United States, was much more radical than
Eastern Canada. In 1898 Nanaimo elected British Columbia's first
socialist Member of Provincial Parliament (MPP), a mine worker. The
first miners' associations and the first strikes failed miserably, until
island miners organized in 1902 under the militant American-based
Western Federation of Miners (WFM). The WFM under the legendary
Big Bill Haywood encouraged not only direct action such as strikes,

but armed defence against company and government abuses. A WFM convention in British Columbia resolved, in part:

> . . . capitalism can never be dethroned and wage slavery abolished until the natural resources of the earth and the machinery of production and distribution shall be taken from the hands of the few by the political power of the many, to become the collective property of all mankind, to be utilized for the use and benefit of all humanity. . .

From its birth the WFM saw socialism as the only political means of securing this redistribution of wealth and resources, and eventually endorsed the Socialist Party of Canada. Exploitation of both picket line and ballot box characterized the emerging generation of British Columbia radical labour socialists. Among the most active and outspoken, even in 1903, were coal miners in Union and Cumberland.

A WFM coal strike collapsed that year. The subsequent royal commission into British Columbia labour problems—its secretary was federal deputy labour minister William Lyon Mackenzie King—decided that the WFM was a political organization, not a legitimate union, and that recent strikes were a socialist conspiracy. Despite the strike's failure, island miners were getting used to organizing and taking direct action. In a pinched labour market flooded by new immigrants, with petroleum steadily threatening coal markets and prices, island miners organized again. This time they didn't raise the banner of the ultra-radical WFM. In 1911 Cumberland and Extension mine workers invited a powerful international union, the United Mine Workers of America, to undertake an organizing drive; Vancouver Island became the union's District 28. One of Cumberland Local 2299's members, soon one of its leaders, was a tall burly coal digger with light blue eyes and dark hair.

Joe Naylor was thirty-seven in 1909 when he arrived in Cumberland via the West Kootenays hardrock mines where, Mrs. Eggar's uncle told her, he'd organized for the WFM. Born in Wigan, he spent his boyhood and young manhood in the Lancashire coal pits. Naylor was self-educated—Cumberland people still remember that he read two newspapers a day, the *Vancouver Sun* and *Seattle Times,* plus Tolstoi's works and various labour and political publications—and his knowledge ranged across the spectrum. A radical labour socialist to the bone, he was also a resolute pacifist. In 1912 he and two other men wrote a letter to the *Cumberland Islander* and the *Western Clarion* on behalf of the UMWA and Socialist Party of Canada, opposing the formation of a Cumberland Boy Scouts troop. They said boys could be expected to kill their own mothers or fathers at the order of a superior officer, as in the army.

> It is quite obvious that the boy scouts movement is only another way of using one portion of the working classes to keep the other portion in subjection. To order a man to go to war, whether with the workers of another country or with the workers of his own country, as in a strike, is like ordering him to take a gun, load it, dig his own grave, crawl into it and shoot himself. Bayonets are made by the working class, nicely polished by the working class, and then patriotically thrust into the working class for the capitalist class.

Joe was a Cumberland character by any criteria. Friends and colleagues referred to his blunt and forthright speaking style, and called him a rough diamond. He favoured natural foods, ate stew for breakfast like many workers who'd spent years on night shift, and consumed impressive amounts of whole wheat bread and beer from John Marocchi's store.

"We had the only bakery around," Elsie Marocchi told interviewers in 1987. "Joe Naylor wanted a special bread made for him. So it was made for him once a week and it was steamed, not baked."

"Joe Naylor, if he saw a fly in the house he'd never go after it or kill it," Karl Coe told me. "He'd let spiders go, and you could see spider webs in every corner of the window, anywhere you looked in that shack there was a spider web, and he would never touch it. I said, 'Joe, let's clean up around here,' one day when I went out to meet him, 'let's get these spider webs.' 'Like hell,' he says, 'they kill the bloody flies. Leave them spiders alone.'"

Naylor is still revered in Cumberland for his tireless day-by-day work to better people's lives, not just through union and political organizing but through educating them five minutes at a time from his porch steps, carrying their groceries, singing them a ditty or slipping them a dollar. Seventy-odd years later, the only negative comment I heard about Naylor was that in the 1920s he relentlessly pushed mule drivers to deliver more empty coal cars to his working place. More cars meant more coal loaded, more money earned. Why did he need the money, a coal digger then batching alone at Comox Lake? It seems he'd reached into his own pocket to buy a house for a woman left homeless by her husband's death—she was his only love and finally declined to marry him, but that's another story—and he was paying her mortgage.

"Many a time when I'd be sitting out there with Joe he'd get me to talk," Karl Coe said. "We'd get to arguing about it, and he'd say something about, 'What would you do if the company did this, took over this?' And I'd give him my impression and raise hell about the company and all this, call them this and call them that. And he'd say, 'That's not right. You've got class hatred. You shouldn't have that if you want to be unionized. You've got to have class consciousness.'"

"He did try to tell us. He'd talk to anybody like that about conditions and policies and what not." As a young man Coe didn't pay much attention. "He described the moon and the sun to me one time. He was calling them stable mobility and mobile stability. He knew all that kind of stuff. But Christ, it was too deep for me."

"He was very strong on the red side," Roy Genge told me. "I don't like to call people reds, but he was. . . a hot one. A real hot one."

Did Joe Naylor truly want a revolution? I asked, and Roy laughed. "You'd think so the way he talked. But there's no use answering what you just think, because it's not always true, is it?"

The 1912 letter about the Boy Scouts stated Joe's beliefs clearly enough.

> . . . there are no foreigners in the working class, the only foreigner to our class is the capitalist class. . . . we have nothing in common with the capitalist class, who by virtue of their ownership of the means of life hold the working class in slavery. . . . our ultimate aim is to bring about a state of society where universal peace and brotherhood will reign. . . . this end can only be accomplished by the complete overthrow of the present form of society. . .

His egalitarian acceptance of "foreigners" stumbled when they deserted the labour ranks. Within a year of the letter, Chinese mine workers intimidated with threats of deportation became targets for racist slurs, although he claimed he objected to Chinese strikebreakers only, not all Chinese. Yet for his era he was a model of racial tolerance.

Joe liked children, and always had a song or joke for them. Josephine Bryden told an interviewer, "I remember rowing Joe Naylor around the lake as a little girl, and I came home singing, 'We'll keep the red flag flying.' I heard my father say to my mother, 'Do you hear what that child's singing?' And my mother said, 'That's Joe Naylor.'"

"Joe was a great guy, too," Jimmy Ellis said. "He was a great socialist, and he was a great man, a good talker, a great organizer, and a man who knew what he was talking about."

Naylor was one of many working men and women who strove lifelong to "bring to birth a new world from the ashes of the old." He would be quick to deride any special claims that smacked of the cult of personality. Naylor organized, picketed, educated any who would listen, counselled friends to acts which the government found seditious, served prison time for his beliefs. So did many others. But Naylor had more effect.

"To me he was just as good an organizer as Ginger was. It's just because Ginger was shot they made a martyr of him. There was so much fuss about it, like causing that general strike in Vancouver for a day," Karl Coe said. "He did everything as good as Ginger."

Mobile stability and stable mobility, the words Karl remembered so long, suggest a planetary motion. Joe and Ginger: did one exert a gravitational pull, the other follow as a satellite? Or were they bound together, unlike on the surface but at the core like-minded, in the motion of binary stars? Across time's gulf we see the steady dark one keeping to shadow, the volatile bright one always passing into sunlight.

First we walked out . . .

Alex Rowan was Cumberland's fleet-footed pride. A distance runner, a marathoner especially, he worked evening shift in Number Four mine as a rope rider. His job was hooking loaded coal cars and unhooking empties to the steel cables that winched them up and down the main slope to the surface. His strenuous labour underground every day made his athletic eminence all the more remarkable; he trained daily on the roads and playing grounds of Cumberland.

One Saturday morning he trained for the Cumberland-to-Nanaimo relay race only three days away, then reported to the pithead for work. What occurred on his shift, at 9:15 p.m., was nothing exceptional for an island coal mine.

Alex jumped on a coal car and caught hold of the brake lever. It wasn't properly secured, and sprang back with enough force to knock him off the car. He lay stunned on the track while coal-laden steel cars crushed his right foot to bloody pulp and came close enough to his left foot to tear the heel from his boot. In Cumberland Hospital his right foot was amputated two inches above the ankle. He might walk again, with crutches or one of the crude prostheses a young working-man could afford, but the lad who lived to run would never run again.

Several Cumberland people told me of Alex Rowan, the brilliant runner, whose foot was crushed in the pit just before his great breakthrough race. So poignant and fresh was the tragedy in their memories that at first I believed this was an accident of the 1950s or the 1940s. It happened the evening of 9 July 1910.

Not much imagination is needed to fill in the rest of the story: slow painful healing, financial worries with no wages coming in, inevitable anger and anguish over a needless accident. But we have no need to exercise imagination; The *Cumberland Islander*, in tones of uneasy compassion, charted every harrowing step over the following weeks and months.

Alex's parents lived in Nanaimo. His mother reached Cumberland by steamer within a few days of his accident; his father arrived soon after, but could stay only briefly. Five weeks after the accident, the paper reported anxiously that Rowan was suffering from shock and despondency, brooding over his accident. Already it had stolen his livelihood and his life's great pleasure. Now his brother, in a nightmare coincidence, lost his own foot to blood poisoning and amputation after a logging accident.

The *Islander* mentioned Rowan in a bright, cheerful tone through the fall and winter, obviously fearful for his will to live. Visit Alex in the hospital. You can buy your tickets for a charity event from Alex. Still active in sports from the sidelines, Alex was soon promoting a professional boxing match (Cumberland produced avid fight fans, and several first-rate boxers). The paper later suggested this "hugging match" was fixed, with "a great deal of whispering between the contestants during their numerous embraces." Soon little more appeared. The *Islander* apparently decided that Alex, having recovered sufficiently to fix fights, needed no more sympathy.

Alex Rowan was left alone with his mutilation and his depression, like other injured mine workers, once the community had done its best to raise funds and console him for inconsolable loss. Left alone, such men and women could only steep in their own bitterness. Their grievances swept many into the strengthening labour movement. Anger and helplessness fused into a powerful resolve. Alex Rowan's next significant acts were as an officer of the miners' union.

The making of a union man, a union woman, in those years often sprang from personal suffering rather than from philosophical evolution. Certainly British Columbia had its intellectual white-collar socialists and labour supporters such as Vancouver lawyer Wallis Lefeaux, enthusiastically endorsed in the 1912 provincial election by Cumberland and the upcoast Finnish utopia of Sointula. But mainly workers made up the front lines of the labour movement. Many had stories like Alex Rowan's, perhaps not so heart-rending, but cathartic enough to spur them into an all-consuming and often perilous activism. Their stories served as personal creation myths.

Joe Naylor's revelation came on an English turnpike in the 1880s. Years later he told the story to Donetta Rallison. When Joe was a young pit lad, made jobless by his Lancashire mine's closure, he and his friends travelled from one dreary coal town to the next seeking work. One day as they walked hungry and sore-footed, a richly appointed carriage came alongside. The driver reined his splendid team in a spray of mud. A coachman opened the door, and an elegant gentleman leaned out to wish them good day. One or two of the young men doffed their hats and bowed, but plainspoken Joe Naylor told his friends they were fools. Why should starving men bow and scrape to this popinjay? If he truly meant well, he would work to right the country's wrongs, since he was England's king. The door slammed and the coach skewed forward. The pit lads walked on, a little colder and hungrier. This meeting with the king on the king's highway helped to shape Joe Naylor's philosophy.

Ginger Goodwin's own creation myth speaks from shadow, understood only in its essential passion and compassion. He left no written blueprint of any one experience that transformed him into a powerful organizer, but we may have an anonymous clue. Was he "Yours In The Struggle" who wrote to the *United Mine Workers Journal* in July 1913? The correspondent claimed that he had been forced to leave England by economic conditions. "Since the industrialization of Great Britain our bravery has gradually been forced into cowardice and submissiveness. . ." But Goodwin, ultimately to his destruction, was neither cowardly nor submissive.

Or Nova Scotia's devastating UMWA strike may have been his personal ordeal, the trial by fire that tempered him. The Cape Breton mines drove out his friends and travelling companions, scattering them across the Alberta coal fields and British Columbia. They arrived together in Cumberland: the Weirs, the Walkers, the Pattersons, the Boothmans, many others. Economic conditions possibly forced them from Britain; economic conditions intensified by blacklists and company discrimination certainly forced them from Nova Scotia. Some friends he left behind. Eight years later, the British Columbia Federation of Labour received queries and protests over his death from Cape Breton Island.

Acquaintances later remembered what Goodwin told meetings as an organizer—of his own experiences as a worker, a slave as he sometimes called himself, trying to survive the owners' crushing injustices—but maddeningly they failed to recall his examples. Did he speak of going to work for a colliery at fifteen, scarcely out of childhood, as a trapper or rope rider or his dad's backhand? Did he describe the dust and clammy damp and gas underground, the mean bunkhouses and boarding houses, that made lung disease endemic among mine workers? Paradoxically, he never told good friends in

Cumberland even his birthplace. The death certificate issued by BC's vital statistics division to this day remains incorrect and incomplete, like the story of his emergence as an ardent trade unionist.

By 1910 Cumberland's mine workers were angry and frightened enough to support a major unionization drive at any cost. Their fate hung in the balance thousands of miles away—in Toronto, in Germany, in San Francisco and Indiana and Oklahoma—and especially in a tropical rainforest where other workers sweated to clear a waterway that would revolutionize global patterns of trade and migration. All who played the international power game were watching the almost-completed Panama Canal.

Emigrants would pour into Western Canada, swamping the workplace with cheap labour and threatening both wages and jobs, predicted trade unionists including the United Mine Workers executive in Indianapolis. In a system without safeguards against summary dismissal, employers could and frequently did fire seasoned workers to take on younger, more easily intimidated workers at lower wages.

A member of the British Columbia legislature in 1911 wanted Ottawa to immediately create a Pacific fleet to protect Canadian shipping in light of the new canal and the "tense international situation." Germany could go to war to distract attention from its own internal unrest, he said, and BC's many inlets would provide ideal cover for German warships. This might sound far-fetched, as might Premier Richard McBride's belief that Japan and the USA would become German allies and bring submarines into Puget Sound to attack Victoria. These fears would soon appear not to be the product of late-night indigestion but of chilling intelligence reports about Baron Alvo von Alvensleben, president of a Nanaimo coal company, alleged spy for the Kaiser. And Germany, in 1913, said that indeed she would send warships to attend the opening of the Panama Canal.

Cumberland miners, scarcely aware of this vast tide of international power, stirred restlessly in its crosscurrents. Canadian Collieries under Dunsmuir management had lost its grip on the all-important San Francisco market for Vancouver Island coal, and petroleum wells in Oklahoma and a dozen other fields were providing quantities of a cheap, clean new fuel. "Slack time" was the norm in Cumberland's four working mines. Most miners worked a day or two a week in 1910, though some lower-paid Chinese miners worked daily. Job safety—in mines where four workers per thousand each year would die—was horrifying. Job security, threatened by favouritism and discrimination, was equally alarming. To top everything, the Cumberland mines had been sold by the Dunsmuirs who, appalling labour practices notwithstanding, were at least Vancouver Islanders. The mines now belonged to the Canadian Northern Railway promoters William Mackenzie and Donald Mann of Toronto.

In a June 1910 *Montreal Gazette* interview, company president William Mackenzie made an ominous claim "that the King's death was solely the cause of the failure of the public to subscribe for the Dunsmuir coal mine flotation." It was perhaps the first hint that the stock issue to raise funds for construction of the new transcontinental railway was under-subscribed and inflated in value. Mackenzie and Mann bought the Dunsmuir interests for $11 million, then released a stock issue for $25 million, according to Paul Phillips in *No Power Greater*; the strike covered the company's inability to pay dividends on this watered stock.

Cumberland miners and merchants, in a full-blown panic over the mines' future, tried to read every omen. The Bank of Commerce erected a prefabricated bank building—did this mean it intended to shut down within months? Mackenzie and Mann made extravagant claims: the Cumberland mines would double their output, increase their employees from 1,800 to 3,000, boost their monthly payroll to $100,000 and replace mules with mechanical haulage. The miners remained skeptical.

"You mule drivers, pushers, rope riders, drum-runners and punks of the City of Cumberland come along to the old ball grounds next Sunday," a July 1910 notice invited, ". . . so we can have a little talk among ourselves concerning the present system."

First responses were undecided. "No work was done in the mines on Monday afternoon or Tuesday, and for a while it was feared that a strike was brewing," the *Islander* reported. "Several meetings of the miners were held, but both the company and the men showed a disposition to view the situation from the other fellows viewpoint as well as their own." The mule drivers got their demand, the same pay as Ladysmith drivers, and went back to work. Ginger Goodwin, still raw from the brutal Nova Scotia strike, may have been one of these mule drivers.

All was not well, however. These protests were not aftershocks from the Mackenzie and Mann takeover, but first tremors of a cataclysmic upheaval.

Who was to defend the workers' interests? Small Canadian unions came and went with little effect; the militant Western Federation of Miners had been outlawed for its revolutionary socialism. Island miners in early 1911 invited organizers from the more powerful, but more moderate, United Mine Workers of America, and within a year were organized into both local unions and UMWA District 28. Secretary of the new district was A.H. Rowan.

Island miners' well-being, however, was not the only item on the UMWA agenda. Minutes of its international executive board show the union worried as early as 1910 that the unorganized island miners were in direct competition with the miners of UMWA District 10, Washington State. The board noted that islanders got higher wages than their USA neighbours, but suffered from docking for rock in their coal. They also paid the company more for their powder and dynamite. The UMW *Journal* letter from "A Driver in the Mud Hole" (page 47) complains of exactly these injustices.

Equally disturbing, an international board member soon suggested that island coal threatened coal dug in the eastern United States by more numerous UMWA miners. Frank Farrington wrote ". . . we will find this coal bidding for markets on the Atlantic seaboard as well as on the Pacific coast. This feature in itself would not be so bad if there could be an interchange of competition but that cannot be, for the reason that the much superior quality of this coal will always bar outside competition from its own zone."

Except during a strike. A strike long enough to allow United States–mined coal to capture Canadian markets, as a Nova Scotia newspaper warned a few years earlier. And who would benefit most from such a coup? United States consumers (especially industrialists who owned coal-fired plants and transportation systems), United States mine owners and United States coal miners who belonged to the UMWA.

Collusion between these interests stretched credibility, but one thing became increasingly clear. Island coal miners could conceivably benefit from labour action, but their welfare was not any other interest group's prime concern. At least one union miner, a friend of Ginger Goodwin's who also went through the strikes in Glace Bay and Cumberland, would soon bitterly accuse the UMWA of callous manipulation. The miners were expendable gamesmen on a global playing board.

Strike talk, buzzing up-island and down-island for a year or two, now reached Vancouver. The Coal Mines Regulation Act of British Columbia required that an employer make up a contract miner's wages, if he were working in a difficult area, to $3.30 a day. Only a few favourites received this. "This law is treated by the operators with contempt," the *British Columbia Federationist* said in a July 1912 story about overall island mine conditions. "If the miners go on strike to remedy these things they will be choked with quotations from law which is broken daily by the owners."

By August, UMWA meetings in Cumberland were drawing up to five hundred mine workers and sympathizers, and the district president was saying that although miners wanted a peaceable working agreement, if their demands were not met they would fight.

An article by Ginger Goodwin appeared in the *Western Clarion* August 10, 1912 under the heading "The Iron Heel," the title of a Jack London serial story popular at the time. The letter makes no direct mention of Cumberland working conditions or union plans; instead it is an earnest but unpolished socialist broadside addressed to "Mr. Workingman."

"Wherever you go you see the same revolt implanted into the workingmen, and as this thing is gradually increasing why soon things will have to come to a climax.

"If we study the condition of the workers it is only logical that this spirit of revolt is existing among them, for wherever we go we see the same miserable conditions and the same competition for jobs in order that they may live.

"Now, then, we know that all this misery is the outcome of someone's carelessness, and that someone is the capitalists, those who own the machinery of production. Now, as this class of parasites have been living on the blood of the working class, they are responsible for the conditions existing at the present time.

". . . this tool-owning class are the masters of the situation, for in order for you to gain access to the means of life you have to go to an employer and sell yourself. Now, as you go to the boss and say 'How are chances?' he will retort in this manner: 'Come around in a few days and I might have a vacancy.' He means by that you will have to wait until he can hire you and make a profit of you.

"In order to throw this system over we have got to organize as a class and fight them as class against class.

"And so I say we have got to back our forces against them, and our weapons are education, organization and agitation, and read and study up on the principles of Socialism, for it is necessary that you know when to strike and how to strike, and if we have not these weapons when the times comes we shall not be able to predict the outcome of the fight.

"All I know is this, that in every phase of society, whenever a change took place it was the outcome of force which determined the winning side, so what we want is to educate you to your power, Mr. Workingman, and when we realize it we have the power and the lever to overthrow the existing society."

Cumberland's union miners readied themselves to put theory into practice.

In this highly-charged atmosphere few were surprised when, on

September 15, 1912, the fledgling union miners of Local 2299 laid down their tools and left the Cumberland mines.

Their decision ignited one of Canada's longest, most expensive and most rancorous labour actions — identified by miners as a lockout and by owners as a walkout — still remembered as the Big Strike. It started in Cumberland, spread immediately to Ladysmith, and eventually affected the entire island coal field. Bombings, shootings, sickness, hunger, severed families and friendships, and violent military intervention would make front-page news for two years.

Mine safety and union recognition inspired the impromptu "holiday" to discuss working conditions. At Extension mine down-island, miner Oscar Mottishaw was a member of a union-endorsed and worker-funded committee which checked each working place before a shift for dangerous gases. When he reported gas, the company did not renew his contract. He went to Cumberland, but drove a mule in Number Four pit for only three days before the company had him dismissed. The event is still remembered in the song *Are You From Bevan?*:

> It was away back in nineteen and twelve
> our gas committee was put on the shelf.

Canadian Collieries wasted no time in declaring the holiday an illegal walkout. They ordered the men to remove their tools from the mine, and refused their workers re-entry.

Union organizers, working steadily for the last year to build membership and commitment, threw themselves into full gear. The UMWA sent Chinese organizer Mr. Wong and Italian-speaking Joe Angelo, knowing from hard experience in other strikes that a division in the ranks meant their downfall. The WFM a decade earlier had tried — and failed — to organize Chinese workers. The UMWA knew their importance to a strike effort. All had to stand together. Recognizing their importance was not the same as welcoming them with open arms; the *UMW Journal* printed blatantly anti-Chinese comments at the same time the union was trying to organize Chinese workers. The Canadian government tried to block its efforts by refusing entry to Chinese organizers from Wyoming; the UMWA eventually got Mr. Wong of Seattle into the country by posting a huge bond of five hundred dollars. In October the *Journal* reported, "he is doing good work." His work was immensely difficult, since the Chinese were extremely vulnerable under discriminatory Canadian law, but Chinese workers promised to maintain the strike as long as their UMWA brothers. Italians and other non-British immigrants were almost as defenceless as the Chinese. Everything would depend on the persuasiveness of Wong and Angelo, among other organizers.

Frank Farrington of Indianapolis, an international board member, was head organizer for Vancouver Island. Johnny Marocchi remembered him as a big handsome man, a smart dresser, who courted a local girl. In the *Journal* he had a chequered reputation; one correspondent in 1909 wrote, ungrammatically if emphatically, "Judging by the venomous manner in which Frank Farrington blusters and scolds... he must imagine that readers are unable to distinguish between noise and sound argument, wheat and chaff, right and wrong, and seems to think that if plenty of rocks are thrown someone is sure to get hurt. His offensive language, not to say that of the slums, I will unheed, being like the fellow kicked by a mule, ready to consider the nature of the animal who done the kicking." Yet the *Cumberland News* reported in November 1912, "He is a fine speaker, and gave some excellent advice, advising order and coolness during this strike."

Other organizers were better known locally. Joe Naylor was involved from the start, as chairman of the local union, organizing the strike effort and negotiating with city council. Today Cumberland folklore paints Ginger Goodwin as a prominent organizer; in truth he was relatively insignificant during this strike. Yet he certainly talked union — in the poolrooms, on the soccer field, in the roaring saloons, in the sanctuary of the socialist hall — and people listened.

"When he first came to notice in this area, in Cumberland, was when he first started working in the mines, and the raw deal the miners had at that time, you see, he started to try and organize the union, which was the IWW," Harold Banks said. In fact the UMWA had a nodding acquaintance but no formal ties with the Wobblies, then active in a Canadian Northern Railway strike on the Fraser River, and soon distanced itself from IWW militancy.

Canadian Collieries took action. At an October meeting, organizers announced that the company was suing union officials for inducing employees to break their individual contracts. The suit apparently went nowhere but, in addition to several international organizers, named a Cumberland who's who of the Big Strike: Joe Naylor, John McAllister, William Greaves, James Smith, Peter McNiven, Barney Farmer, Oscar Mottishaw, Robert White and Chas Walker. The list didn't include Ginger Goodwin, probably still an apprentice organizer.

Strikers were kept busy — though the incorrigible *Islander* tagged them all "idlers" — picketing and planning a round of social activities to keep spirits high and minds off disaster. They built a new football field—still used in Cumberland's city park—when the company denied them access to the Canadian Collieries playing field. At Christmas they held a children's party with presents for all. Dances, masquerades, meetings and lectures occupied many evenings. Ferocious Mother Jones, the UMWA's most formidable crowd-gatherer, in 1913 shared a Cumberland platform with local dignitaries and organizers; Johnny Marocchi remembered the tiny old woman well. "She was a fiery one. I think she was four foot five or something, a short woman, but by God she was something."

Soon the strikers would be even busier building emergency accommodation. Within weeks of the strike, Canadian Collieries ordered families out of company housing by October 31. Even families who owned their homes on land rented from the colliery were evicted. Those who resisted reportedly saw company men drag their furniture out into the muddy street. "At that time that was all the houses there were because they were all Canadian Colliery built," Elsie Marocchi said. "You had to live in one of their houses. So, of course, as soon as the men went on strike—everybody out, get out of our houses!"

Many regarded the company houses down camp as marginal accommodation at the best of times. ". . . when one sees the shacks they have to live in one has to marvel that they endure so much. At Cumberland one sees rows of wretched, one-storey houses which a colliery owner would not use for woodsheds," a *British Columbia Federationist* story had said in July 1912. "Nanaimo would not be so bad if it was not Nanaimo, but Cumberland could not be worse than Cumberland."

Then we were locked out . . .

First we walked out, then we were locked out,
then by a foul we were all but knocked out.
Are You From Bevan?

A few evicted strikers were able to crowd in with friends or relatives. A steady stream, refusing to scab, left Cumberland for other coal fields as far away as Australia. Strike pay of four dollars a week, with a little more for wives and children, barely covered food costs. The unfortunate with nowhere to go, no one to take them in, huddled in tents and shacks wherever they could beg permission or settle as squatters. Some of them survived there winter and summer, rain and snow and dust, sickness and near-starvation, for two years.

Cumberland merchants, including the anti-union editor of the *Islander*, drew their own sustenance from miners' pay packets. Strike pay, a bare trickle, went mainly to suppliers of food staples. One of these in 1912 was Campbell Brothers. Old-timers still remember their marvellous device that shot a cylinder along a pulley system, carrying cash from congenial Red at the front counter upstairs to reticent Black who kept the books in the office. Change would then whiz back down to the counter. Children, revelling in this 1912 high tech, enjoyed their errands to the shop.

Quietly, and at enormous personal cost, the Campbells played an important role during the strike. When other merchants cut off strikers, the Campbells continued to supply them on credit. By the

end of the strike, one Cumberland man estimated, they had lost about
$80,000 in unpaid credit which they had no expectation of recover-
ing. In 1990 currency the figure would probably be well over a million
dollars.

"They were very good during the strike. They saved a lot of
people," Karl Coe said.

Johnny Marocchi agreed. "They were too good. They gave credit,
credit, credit."

As if food and clothing were not enough, they also provided refuge.
Elsie Marocchi recalled the strikers "couldn't go anywhere else because nobody had anything—and Campbells said, 'Put up tents, put
up shacks, do anything you like anywhere on our property.'"

The Campbell ranch, where shy Mary Campbell kept house for her
three brothers, stretched from the outskirts of Courtenay south
almost to Roy's Beach. Their gracious house still stands on the west
side of the highway. The ranch's fresh water sources included Millard
Creek which drained from Minto district into sheltered Baynes Sound.
In this area, the Campbells allowed strikers to break ground for
vegetable plots—families evicted from company houses could no
longer harvest the fruit and winter vegetables they'd planted in their
steep back gardens—and to pitch tents or build cabins. This was
known as Strikers' Beach.

Other evicted strikers made a smaller Strikers' Beach at the near
end of Comox Lake, and a few Italian families with boats built
squatters' cabins farther along the south shore. Cabin owners of
"Little Italy" carefully guard their longstanding family squatters'
rights even today.

"The whole lake actually was camps here and there," Ben Horbury
said. "A lot of Italian fellows stayed up the lake. Lots of miners
camped up there."

Single men were little better off than families. In Cumberland,
strikers invested in seven hundred dollars' worth of lumber and
fittings for a new hall on "church street" or Penrith Avenue. Hired
carpenters and more than a hundred men turned out for the construction bee. The union hall doubled as a single men's barracks for the
duration of the strike, neatly solving problems of housing and commercial hall rental, and providing a strike headquarters and gathering
place. It also sent a clear signal that the UMWA was digging in for a
long campaign.

Ginger Goodwin probably lived in the hall with other single men
when it was ready, but also around this time he boarded with Mrs.
Andy Williamson, sister of Scots mine worker Robert Rushford. Mrs.

Louvain (Rushford) Brovenlow, born in 1916, grew up on stories of the strike and Ginger Goodwin.

"When my mother arrived there the strike was on," she wrote. "She always told me those years were some of the happiest of her life. The people all stuck together, they ran concerts, dances, soup kitchens, etc. all the time the strike lasted."

One of the stories reveals Goodwin as a poker-faced practical joker. "It was at one of these parties at my aunt's house that Ginger Goodwin bought a new chamber pot, filled it up with ginger snaps and beer and put it below one of the beds," Louvain Brovenlow wrote. "When everyone was having a swell time he fetched the subject up and bet them all he would sup what was in the pot below the bed. Anyway, he pulled it out and started supping it and had all the company sick to the stomach."

Hilarity and comradeship carried on through the darkest days of the strike, which soon seemed endless. The union was prepared to finance a long struggle. If the company was prepared to hire strikebreakers, the UMWA was equally prepared to fight to the bitter end. The *Journal* explicitly called the strike "the crucial point in the history of the coal miners' organization on Vancouver Island." The newspaper was not alone in this understanding. The strike's direct action created a make-or-break situation, with intense pressure on each side for triumph. Neither side could afford either defeat or impasse.

Dissension in the strikers' ranks didn't bring down the strike as Canadian Collieries assured stockholders; it did sunder families and friendships. Canadian Collieries was determined to continue coal production with non-striking employees, later with imported strikebreakers. Chinese workers, threatened by company lawyers with deportation, within weeks were again working the coal face. Most immigrant European workers held fast.

"It's not remembered who was on strike mostly, what's remembered is the guys who worked. And they're never forgotten. Everybody knows them," Peter Cameron said, seventy-five years after the Big Strike. "There were some of them that weren't to blame for it, either. There were some kids whose dads made them go to work. But I can't remember their names now."

Strikers bitterly resented the "traitors," replacement workers who enabled the company to maintain coal output, limiting the effect of the strike. Some enthusiastically took up scab-baiting.

"I used to play dirty tricks on the fellow who lived next door to me, he was a scab," Karl Coe said. "At that time we had a couple of instruments at home, one was an accordion and one was an old

ukulele. Every time he was on night shift he had to come home and
sleep all day. Well, we'd get out in our yard and slam those things
around and play that thing all day long. Mother said, Get out and
wake him up! Don't let him sleep! God, it was awful."

Crowds of Cumberland women would accompany strikebreakers
to and from work, singing *The Marseillaise* and more raucous ditties—they formed a kind of marching band with fiddle, accordion and
trombone—and jabbing at them with umbrellas. By November tempers were on a short fuse.

Joe Naylor, John McAllister and other leaders urged strikers to stay
at home, keep within the law and avoid unruly street gatherings. Alan
Wargo points out in his thesis *The Great Coal Strike*, "Violence was
not in the interest of the strikers." It occurred anyway. Someone tried
within weeks of the "holiday" to bomb the Trent River railway bridge
between Cumberland and the coal shipping port of Union Bay, and
in December to blow the powerhouse at Number Four mine. The
powder failed to ignite both times. Strikers scoffed at the inevitable
accusations. They said if they'd set the charges, with their long
experience in setting mine "shots", the powder would have exploded
properly.

"Things got pretty rough up there. My father said to my mother,
you don't go up there at night any more if you want to get the mail,"
said Margaret Eggar, then a Minto farm girl. "I can remember now
his renting a livery horse in Courtenay and a buggy, and driving up
to Happy Valley and loading up the eggs and other supplies that Mum
would sell, and taking them up on his half-day off. Because he didn't
want Mum and me going up to Cumberland and being there after
dark."

Violence, when it came, carried the name Goodwin.

Richard Goodwin—coal miner at Number Six pit, householder,
amateur boxer—remains a mysterious figure. In May 1911 he wrote
a letter to the *Islander* challenging a Johnnie Dixon to a boxing contest
for stakes of fifty to one hundred dollars. Dixon, instructed to reply
through the newspaper, apparently declined. Was this an attempt to
settle a longstanding dispute with a poor man's duel? A year later, in
July 1912, the *Islander* printed an even stranger notice under Police
Court Happenings:

> Alex Black laid an information against R. Goodwin for
> assaulting him while working in No. 6 mine. The two had
> their coats off, and seemed determined to prove which was
> the better man. The magistrate [Police Magistrate James
> Abrams] gave them a good dressing down, and informed

them that they both ought to be fined for fighting in a coal mine. He dismissed the case with a warning.

Richard Goodwin was in trouble again in November 1912, the month when strikers' tempers first detonated into open conflict with strikebreakers. Goodwin was one of four men who went to the home of a strikebreaker and, in an attempt to dissuade him from working further, allegedly beat him in front of his family and knocked down his wife. The four strikers said their host, a former boxer, ended the conversation by attacking them with a baseball bat. Although the courts were generally unsympathetic to strikers, a New Westminster jury acquitted all four men.

Who was this Richard Goodwin? Interestingly, Johnny Marocchi thought Ginger's given name was Richard, and a *Federationist* story likewise confused the two men. Were they brothers? Cousins? Strangers? Both were coal miners, both were Yorkshiremen, both were described as young men, both suffered poor health, and both took part in the Big Strike in Cumberland. A Richard Goodwin of about the right age claimed a Scottish birthplace, but the Scots Registry Office can find no trace of him. Albert Goodwin's Yorkshire birth certificate shows no middle name or initial. The mystery demands further investigation.

Distressed union officials and city police commissioners agreed to co-operate in maintaining order as they had done until the street fracas. But the provincial police now stepped in, and put Chief Constable Albert Stephenson in charge of Cumberland's policing. He immediately closed the brewery, the Union Hotel and any other places selling liquor. This dammed the flow of alcohol, but by no means dried it up. Within days, perhaps coincidentally, thirty special constables and forty strikebreakers arrived in Cumberland from the USA and Britain.

Strikebreakers began to take over company housing. Labour contractors didn't always tell the newcomers what they faced, Doll Williams told an interviewer. She was a girl of ten at the time. "When Naylor and somebody else met the train and the miners, he told them what they were coming into, they stopped dead, they wouldn't come, but my dad with seven in the family, he had to come right through," she said. "I remember my dad saying to [the contractor], If anything happens to my wife and kids, you'll get killed."

"They put my father in a house a long way down in the Camp. I realize now that my dad did wrong, he came and worked when the strike was on."

Over the next few months the provincial government obligingly sent 107 special plainclothes constables to Cumberland, most without police training, to "keep the peace." On foot and horseback, armed with revolvers and billy clubs, they swaggered through the city streets provoking strikers and making vulgar comments to their wives; some created incidents while drunk. The British Columbia Provincial Police ultimately dismissed nearly a third of the "specials" for misconduct. Instead of inspiring peace, they stirred violence. A rowdy element on both sides eagerly took up the challenge by drinking, brawling and harassing each other.

The specials, Karl Coe remembered, "were awful. The things they used to do around here! Parade up and down the town on their horses.... You couldn't hardly do a thing without they'd come up there and ask what you were doing, where you were going and all this sort of stuff."

"Charlie McTaggart the big one's name was, he was the one that damned near broke old Milly Brown's wrist when he grabbed her so hard and squeezed it. Right on the street. She was giving him hell, when he grabbed her just like that and damned near broke her arm one time. A little old lady. I tell you, it was really hot and heavy at times. I can't yet figure out why there wasn't some bloodshed."

Karl and other strikers' kids played their part, and not just with off-shift accordion serenades. "I had a slingshot in those days, and I'd be hiding behind my gate down there, and when they went past I'd smack their horses. Then you'd see something. One guy had to fall right off his horse after I hit it, it jumped so great, it knocked him right off his bloody horse. Did I go, though, I was just running my legs off getting the hell out of there."

Hardship soon overtook the strikers and those who depended on their income. On March 29, 1913 the *Western Clarion* printed Ginger Goodwin's letter about dwindling Cumberland subscriptions.

"Owing to economic conditions there is a limit as to how many people are able to subscribe, owing chiefly to the strike in this community." He signed himself, "Yours in Revolt, Com. Goodwin."

Things remained quiet in "dry" Cumberland until well into 1913. Strikers settled into their barracks and shanties; strikebreakers settled into work, accompanied to and from their shifts by special police and a raucous mob of strikers. Picket lines paced. Delegations, numbering not only miners but a socialist MPP, petitioned unsympathetic Premier Sir Richard McBride for mediation. Like the Canadian Collieries managers, he refused to meet with them. Union workers had been off the job for months. The strike, with Nanaimo mines still turning out their usual coal production, was at an impasse.

In late March, Mackenzie and Mann wrote to William Bowser, the British Columbia attorney general, enclosing a report from one of the company's "secret service men" in Cumberland. Agent 17 wrote that he had spent the previous Saturday, as usual, mingling with strikers at the King George, Cumberland and Waverley Hotels and in several poolrooms. There a striker told him that too much coal was coming out of the mines and the strike had a poor chance of success against one of Canada's strongest companies. But that would change soon.

". . . from information which he had obtained the other day from one of the leaders of the strike here, he stated that the Industrial workers of the World are going to mix into this affair shortly, if their permission is granted, having at present written to Frank Farrington of the UMW of A. . . ."

The IWW would stop all steamship crews from docking at Union Bay to haul coal, thus forcing Canadian Collieries to recognize the union.

Bowser merely acknowledged receipt of agent 17's information, but a strong reaction came from another quarter. Malcolm Reid was a federal immigration officer in Vancouver, a virulently racist political appointee who would soon become infamous for his brutal handling of the 1914 *Komagata Maru* incident, in which Sikh immigrants were denied permission to land in Vancouver. Lives were lost and diplomacy was upset over the ugly incident. Now Reid appeared to greatly exceed the authority of a simple immigration officer in his May 10 rush wire to his superintendent of immigration in Ottawa.

Frank Farrington was about to visit Nanaimo, he was informed, as the representative of the United States–based union which had caused a serious colliery strike. His visit could only be for the purpose of agitation.

"I therefore strongly recommend in public interests that he be refused permission to land in Canada. . . . Under these circumstance would you instruct border points to reject," Reid wired.

Reid's role appeared to lie more in the realm of intelligence than of immigration matters, and his name would surface ambiguously throughout World War One in connection with labour activism among other things. This time, he quite literally missed the boat.

Farrington had arrived in Nanaimo before April 30, and had emphatically rejected any involvement by the IWW in a UMWA strike.

On the last day of April, he instructed the UMWA locals to declare a general strike on May 1, 1913 – the original Labour Day – for all Vancouver Island coal miners. He wrote, "You should also exert

every effort to prevent unlawful or abusive tactics by the men. . . ."
Earlier, he'd told Ladysmith strikers that the international union
would immediately withdraw its support if they engaged in violence.

Some grumbling followed the strike call, since only union officials
and not members had voted, but Nanaimo mine workers downed
tools as instructed. More than seven hundred new members joined
the union. Cumberland and Ladysmith strikers had managed nearly
a year of mainly disciplined restraint. At last, the strike affected every
Vancouver Island pit. Union recognition seemed possible, briefly.

That hope died with the July and August 1913 riots.

Strikebreakers, special police, isolated outbursts of violence and
lurid rumours all played their part in touching off the riots, but
probably the biggest factor was sheer frustration. The non-fatal
stabbing of a striker at Extension, special police taunting of strikers
at Cumberland, new specials pouring into Nanaimo: minor provoca-
tions now exploded into chaos. The strife and destruction at Nanaimo, South Wellington and especially Extension reached
catastrophic proportions. In Cumberland union officials and police
kept better order. Yet up-island and down-island, there were stab-
bings, bombings, a pithead shootout, widespread arson and vandalism, and an impromptu cavalry charge through the streets of
Cumberland.

"I remember one fellow, they called him Red George," Ben Horbury
told an interviewer. "There was I don't know how many there was,
but it looked like quite a bunch of men on horseback, and they came
up from the company office. He pulled a paper out and unrolled it,
and he read something off it. I don't know what it was. I was on the
corner just below. Then he hollered, 'Charge!' The horses charged
these men on the corner. Next thing I knew I got a boot in the arse,
and father was behind me and he says, Get home. I didn't argue about
it. I headed for home. There was quite a battle. I would have liked to
have seen the whole thing."

On July 19, strikers filled the streets in response to a special
policeman's threat. Joe Naylor kept order until one man gave in to
the provocation and clashed with a strikebreaker; the strikebreaker
was later charged and fined. This touched off Cumberland's minor
riot, which consisted mainly of shoving and fist fights in Dunsmuir
Avenue. Blood briefly settled the coal dust.

Cumberland police collared Richard Goodwin, out on bail, for
allegedly assaulting a Special Constable McCarville during the riot.
They also arrested the foremost voice of law-abiding calm, Joe Naylor. He would later remember marching, with all the arrested strikers,
through the streets of Nanaimo between fixed bayonets:

> Our union miners faced guns and jail,
> hundreds of us were held without bail.

In Ladysmith, soldiers hauled young Sam Guthrie, president of the UMWA local there, out of bed in the small hours of the morning. Police arrested socialist MPP Jack Place of Nanaimo for receiving a stolen police firearm; he'd taken it from a striker when things got rough on the steamer docks.

Military action—having refused peaceful intervention—was the provincial government's immediate response. In August 1913 militia—complete with artillery and field hospitals—marched into all the island coal towns. The militia units included the Seaforth Highlanders, the Victoria Fusiliers and the Royal Canadian Artillery. Sending them was like pouring oil on the flames.

When the smoke cleared, long before the damage was tallied, all the key strike leaders were in custody. Their whereabouts or peacekeeping efforts during the riots carried no weight. Karl Coe said, "That's the kind of guys the looked for, especially all the organizers, that's all they wanted, to shut them up and put them in jail."

"Brother Naylor," wrote "A Striker" in the *Journal* in August 1913, "was without doubt the most popular and most powerful man belonging to the UMW of A in Cumberland and was respected for his integrity even by the scabs, but being a class-conscious man he was naturally a thorn in the side of the capitalists, and it is obvious that he was the prey of the rapacious thugs that are at present infesting the island. Previous to his arrest he had conducted affairs here from the beginning of the strike and had practically come to be look upon as a father for his wisdom and judgment in all matters was asked and worked upon.... For nearly 11 months the powers that are had been anxious for his arrest..."

Ginger Goodwin (quoted in *Builders of British Columbia*) wrote in protest, "Strikers are given the maximum penalty while those who are helping the masters to defeat the strikers are let off with the minimum.... Stop appealing and praying.... Line up in this great worldwide movement of socialism and use the concerted action of all workers to wrest from the master-class the means of wealth production."

The riots and especially the resulting arrests crippled the strike effort as intended. Strikers railed at the imprisonment of their leaders, formed committees and petitioned the government, all without effect. In Cumberland a number of their cases were heard by Police Magistrate Abrams, a man so hostile to strikers that the government itself eventually withdrew him. Nearly three hundred striking mine workers

awaited hearings in overcrowded and unsanitary conditions in Nanaimo jail and later New Westminster jail. One young man died there
of the miner's nemesis, tuberculosis. Few strikebreakers faced charges.

On November 22, 1913 the *Western Clarion* printed an article by
Goodwin which was angrier, more outspoken and more eloquent
than the one written on the eve of the strike. After describing the
evolution of capitalism from feudalism he wrote that capitalism had
run its course.

"The Time for the Revolution is Rotten-Ripe," a sub-heading
stated, "but the mind of the vast majority is not ready and the struggle
takes on the form of an intellectual one for the possession of the mind
of the working class.

"The forces that make for this struggle are represented for the
capitalist class by the institutions of the pulpit, press, army and navy,
YMCA's and so forth. The proletarians have at their disposal the
teachings of Socialism, the Materialist Conception of history . . . "

Joe Naylor, out on bail in late November, addressed a Vancouver
crowd at the Princess Theatre about the strike. His July 19 rioting
charge had effectively removed him from strike leadership for four
months, although it was ultimately shown to be without substance;
when his case finally came to trial he was acquitted.

Richard Goodwin languished in New Westminster jail, and was so
sick at his trial that he nearly fainted in the stand, causing an
adjournment. Finally "G. Goodwin" (as the *Federationist* called him)
and three others were acquitted of intimidation and assault. Goodwin
was not free, however. Although a J. McAllister had confessed that it
was he who assaulted McCarville during the Cumberland riot, the
judge said it was too late in the process to withdraw charges. As a
result, "R. Goodwin, who is also popular with his fellow miners, went
down to the cells to be returned to the provincial jail . . . "

The Big Strike had now faded to almost nothing. One international
board member said in January 1914 that the union was blundering on
Vancouver Island as it had in Nova Scotia; both strikes were unwin-
nable from the start. The UMWA took steps to withdraw its support.
With other strikes in progress, having poured an estimated 1.5 million
dollars into strike funds, its treasury was depleted.

The United Mine Workers finally cut off funds in August 1914. But
the real end of the Big Strike was the long-expected war in Europe:

> In August nineteen-fourteen
> our labour they were courting,
> but they blacklisted me.

Most socialists in the labour movement thought the war was a cold-blooded profitmaking venture. As Joe Naylor and others had demanded, why should German workers and Canadian workers kill each other to further enrich arms manufacturers and other wealthy elites?

The British Columbia Federation of Labour resolved, at its January 1915 convention, "That all labour bodies throughout Canada and the United States take up the discussion of anti-militarism, general strike, and organization work, so that they will be in a position to take definite action in such a way as will make war impossible."

Yet in 1914 many unemployed workers enlisted. Ironically, some striking miners joined the units keeping order in the coal towns. Cumberland men joined the Seaforth Highlanders they had recently jeered and heckled in Dunsmuir Avenue. Many worried that this European adventure would be over before they had a chance to take part. Names on Cumberland's cenotaph show this fear was groundless. World War One—monstrous, unfathomable, unspeakable in its degradation and horror—would long outlast any Canadian's desire for war.

Coal companies seized on the war for its market opportunities, and exhorted miners to do their patriotic duty. But at least one island coal company neglected to practise what it preached, according to William Bennett in *Builders of British Columbia:* "A photo in the San Francisco *Bulletin* showed the [German warship] *Leipzig* being coaled with coal dug by Nanaimo miners, from Western Fuel Company barges in 'Frisco harbor after the outbreak of the war. Capitalist patriotism!"

What did the Big Strike, with all its passions and privations, actually achieve?

British Columbia's economy staggered. A federal investigation team arrived, interviewed mainly managers and strikebreakers, and departed without discernible effect. The UMWA spent an enormous sum in organizing costs and strike pay. The International Workers of the World—Joe Hill's radical industrial union—marched in the Vancouver streets. British labour leader Keir Hardie demanded government intervention. Preachers stepped down from their pulpits to speak for their suffering congregations. Starvation became so serious in Cumberland by the end of the strike that the provincial government sent a health commission and, unthinkably for the times, food aid.

Joe Naylor wrote about the strike's aftermath three years later in the *Federationist.*

"Men were kept out of employment for the purpose of bringing them down to the level of starvation, to make them cringe and crawl and promise never to repeat again the spirit of unionism. We also know how Bowser was forced to deal out beans to these same workers to keep body and soul together. After having helped the operators to beat the men he was later forced to feed, to keep them from dying of starvation. We haven't forgotten the march of the kilties, nor the glistening of bayonets, the muzzle of machine guns, sent to the coal camps on the island by the then attorney-general Mr. Bowser, to terrorize, intimidate and deprive the miners of the right to organize.

But miners now said even harsher things of the UMWA's role. Robert Walker, a Cumberland miner and Socialist Party member, like his friend Ginger Goodwin had endured both the Glace Bay and Vancouver Island coal strikes. Walker wrote a series of articles for the *Western Clarion* in September 1914 comparing the two strikes. His bitterness was mainly for the "single individual allowed to declare the strike on the island off," probably the Illinois organizer Frank Farrington.

"In both cases the officials controlled. The tactics were the same, only a part of the miners being called upon to strike; in both cases the men were sold, the only difference being that the miners on the island know they are sold, while the men in Glace Bay did not realize until the strike was well over.... The results in both cases are similar—a list of killed and wounded, some still suffering in jail, a black list four or five feet long, and the conversion of many loyal adherents into avowed enemies...

"And now, you gods and would be's, I have stood aside and allowed you to flim flam and hoodwink the island miners with your sentimental junk and bourgeois economics for the last two years.... I intend to reveal certain facts pertaining to trade unionism in general and the UMW in particular." Over the next few issues, Walker savaged the union for its betrayal. His censure can have provided little consolation to starving miners.

On a personal level, organizer Joe Angelo received a staggering four-year sentence for riot. Classed as a "foreign agitator," he was immediately deported to the USA.

During the strike the British Columbia Provincial Police had hired at least one undercover Pinkerton's agent from Seattle. The dispatches of agent 17 in Cumberland and agent 29S in Nanaimo routinely laid out infiltration techniques, disruption efforts and intelligence reports. Agent 17 reported to Mackenzie and Mann; agent 29S reported to the Provincial Police. Cumberland radical socialists, above all Joe Naylor, remained under intense federal surveillance for decades.

Mine owner Baron Alvo von Alvensleben, a 1913 *Federationist* story said, was "A man of winning personality, great force of character and extraordinary magnetism... not only a credit to the German people, but also to the country of his adoption." The Vancouver "merchant prince" and president of the Vancouver Nanaimo Coal Mining Company Limited had earned the federation's favour by recognizing UMWA miners and offering them a decent contract. No other mine did so. His liberal-minded manager Harry Freeman was under surveillance by a Pinkerton's agent, who decided he was socialistic. Von Alvensleben himself would soon be under surveillance by military intelligence as a suspected German spy. His control of a west coast coal company able to fuel enemy ships, his planned Queen Charlotte Islands fish packing plant which looked strangely like submarine pens, his alleged clandestine night signalling to unknown ships standing off Victoria, his investment of eight million dollars of obscure origin: certainly these raised questions.

Was von Alvensleben indeed investing the Kaiser's funds in an attempt to ensure fuel and secret docking for German war vessels? Did he see organized labourers, his admirers, as a wedge he could drive into a viciously hierarchical colonial society? Or did he recognize the union to prevent dangerously close scrutiny of his actions? Did he flee to the neutral United States to escape prosecution, only to be interned in Salt Lake City in 1917 as an enemy alien? If the truth can be known, it probably lies deep in a German government archive. Von Alvensleben denied all complicity even as an impoverished and embittered old man in Seattle years later.

Less tangible effects of the Big Strike have been discussed by other writers: the hostility and fear between British Columbia labour and capital which persists today, the lingering bitterness between families and former friends, and the last gasp of King Coal before the advent of fuel oil.

One achievement certainly was the personal development of a young union organizer until then better known as a footballer. Lifelong friendships and an applied education were the strike's greatest payload for Ginger Goodwin.

One East

O n Vancouver Island the Big Strike broke the United Mine Workers' cohesion. The international union withdrew support and
disbanded District 28. Cumberland's Local 2299 and the other or-
phaned locals struggled on for a few years, and died.

Hundreds of miners had lost their jobs, their houses and all hope
of a better future. They still lacked union recognition. Mine safety
was still dreadful. Canadian Collieries ultimately betrayed friends
and foes alike. It dismissed many workers it used as strikebreakers,
leaving them with a lifelong stigma for scabbing in a close-knit and
strong-minded community. Despite promises to the provincial government it refused to rehire many former strikers. Instead it wielded
the dreaded blacklist.

Joe Naylor had been a coal digger in Number Four pit, travelling
by company train to and from the pithead near Comox Lake for his
night shift. Now he walked three miles out and three miles back every
day to stand outside the mine manager's office waiting for work. He'd
given coal digging his best since the 1880s. He'd given the strike his
best for two hard years, never yielding to violence, always counselling
level-headed and law-abiding restraint. His efforts failed and his strike
failed. Now he was again ready to give coal digging his best. He would
stand at Number Four pithead waiting in vain for work, day by day,
rain or shine, for years. He was one of many.

Ginger Goodwin was another. Blacklisted, he hadn't worked for
two full years. The strike had taken its toll on his hopes and peace of

mind, no doubt, but certainly on his physical wellbeing. Goodwin's health became a matter of public record for the first time in early 1915, a few months after the strike crumbled, when he was forced to spend several weeks in Cumberland Hospital. J. Goodwin, twenty-six, male, spent several weeks in Cumberland and Union Hospital with gastritis and diarrhoea, in October 1914 and January 1915. In February 1915 A. Goodwin, twenty-eight, male, spent three weeks there. Who was this J. Goodwin, otherwise unmentioned in Cumberland records? Given the variable accuracy of these accounts, this may also have been Albert Goodwin. Both entries were rather cryptically marked *free, paid*; this apparently meant that a patient subscribed to the hospital fund through the UMWA, which paid his fees in full.

Gastritis, in 1914, probably described a stomach ulcer. Andrew Waldie later remembered that Ginger Goodwin had an ulcerated stomach. Diarrhoea was a common consequence of poor diet or malnutrition over a length of time, for example, throughout a two-year strike. Friends recalled Ginger as a light-hearted, easy-going companion with a joke or a kind word for anyone. Anyone but himself, it seems. Outwardly he was friendly and sociable, but if he indeed had an ulcer, inwardly he may have been tormenting himself with despair and guilt over the failed strike. Should he have done things differently, worked harder, kept more strikers off the job, given more help to Joe and other organizers? Thoughts like this oppress both mind and body.

This hospitalization was probably the first overt sign of Ginger Goodwin's physical debility, which was to progress over the next few years until others commented on his obvious affliction. Until the strike he had been active—playing football, swimming, hiking, fishing—but now he was bedridden. Many people have recalled the unhealthy living conditions of miners and their families during the Big Strike, and the endemic sickness at squatters' camps such as Striker's Beach. Living in tarpaper beach shacks, lean-tos, jerry-built cabins, and tents created exactly the right conditions for the deadly "white plague" of tuberculosis: overcrowding, damp, chill, poor water and sanitation, with inadequate food and nutrition. It may be that these conditions not only aggravated, and drew attention to, but caused Goodwin's ailments.

"Ginger was a thin sickly red-headed fellow. He actually did not interest me too much. They talked about the mines and things which weren't interesting to me at the time," Winnie Williamson told an interviewer. Her father Ed Calnan worked at Number Four but had a few acres in Minto or Happy Valley, halfway between Cumberland and Royston beach on the old "goat track." "I remember him well because when I went to high school he used to stay in some rooms where I was staying with my grandmother. He had miners' TB or whatever it is..."

Hardship went on long after the strike ended.

"My father was a socialist, and during the big strike he let the miners have their gardens at our place in the valley," Winnie said. "I remember the patches of cabbages, turnips and potatoes."

Farmers and stump ranchers like Ed Calnan now gave up some land to let blacklisted union miners, instead of strikers, build shacks and scratch vegetable gardens. One great character was a mine worker who had lived in the Union Hotel until the strike, but afterward was thrown on his own resources. An American who retained his Norwegian accent, Ole Oleson was a short stocky man with a big black moustache. He was a lifelong socialist and a skilled all-around craftsman.

"He built all the buildings right here. My dad bought this property here for five hundred bucks...and he measured off an acre or two for Oleson. He did all the carpentry work, and for the collieries and for everyone in the district," Winnie's brother Harold Calnan told me. "He always told Dad about the Russian Revolution—God, she's a-coming, Ed. But it never come."

On the Calnan homestead Oleson built himself a small cabin and set up shop as a jack of all trades. It was an old bachelor's life, punctuated by tub-thumping socialist meetings and regular binges in town. Instead of a vegetable garden, Oleson installed a mobile stump puller outside his cabin door. He was full of wonderful schemes, two of them still visible: a water ditch travelling hundreds of metres through the woods from a creek, and a rectangular depression about ten metres by twenty metres and a metre deep. This was to be Minto's socialist hall.

Minto, with its miners who farmed and farmers who dug coal—there were both—and its collection of local characters, had always been a gathering place for Cumberland area socialists. After the strike their activities didn't falter. The new war in Europe, though no one thought it would last until Christmas, reassured many of imminent world revolution. Old-timers remember the red flag flying atop farm silos in Minto, and the strains of *The Internationale* and *The Workers' Flag* floating over the rich Happy Valley pastures. A brilliant new world would rise on the ashes of the evil old world, and Minto district was as good a place as any to lay foundations. Ole Oleson collected donations, bought some lumber and prepared to build.

The socialist hall remained—and remains—at the excavation stage. On one truly magnificent bender in Cumberland's bars, Oleson spent all the money he'd raised for building materials. This wasn't Ole's last disappointment. He returned from another binge in the early 1920s to find his cabin vanished. Local boys had stuffed his chimney with rags to fill the cabin with smoke, but the prank backfired. The cabin burned to the ground, and unlike the socialist dream, failed to rise from its ashes. Local people were impressed, if saddened, at how reams of radical literature in Ole's rafters fuelled the blaze. The socialists continued to meet elsewhere and plan.

Oleson took on many construction projects around the area. Many of the company houses out at Number Eight mine were his work. He dug wells, built foundations, laid bricks, pulled stumps to clear farm land, and undertook precision demolition work; when Canadian Collieries needed to dismantle an obsolete brick chimney surrounded by other important buildings at Union Bay, Oleson used fire to weaken the structure before he dropped it in a neat pile of bricks leaving the other buildings unscathed.

"If the collieries needed any intricate work done they always got hold of him, because he was a clever old guy. Harry said he could turn his hand to anything, especially hewing or anything like that," said Harold.

Oleson's odd jobs often called for extra hands, occasionally including Joe Naylor, Harry Williamson — a Minto farm boy who married Winnie Calnan after many years in Tasmania — and Ginger Goodwin.

"He used to have people come and sit with him, especially anyone who was a socialist, and Ginger used to come to his place all the time, and they used to eat at our place," Winnie said.

Minto folks are unclear now whether Ginger lived with Ole after the strike when he was blacklisted, or a few years later, or both. Harold Calnan said, "I think maybe over a period of eight or ten years between the Comox Lake and here, Oleson's cabin was ideal for him."

Ginger's habit was to live with socialist, UMWA or soccer friends here and there around Cumberland. At different times he stayed with Bob Rushford's sister Mrs. Williamson, at Clark's boardinghouse, with the Andrew Clarke family, and Peg and Meg Westfield. He batched with a group of other men including Joe Naylor. Probably there were other arrangements, few of them guaranteed to improve the physical wellbeing of a young man with an ulcer, bad teeth and lung disease. If he ever owned or rented accommodation on his own, as Joe Naylor later did by 1918, no record remains. Ginger was outgoing and companionable, not inclined to live alone.

In Minto the jobless mine workers and their friends kept the faith. After the international headquarters of the United Mine Workers in 1914 withdrew support from the Vancouver Island local unions, the locals struggled on alone under the unflagging leadership of men like Joe Naylor. Someday, they believed against mounting odds, the coal companies would have to recognize the UMWA and yield fair working conditions. And the socialists believed a better time was coming soon; they had only to muster support, and maintain hope, to bring a new day. This was no time to slack off on meetings and organizational efforts. They lacked money, even roofs over their heads, but they didn't lack spirit.

"Oleson and my dad and them were great union men and good socialists," Harold Calnan said. "My dad was a socialist to the day he died."

Organizing the Cumberland mines might not look hopeful just now, but other west coast workers also badly needed union representation. Fishing and logging drew heavily on immigrant workers, the greener and more cowed the better, for their heavy labour. These were some of the coast's most abused and exploited workers.

Logging relied mainly on "tame apes" hired on a seasonal basis, often paid and supplied through chiselling company stores. Many men spoke little or no English; many were illiterate. Scandinavians and Slavs predominated, but there were also Japanese and Irish and Italians, all thrown together in polyglot isolation to harvest mostly virgin forest. Fishing was a more individual, free-enterprise opportunity. Any man or woman with basic gear and the use of a rowboat could at least handline salmon, so plentiful there were tales of people walking across inlets and bays on their teeming backs. Larger boats, many of them skippered by Japanese and Scandinavians and coast Indians, also hired crew.

On *illahie* or *chuck*, land or water, isolation kept these men powerless against buyers and bosses. A union could help them by negotiating wages, fish prices and working conditions.

The radical American-based International Workers of the World, like the later all-Canadian One Big Union, was not a trade or craft union but an industrial union. In a coal mine, for example, all colliery workers would join the IWW rather than miners joining the UMWA, firebosses joining their own union, electricians joining another union and so on. Anyone could join the IWW. Joe Naylor was said to be an organizer for the IWW after the Big Strike. Karl Coe said, "Joe was organizing the coast here, as far as I can remember, he'd run up and down the coast organizing the fishermen and what not."

Ginger Goodwin, during his blacklisting in Cumberland, reportedly went along on these trips upcoast. Fish camps and logging shows were scattered from the outskirts of Vancouver all the way north to Alaska. Small, haphazard, often "haywire shows" of gyppos or fly-by-nighters, they came and went yearly. Few left any trace, after lush growth erased their scars from the rainforest landscape, and almost none left written records. Even their songs have drifted away like smoke from their slash fires. A few years ago I saw music historian Phil Thomas pursue an ex-logger from a dinner to capture him on tape—all for two stanzas and the refrain of a forgotten ditty that starts, *Ay bin Swedish falling logger on the boat to Campbell River*... A few settlements did leave traces, though not of Ginger and Joe. One was the Finnish utopia of Sointula.

Harmony, the meaning of *sointula* in Finnish, was a badly needed quality in the 1901 colony within a country. Draft dodgers from the Russian tsar's army, religious nonconformists, free thinkers, pacifists, revolutionaries and socialists made up the determined band of colonists on Malcolm Island, far north in Johnstone Strait. The utopia needed skilled farmers and fishermen and carpenters; it got professors and poets. Sointula's tragic and splendid history occupies several books (see Works Consulted). Disaster and near starvation sent some colonists back to safer shores, but the hardy struggled on, with help from the Kwagiut people of nearby Alert Bay. By 1914 the community was predominantly socialist. Although strangers were interrogated at the docks and often refused landing permission, Sointula warmly welcomed leftist speakers. Surely such fertile ground would not escape any IWW organizers, including Joe and Ginger.

In February 1917 the *British Columbia Federationist* reported a recent mass meeting in Sointula to organize the fishermen of Rivers Inlet. "The aims of the organization will be the protection of the fishermen against exploitation by the cannery owners to secure better prices for their catch, to raise a protest against restrictions which now inconvenience the fishermen and, in general, to better the conditions under which the men are operating."

Organizing was a labour of love, however, which provided little in the way of daily bread. Cumberland's blacklisted union men found no work at Canadian Collieries, despite the European war's boost to the Canadian economy, and might never find work. Family by family and one by one, with sick children and mounting debts, blacklisted mine workers finally had to choose: stay in Cumberland or leave.

Many walked away from their beach shanties and their unpaid grocery bills at Campbell Brothers and Frelone's and the Big Store. Some sought out recruiting sergeants and went to Flanders, hiring on for another dirty and underpaid job while it lasted. At least the army wanted them; the mines didn't. Even the war soon seemed less like a valiant adventure than a reeking slaughterhouse. One Cumberland former miner was called up from the reserves for active duty, though

Canada had no conscription, because he had served in Britain's Black
Watch Regiment fifteen years earlier during the South Africa War.
Friends, possibly including Joe Naylor, advised Robert Rushford to
"head for the hills" rather than go to war. But he and his wife Jessie
had two small children and another on the way, and a fugitive's life
seemed even less attractive than army life.

Lance-Corporal Rushford served only briefly, wrote his daughter
Louvain Brovenlow. "They took him all the way back to Scotland to
pass the doctor before he went to the front. He was shot through the
chest, the bullet passing right through him, so he was invalided back
to Vancouver Island." He was Cumberland's first war casualty, but
far from the last.

Rushford returned home in spring 1915. A photograph in the
Cumberland Museum files shows Station Cumberland decked out in
flags and bunting, and a large crowd waiting on the platform to
welcome him home.

"The school children got a holiday," Mrs. Brovenlow wrote. "The
engine of the train [was] covered with the Union Jack and all the
people [were] waving flags." Her father "wondered what it was all
for, not thinking it was for him."

The accolades didn't end there. Cumberland's mayor at the time,
mine boss Charles Parnham, presented Rushford (and later other
returned soldiers) with a modest donation and a floridly-worded
"address of welcome."

"Your recollections of the enthusiastic loyalty of Canada, the
throbbing patriotism of the British Isles, the stirring scenes of France,
the Battle of the Aisne, the desolation and spoliation of Flanders, may,
in years to come, grow dim and fade from your memory, but the
screech of shells, the shock of arms, and the smoke and din of
battle-wracked Ypres will never be forgotten, and this Flemish town —
of immortal fame — has fittingly given a name to the little girl who
came into this world while her father was bravely striving for King
and Country," the proclamation reads in part.

"In presenting this purse, we ask you not to guage [sic] our esteem
or our gratitude by its size. Services such as yours are not remunerated
in gold; rather you will find your recompense in the respect and regard
which all will offer to one who has so bravely fought and bled in his
Country's service."

This purple jingoism confirmed the worst fears of pacifist socialists
like Joe Naylor. Though Rushford remained proud of his war service,
significantly he later did his utmost to spare other young men this kind
of "immortal fame." As Cumberland's chief constable, he would play
a lonely and courageous role in Ginger Goodwin's last days. And —

soon after his little girl Ypres, named for the battle in Flanders, died in the great 1918 influenza epidemic—he would be dragged through the courts as a witness in Joe Naylor's case, with the insinuation that he was incompetent and a traitor. He remained proud of his courage too, though it cost him his livelihood, his government's "respect and regard," and even his new country when he took his despondent family back to Scotland.

Some blacklisted miners left Cumberland for other coal fields in Canada and the United States; some drifted as far as Australia. Few ever came back. Canadian Collieries no longer promised doubled mine output or huge payrolls; Mackenzie and Mann's Canadian Northern Railway was steadily approaching bankruptcy. Cumberland was a quieter town for those who stayed. Joe Naylor decided to stay.

Ginger Goodwin decided to move on in the spring of 1915. In Cumberland he'd won some glory as a football star, dropped a few balls in corner pockets, laid a line across some of the continent's best trout streams, taught himself the art of public speaking, danced up a storm, worked down pit, helped found a socialist group, served his apprenticeship as a labour organizer, and made the best friends anyone could have. It was time to move on.

Merritt, where the coal seam still smoulders on the outskirts of town, in 1914 was the most isolated coal town in British Columbia and maybe in Canada. Its handful of mines lay deep in the mountains south of Kamloops, beyond electricity and telephone and even telegraph. When mine disaster struck—regularly—days passed before Vancouver newspapers knew. Isolation and the usual poor working conditions made it difficult to find miners. What better place for a blacklisted union mine worker to try his luck? Ginger Goodwin worked as a miner in a Merritt pit in 1915, accumulating fresh work experience. At least he claimed that he worked in a Merritt mine; the same qualities that made Merritt ideal for a new start also made it ideal for a man who needed to fabricate a work record. No one was likely to check his references. The coal companies' few surviving records show no trace of him, but probably he did as he said. Nothing in the sparse documentation of Ginger Goodwin's life suggests that, however rousing his rhetoric, he told anything but the truth.

By December 1915 he'd moved on again, southeast to the coal towns of the Crowsnest Pass. On the British Columbia side of the provincial boundary, he was only about fifty miles from the coal-mining Goodwin family in Bellevue, Alberta. Members of this family had arrived in Nova Scotia with Ginger on the SS *Pretoria* in 1906. Derbyshire born, Salvation Army members, flower fanciers, gifted musicians, hobby ranchers, staunch supporters of the war effort, soon in mine management, they were anything but radical labour socialists. Cousins they may or may not have been; in every way they were worlds apart. Goodwin is a common name in the English midlands, and I found no family ties. One thing precludes dismissing them outright as relatives—their photographs in *The Crowsnest and Its People* reveal a striking physical resemblance.

Ginger Goodwin hired on at the Coal Creek mines December 18, 1915, in the mountains seven miles southeast of Fernie. The Crow's Nest Pass Coal Company took him on as a mule driver for one of its dozen Coal Creek mines, One East.

Fernie in 1915 was a town with fire in its eyes. Crime was rampant, much of it the result of drinking and gambling among transient single men of a dozen nationalities. The British Columbia Provincial Police struggled to keep constables in the town; sometimes two or three resigned each year. It was easy to spot at least one socialist household; the house was painted revolutionary red. The UMWA owned and operated one of the two newspapers, the *District Ledger.* Some of the most prosperous people in town were the whorehouse madams, Torchy Anderson told me, and these were no shrinking violets. One threw her lover's steamer trunk from her balcony into the main street—shouting instructions on what he could do with it, himself and his new woman—when he returned from his honeymoon. Fernie's brothels were no secret; town council had voted openly in 1910 to let them reopen after a closure. Rumour has it the madams paid a strictly unofficial business tax in the form of police fines every month-end, a day after the local payday.

Other Fernie whispers said the "black hand" or Mafia was ascendant. Italian immigrants, downtrodden in many predominantly English communities, here found a saviour in the unlikely guise of an ice cream peddler. By 1914 Emilio "Pic" Piccariello, the Emperor Pic, was a prosperous businessman and, allegedly, a strong *capo* who gave grocery hampers to the poor but meted out punishment to betrayers. During Prohibition his fast cars carried out a lucrative rumrunning business. In 1923 he was dead—hanged for the murder of an Alberta policeman whom Pic mistakenly believed had killed his son—if any legend is ever quite dead. Recently two Italian women told me, sitting on the porch of a Crowsnest Pass old folks' home, that Pic was not only alive but still rich and powerful, driving "a shiny black car a block long. It wasn't true that they hung him, you know. He bought the judge and got away to Brazil."

Coal mining dominated Fernie's economy from the start. Other industries—logging, hardrock mining, pack trains, farming, even the railway—remained less significant. Coal gave rise to virtually all of the twenty-odd Crowsnest Pass towns, from Fernie east to Hillcrest, though some now exist only as memories or ghost towns. In their heyday they were thriving commercial and residential centres, but most of their buildings were erected on skids or blocks. When the mines closed everything vanished almost overnight. One of these portable towns was Coal Creek.

In 1915 the well-established community of Coal Creek nestled on a plateau between two wooded whaleback ridges high above Fernie. Old-timers remember Kutenai Indians silently riding their ponies down the north ridge on their way to winter camps in Montana. Coal Creek's residential districts of private and company houses reflected the ethnic divisions—Welsh Town, French Camp, Slav Town, and so on—and the business district had a hotel, boarding houses, theatre, pool hall, bank, merchants, a miner's hall and library.

Upstream from the townsite the creek deepened into a fine swimming hole, and a first-rate playing field now given over mainly to wildflowers. On this field, between shifts, Ginger Goodwin played football. Maybe it was here that he and his Coal Creek teammates won his gold medal in the five-team Crowsnest Pass league which, like the Vancouver Island league, achieved near-professional soccer with hand-picked and imported players. Beside its tawny mountain stream, the soccer pitch is the only flat ground for miles. Sometimes players lost the ball there, and lost it for good; the creek was too swift for a rescue.

This is the one part of Coal Creek still in regular use. We arrived one summer afternoon in time for the annual Coal Creek Old-Timers' Picnic: children splashing in the creek, women walking arm in arm, teams forming for softball. Octogenarians whipped Stephen at horseshoes while retired miners plied me with beer—it's always beer—and demanded to know whether I was writing one of them women's books about the men's business of mining. They agreed to reserve judgment. We left laughing a few hours later, full of homemade pasta and sausage and potato salad, replete with stories about the old days. Coal Creek remembers how to welcome a stranger.

The town of Coal Creek has vanished, hotel and boarding houses and shops. Coyote Street has gone to grass. One East mine is a shallow hole in the mountainside posted with warnings. Only the soccer pitch remains, and the wind on the green hillsides, and the stream. Coal Creek runs clean again now, like most of our coal creeks.

In late 1915 One East was going full bore; it needed mule drivers, coal diggers and other mine workers. Men were enlisting in the 107th East Kootenay Regiment, and the government was interning Germans and some Slavs as enemy aliens. "Interning" was a euphemism for being marched into detainment camps; some would later be freed to dig coal in the mines they'd been forced to leave. The Crow's Nest Pass Coal Company hired several experienced Cumberland men, almost certainly former strikers. Those with miners' certificates generally hired on as contract coal diggers, while Ginger and other mule drivers signed at $3.03 for an eight-hour day.

Ginger's Crow's Nest Pass Coal Company work record sheet gives scant information compared to some others. The company assigned him the working number 2771, which may also have been his tag number for a company-owned safety lamp. A clerk filled in the form: Albert Goodwin, English, twenty-eight, single, no children, father Walter Goodwin of Silverwood in Yorkshire as next of kin, last employed as coal miner in Merritt, thirteen years' experience, hired as driver, 1E, wages $3.03 for eight hours. Cold (there were record snowfalls that winter) or in haste or without a writing surface, perhaps, Ginger signed in an angular scrawl barely recognizable as his signature. The only other remark, noted on every such work sheet, is "Received a copy of special rules." The 116-point booklet outlined safety practice, duties and penalties for every mine job from rope rider to overman. His sheet bears no miner's certificate number in the remarks space.

Goodwin didn't return to the island, but he didn't work long at Coal Creek. When he wasn't playing soccer, he spent his off hours organizing for the UMWA and the Socialist Party of Canada. He was one of about twenty socialist and labour speakers who regularly travelled through the district, barely covering their expenses with collections at meetings. Another of these speakers played billiards for money with some desperation, former UMWA official David Rees later recalled, since he couldn't cover his bets. An acrimonious UMWA strike in 1911, hard on the heels of a 1907 strike, had brought violence and armed militia as on Vancouver Island. Fernie had become the UMWA's first Canadian local when District 18 formed in 1903, but conditions and wages were still far from ideal.

One East was gassy and unstable, prone to dangerous blowouts and bumps. Blowouts resulted from gas pressure in the seams, and shifted tons of coal dust at a time; drilling the face could relieve the pressure. Bumps or tremors heaved the entire coal seam many feet upward, and were uncontrollable; miners learned to predict bumps and save themselves by leaving the mine. Coal Creek's worst disasters — 128 dead in 1902, 34 dead in 1917 — occurred in theoretically safer pits.

Wages doubled during the First World War, commentators like to point out, but unchecked wartime inflation meant the cost of living rose even more steeply. Mine workers struggled to keep up, and failed. The IWW and later the One Big Union challenged UMWA representation before and after the war, but it was the UMWA that signed a contract with the Crow's Nest Pass Coal Company.

"I went up to Coal Creek on the train," Vancouver labour organizer Bill Pritchard told an interviewer. "I met the fellows going off shift, and Ginger jumped up in the coach, introduced me, and made a flowery speech on coming down to the meeting that night, and so on. Yes, he had a kind of what you might call uncultured eloquence—"

Pritchard couldn't remember the exact content of Goodwin's speeches. "He'd just tell about his experiences as a worker... the matter of working for wages and what it meant—and general soapbox propaganda."

"I remember Ginger addressing a convention when I was in Fernie—Mine Workers convention, you know—for he was an able fellow on the platform, very able," David Rees said. Details escaped him also, speaking six decades later. "There was so much of it... in those days that was similar in a sense—perhaps said in different words—that I can't pretend to remember anything, any particular point that Ginger made, other than he was a good speaker and he would make his points very forcibly, no question about it."

Another topic took on greater urgency. The war in Europe not only failed to end in gentlemanly handshakes but increasingly revealed itself as a hideous charnel house where dead and dying alike wallowed in endless mud. It had to end. Labour socialists in Germany spoke against it and died by firing squad. Labour socialists in Canada were freer to speak against it, they thought, in an attempt to halt Canada's participation in a European war. Rees said one of many outspoken critics of this exercise in imperialism and commerce was Ginger Goodwin. "Ginger wouldn't be speaking for the war—we'd know anything he said would be against it."

Meanwhile, the Canadian war effort in Europe was in serious trouble. Canadian units took terrible losses as English generals squandered their "colonials"; Australians are still bitter over the carnage their countrymen suffered at Gallipoli. Canadians have shorter memories, apparently, though machine gun fire and artillery wiped out entire Canadian battalions. We've largely forgotten that Canadian firing squads under British orders also shot Canadian "cowards," many either pacifist or shell-shocked.

In 1915 the Canadian army alone was using an average of thirty-five hundred tons of ammunition a day. Arms manufacturers in Europe, whether they engineered the war or not, did a brisk business in death.

The United States war industry would prosper for another three years, and Canadian resource suppliers and manufacturers rushed to grasp their share before this marvellous opportunity evaporated.

One supplier—of refined lead and zinc for armaments—would be the Consolidated Mining and Smelting Company in the West Kootenays town of Trail, where in early 1916 Ginger Goodwin went to work as a smelterman.

Sam

Trail at first sight had a feudal aspect. Its citadel, an imposing flat-topped hill at the confluence of a creek and a great river, thrust slab-sided buildings and smokestacks toward a dull, reeking sky. The heights sequestered a powerful elite, governing their town with a firm hand, and secluded an arcane guild of alchemists transforming base materials to precious metals. Far below, on the river flats prone to flood and fire, sprawled the commoners' wooden town of merchants and mansions and shacks. Epidemics regularly scoured out the worst shanties. A commoner could ascend the heights temporarily only by supplying lesser trades or brute labour.

Trail in 1916 was worlds removed from the medieval, of course. It had electric lights, motorcars, daily trains and long distance telephone service. It had Canada's foremost lead smelter and several global "firsts" for metallurgical technology. The mayor, the chamber of commerce and the *Trail News* agreed it was a city of the future. Others took a different view, especially from the base of Smelter Hill.

"When I came to Trail in the early days it was a town of horses, barns, manure heaps and flies and sticky fly paper," said Andrew Waldie in a 1979 interview; he'd come to work as a clerk for the smelter in 1913. Fly paper was the salient feature of the restaurants on Bay Avenue. Big sheets of sticky fly paper lay on the counters, and saucers held fly pads. Long strips of fly paper hung here and there from the ceilings. The reason was easy to find, Waldie said. The alley behind the restaurants was dotted with steaming, fly-infested manure heaps from the livery stables that fronted on the next street. "Flies were predominant, and why not?"

Flies plagued Trail's town centre in particular. Built in wood and threatened several times by forest fire, the downtown area occupied the river flats between Trail Creek and the Columbia River at the foot of a steep south-facing embankment. Consolidated Mining and Smelting Company Limited, by far the town's largest employer, occupied Smelter Hill above. The narrow valley of Trail Creek where it flowed down to the Columbia River came to be known as the Gulch. This area housed the town's working people, mostly recent arrivals from non English-speaking parts of Europe including Italy, Austria and the Slavic countries. Despite the foul fumes that roiled invisibly down from above, the Gulch offered the immigrants companionship, mutual protection and affordable housing within a few minutes' walk of the smelter.

Early Trail attracted more single men than married men. Some batched in shacks right in the hill's shadow on land later given over to a slag dump. The poorest or thriftiest lived two or three to a shack, never letting the beds cool as they worked and slept in shifts. Others lived in rented rooms, boarding houses or hotels, and took their meals among the thickets of fly paper. Some gave Trail a wild-west character, and a reputation as a high-rolling, hard-drinking town it hasn't entirely lost today.

"There was a whole lot of characters landed in this town simply because there was a steady payroll. The odd few used to come around every two months, the gamblers. They'd sit down and play cards. Gambling was the pastime," recalled retired smelter worker Mike Landucci. "Either you'd go to the saloon or to the poolroom to play cards, and they'd smuggle a drink to you. That was bootleg, you weren't supposed to do that at all."

Well away from flies and livery stables lived Trail's leading families, whose travels and entertainments the *Trail News* faithfully reported in its "In and Around Trail" column. Their gracious homes were either in the central area — like the Cedar Avenue house of police magistrate, former mayor, furniture merchant and undertaker Noble Binns — or up on the "benches" of surrounding hills, like the founding Hanna family's house. Bill Devitt was Trail's popular chief constable, later city clerk and police chief. His Provincial Police salary didn't allow his family high living in their Cedar Avenue home, but they did enjoy select company and were favourites of the social notes. Devitt led Trail's 1901 incorporation parade on a grey charger; this was a social highlight, like his 1904 marriage to Sophia Hanna. Devitt, who kept bloodhounds or boarhounds, was known as a crack shot with a revolver. James Schofield, another former mayor and Trail's Member of Provincial Parliament (MPP), made frequent appearances in the *News* socially as well as politically. At the turn of the century Trail's "big four," all Freemasons, were alderman James Byers, Schofield, Devitt and Binns.

Consolidated's managerial and technical staff soon created their own hierarchy of privilege. At first they lived in the company staff house, but later they found a haven upstream and upwind—away from the sulphurous smelter fumes—in the pleasant riverview suburb of Tadanac. The company reserved this neighbourhood for residents of its choice, mainly smelter mandarins.

"They wanted to keep the place exclusive," Andrew Waldie said. "They didn't want any Tom, Dick or Harry in there. They wanted somebody socially acceptable."

Any Tomaso, Ricardo or Enrico was especially unlikely to fit the bill, according to Mike Landucci's recollections. He explained why some newcomers called themselves Austro-Hungarian—a choice they regretted when the Canadian government began interning "enemy aliens" in 1914—rather than Italian.

"Here most people used to avoid Italian nationality, because it was not desired by the ruling group here, a Scottish group. Believe me, they were born by the barrel in Scotland where they got them from. Often as not they became supervisors," he said. They routinely demanded kickbacks for taking on new employees; the preferred gift was a bottle of good Scotch whisky. "It was really something. Class distinction was very prominent."

The Italian workers spent many off hours shouting over the frenetic finger gambling game *morra,* bowling the boxwood *bocce* balls, playing poker, attending the opera, watching boxing matches, arguing about politics and the war. Mostly they worked. Landucci remembered, "My dad used to say, 'That's all this damn country's good for, is work and money.'"

Work and money, however, drew people to Trail in the first place. The city grew quickly from a creek-crossing stopover to a prosperous centre—so quickly, in fact, that there was never quite time for some of the finer points of habitation. In April 1916 the *Trail News* printed a hopeful list:

THINGS TRAIL NEEDS
Better coast mail connections.
Free express delivery system.
Speed by-law for motorists.
Enlarged fire department.

Ownership of water shed.
City building inspector.
Lower insurance rates.
Apartment houses.
Federal building.
More residences.
Steam laundry.
Sewer system.
Creamery.

Many of these items would be available, in a rush of wartime prosperity, before the printer's ink faded.

The Italians soon realized Trail's class-ridden society was inimical to their progress in the new country. If they wanted to enjoy life, let alone achieve a better life, it was up to them to secure it. As a child Mike Landucci was thrown into speaking English, sink or swim, when he translated not only for his midwife mother but for magistrate Noble Binns in court. One lesson was driven home to all Italian youngsters: go to school, study hard, learn English, get ahead. Education was everything. Another self-help solution in 1905 was formation of the Cristoforo Colombo Lodge, which aided Italian members in distress and provided the social life from which Trail's English and Scottish elite excluded them.

Most of the Italians were temperate, though not Temperance tee-totallers. They "baptized" their wine by mixing it half-and-half with water in the Mediterranean tradition. "The Italians always with their meals drank their wine," Mike Landucci said. "Right to this day in the old country style, you go in the home, there's no such thing as tea and coffee on the table. The hell with that, that'll kill you, they say. Drink wine."

Smelter workers, like coal miners, sent their children to the saloon after shift with a bucket for ten cents' worth of beer. It cleansed the system of dust and chemicals, they claimed; certainly it slaked a powerful thirst after long hours of physical labour.

Working conditions at Consolidated were dismal. Wages and job security were immediate concerns in a favouritism-driven workplace, but accident and health hazards could be more serious in the long term. Lead poisoning from the vast quantities of smelter chemicals blighted vegetation and living creatures in downwind areas such as the Gulch and the city centre. One man said he didn't see a dog until he visited Vancouver when he was nineteen. The company warned residents in 1916 not to walk along the Columbia River near the smelter because of material dumped down the bank. There was no suggestion of cleaning up this health and environmental hazard — not until United States farmers a few miles south across the border undertook a damages lawsuit years later — only a warning to "approach at your own risk."

Trail didn't impress Andrew Waldie when he first arrived. "You could stand downtown in Trail and point up the mountainside, and you could tell every birch tree on the mountainside. The birch trees were the first to die out. You could spot every birch tree, miles and miles and miles of them. . . . The birch leaf is spongy and absorbent, and seems to take in the acid. And they're the first to be killed."

Waldie remembered one incident from soon after his marriage. "One morning I'd gone out to work and walked up the hill, and there were half a dozen roots of rhubarb growing by the road. That rhubarb looked so lovely that I went back into the house and asked my wife to come out to look at my rhubarb. The rhubarb leaves were about the most beautiful thing I ever saw in my life, just shining, shining, beautiful. . . . She did. When I came home at noon time I called my wife out again to have a look at those rhubarb leaves and they were absolutely white. I cut one of them and I rolled it out in the palm of my hand and it was spun out like a silk handkerchief. And I turned round to my wife, I says, 'You've been washing today?' She says, 'Yes, the sheets are on the line there.' I says, 'Look, you go up and touch one of those sheets with your forefinger.' 'Why?' 'Never mind . . .' She went up to the line and touched on of the sheets with her forefinger, and her forefinger went right through the sheet."

Consolidated employees who complained of the pollution, he said, were told, "You want your job? Well, you'd best keep your mouth shut. Keep your tongue between your teeth."

Workers were hardest hit by lead poisoning even in the plant's early years. "Leaded" men suffered various agonizing symptoms including stomach and bowel pain.

"Constipation was hardly the word for it," Mike Landucci said. "You almost became like hardened cement. It was terrible the way you'd see them lying on the floor and kicking their legs with stomach pains. And it would affect them in different ways, they went off their rockers, some of them."

Many victims died. The company helped some of their families, though they didn't pay compensation in the modern sense, by offering jobs or buying out their houses or arranging passage back to Europe.

Accidents also claimed lives in an extremely dangerous workplace lacking safety precautions and proper maintenance. The *Trail News* regularly reported accidents and the recommendations of subsequent inquiries, but the plant remained hazardous. Some men caught fire,

Gino Tognotti told interviewers, when they hand-tapped the huge vats of molten metal. Protective clothing was nonexistent. "That's like asking, Did they go for a holiday on the moon. No, there was no such thing as hard hats or safety shoes with steel toe caps. Goggles, never even heard of them," Landucci said. "Mind you, the company tried at the time to bring in any precautions they could take advantage of for the employees, but it was a time in history when people were expendable."

Andrew Waldie remembered, "One man was killed because the rope that was holding a scaffold broke. Now when a rope breaks holding a scaffold, that rope was in poor shape to start with."

At the turn of the century smeltermen worked an eleven-hour day shift or thirteen-hour night shift, but by 1916 men in some positions were working only eight hours a day—theoretically. In practice they might work ten or twelve, retired smelterman Peter Lauriente told an interviewer; on day wages with no overtime their pay packet remained the same for eight hours or twelve. Workers had been demanding an eight-hour day for years in British Columbia, with varying degrees of success, since the earliest days of smelting in the West Kootenays.

Gold and silver strikes first brought independent miners to Trail and nearby Rossland in the 1890s; what kept them there was abundant lead-silver-copper ore with a high zinc and iron content. Montana mining magnate Fritz Heinze opened a four-furnace copper smelter at Trail Creek in 1896 and acquired railway right-of-ways throughout the West Kootenays before he stretched his finances too far and had to sell. The Canadian Pacific Railway, just starting work on its southern line through the Crowsnest Pass, cast an acquisitive eye at Heinze's railway holdings. All or nothing, Heinze offered; in 1898 for about $800,000 the CPR took ownership not only of right-of-ways, trackage and rolling stock but of Trail's new copper smelter. The operation grew rapidly, and soon required specialized staff. In 1899 the new chemist was a freshly graduated engineer from Montreal's McGill University, twenty-year-old Selwyn Gwillym Blaylock.

"Blay" was a good-looking young man, tall and well-built with brown hair and blue eyes, an all-around natural athlete. Born in 1879 in Paspebiac, on Quebec's Gaspé Peninsula, he was the son of a Methodist minister. His father was from Ulverston, Cumbria, in the north of England, and his mother from Quebec City; his two given names suggest a Welsh connection. Friends described him as sociable, hard-working, brilliantly innovative, perhaps somewhat strait-laced, always concerned about his employees' welfare; others said he high-handedly interfered with his workers' personal lives and held grudges.

Soon the company had recognized his extraordinary aptitude for both metallurgical development and management. In 1906 he became chief metallurgist for the newly incorporated Consolidated Mining and Smelting Company of Canada Limited, and over the next few years he managed Consolidated's mines at Nelson and Moyie. In 1911 he became assistant general manager and in 1919 general manager. An entire generation of Consolidated operations would later be remembered as the Blaylock Era.

Arriving in Trail was an adventure that he relished even years later. *Trail, BC: A Half-Century, 1901–1951* printed his recollections:

> . . . As I came down the Arrow lakes on July 29, 1899, the thermometer was about 100 in the shade. Coming down the river from Robson we travelled through heavily wooded country right down to the "Smelter Junction." The clearing was some ten or fifteen acres right about where the zinc plant stands now and the present Tadanac station was there—a fine new building all painted up, with "The Head Offices of the BC Southern Railroad" on top.
>
> Beside the station was a little group of three houses, a fairly large stable and some shops. The general office was a very unpretentious one-storey building. The smelter was not in sight; it was over the brow of the hill.
>
> After considerable fussing the train swung over the hill and proceeded down the side hill to enter the Gulch. Most of Trail was then resident in the Gulch and most of it was foreign. The remainder were in the Bowery, which is the present Dewdney ave., and a few cottages were on Hanna bench—one occupied by Frank Hanna, who had helped locate the townsite.
>
> At the Crown Point [Hotel] I enjoyed an excellent dinner and then started to look for the man I was to work for. I found him in the bar playing solo—it was Sunday, too—so I decided to wait until morning to see him and went to bed.
>
> I had no sooner landed on the pillow than I heard a revolver shot followed by five more in quick succession. In the morning I expected to hear of murders but nobody seemed excited and I had to inquire. "Oh, nobody was hurt. The shooter's aim was poor and a little alcoholic!"

Blaylock and Consolidated's other high-spirited young technical staff threw themselves into their work. After hours they played baseball, then Trail's favourite sport, and introduced a tennis team

and a rifle club. Blaylock was later president of the curling club. But
it was hockey, in the fall of 1899, that nearly got them all fired.

> There weren't many hockey players but there were a
> powerful lot of willing recruits. I sent away and got 18 sticks
> and six pucks. They came in November before there was
> any ice and the boys were too impatient to wait.
> We got a tennis ball and went out at the back of the assay
> office. The game was so good it was continued in the bunk
> house that night. That was disastrous! Before long, we had
> to call the game on account of darkness; all the electric
> lights were broken.
> When we surveyed the damage we found a lot of plaster
> loose and a lot of cuts and bruises. We would have been
> fired if everyone but the general manager hadn't been in on
> the game.
> Later we worked out quite a team. Our power line were
> all over 200 pounds a piece and we gave Rossland some
> good games.

In the seven-man hockey teams of the era, Blaylock played point.
Working 6:30 a.m. to 5:00 p.m. every day but Sunday left little
time for hijinks. Consolidated added an electrolytic lead smelter — the
first in Canada to produce refined lead — and soon added a silver
refinery. CPR's powerful financial backing allowed the company to
either buy or squeeze out all nearby competition; taking over several
mines in the region ensured a steady supply of raw ores. It also
influenced Canadian tariff legislation, ending duty-free imports of
United States lead. Selwyn Blaylock personally innovated a high-
efficiency refining process that reduced lead loss from 20 percent to
3.5 percent per ton. With Kootenays ores to refine and Crowsnest
coal to fire its furnaces, Consolidated grew steadily.

Zinc content in Consolidated's complex ores had always been a
problem at Trail. Slagged out with other undesirable materials, zinc
was yet another obstacle to efficient silver-lead refining. Blaylock's
metallurgical staff had puzzled over ways to transform the zinc from
hindrance to benefit, but this remained as far beyond reach as the
alchemist's dream of transforming lead to gold. The company bought
an option on an electrolytic zinc process in 1912, but soon let it lapse;
it offered no advantage over existing methods. Still, there had to be a
way to pull zinc even from difficult ores. In 1914 an experimental
small-scale zinc plant at Consolidated, using sulphuric acid as a
leaching agent, did produce several carloads of high quality zinc. This

arrived on the market just as it became clear that the war in Europe would last not months but years. Britain, rushing to expand its armaments, desperately needed new sources of refined zinc—a component of brass—to manufacture ammunition. In 1915 Consolidated signed a contract to produce and refine zinc for a British agency in Canada, the Imperial Munitions Board.

The Canadian army needs shells, General Sam Hughes told the country in August 1915, and proposed a "combination of Canadian capitalists" to fund development of a Canadian zinc smelter. While Hughes stressed Canadian needs, Britain was the driving force behind manufacture of Canadian war goods. The Imperial Munitions Board had been created at British insistence (but only after Britain cancelled all Canadian contracts) to end Canada's shoddy workmanship, profiteering scandals and non-delivery of munitions and supplies. Hughes cast a cold eye on labour, too, saying that all strikes were incipient civil war. The antipathy was mutual. A January 1915 *Federationist* commented, "If talk would win battles Sam Hughes would be an army in himself." Now Canadian copper and zinc—instead of being refined in the United States and resold in Canada at higher prices—would be produced and refined at Trail and elsewhere in Canada, said a *Trail News* story.

There was no pacifism in Canada, the same newspaper quoted a *London Telegraph* story; resistance to the war, especially from the labour movement, was growing in Britain with the introduction of compulsory military service. Clearly the *Telegraph's* writers hadn't been reading the views of Canadian socialists, certain religious groups, non-British immigrants and labour activists in papers including the British Columbia Federation of Labour's weekly *Federationist* and the UMWA's *District Ledger* in Fernie, among others. From the start, they portrayed the European war as an exercise in imperialism and profiteering.

Canadian-born men were reluctant to enlist even before the war. Desmond Morton quoted the *Farmer's Sun* view that since three-quarters of Canada's regular army were British-born, "The fact is a tribute to the common sense of our people" for not enlisting. Sir Wilfrid Laurier himself had rejected a philosophy "which wants to bring Canada into the vortex of militarism which is the curse and blight of Europe." Pacifism, and a thorough distrust of other nations' warmongering, flourished in Canada. But so did frenzied support for the war.

Carnival gaiety greeted the first announcement of war in many British Columbia towns. In Rossland, twelve miles from Trail, fifty men had enlisted immediately and half accompanied the first contingent of the Canadian Expeditionary Force. On their departure date, wrote Lance Whittaker, "an impromptu celebration was sparked which lasted throughout the night and ended only when the men had been put aboard their train the next morning" as Trail's smelter whistle blew continuously for an hour. More than five hundred people paraded the streets all night singing and playing patriotic airs. Every Rossland recruit left with a gift of ten dollars raised by their city council and legislative member. Noble Binns gave each Trail recruit — more than two hundred, mostly from the smelter — a watch as a personal gift. He also donated twenty-five dollars to the gun fund; Trail MPP J.H. Schofield donated ten dollars and Bill Devitt five dollars. Mrs. Devitt and Mrs. Binns donated old sheets for bandages.

A year later there was less enthusiasm but more rancour, not toward the war but toward those who opposed it. Men who declined to enlist were castigated as cowards, shirkers and slackers. Society women took time out from knitting socks and wrapping bandages to hand white feathers — symbols of cowardice — to strangers in the street. Heavy-handed sarcasm turned up in print. A *Life* item reprinted in the *Trail News* was titled *The Creed of the Slacker:* "I believe in peace and the obliteration of all feeling of wrath and indignation for crimes against humanity and civilization. I believe in a supine endurance of all insults, and a cringing compliance with the evil forces of bestiality, destruction and lust. I believe in opening the gates to madmen and leaving our homes defenceless. I believe that if a war is to be fought it should be fought by someone else. I believe in milk and water namby-pambyism and flapdoodle, in gush and bunkum, in veiled eyes and in soft heads, in mealy mouths and in fat stomachs, in the encouragement of cowardice, in the forgiveness of everything rotten and in slavery everlasting for the Kaiser's sake. Amen."

But soon the war became a hideous reality to Canadians, even the most fervently patriotic. In June 1915 Sergeant Major Hill wrote to the *Trail News* that he had visited the 7th Battalion at the front. "I am very sorry to inform you that I found very little except the name left. C.P. Jones is the only one of the Trail boys [to survive]. At the battle of Ypres the 7th Battalion lost, killed and prisoners, about 700, including 13 officers, and on returning to billets, could not muster 100 men. . . . C.P. Jones is well except a touch of nerves, and I say the man who comes through an engagement like the one we have come through with nothing less than 'a touch of nerves' is lucky."

Sergeant Jackson wrote, "We were in the trenches 7 days and it seemed 7 weeks, as the Germans were shelling us pretty accurately. We advanced under a hail of bullets and shrapnel. Our company lost heavily. I lost all my section except two men. . . . All of us are pretty well shaken up with the strain. . ."

Prime Minister Sir Robert Borden in his 1916 New Year's message promised Canada would provide half a million soldiers—the war's huge impact had shocked him on a recent trip to Britain—yet the country's population was only about eight million, and voluntary enlistment was dropping off dramatically. War was coming home in every sense. An army garrison was stationed right on Smelter Hill, not far from Consolidated's strategic lead, copper and zinc plants. Canadian casualty lists grew steadily longer until the government banned their publication in 1916; the huge numbers of dead and wounded were too discouraging. Soldiers returned with appalling injuries and neurological damage from poison gases. Many told incredible tales of Flanders mud floating with corpses and seething with vermin. No one could go on believing this European war was a chivalrous passage of arms.

Even romantic Canadian poetry conveyed the awful cost: "In Flanders Fields the poppies blow / between the crosses, row on row. . ." Some British poets were far blunter. The premier voice of imperialism, Rudyard Kipling, after his only son's death in France wrote in *Common Form:*

> If any question why we died,
> Tell them, because our fathers lied.

And in *Dulce et Decorum est* Wilfrid Owen wrote of a friend's death from poison gas:

> If you could hear, at every jolt, the blood
> Come gargling from the froth-corrupted lungs,
> Obscene as cancer, bitter as the cud
> Of vile, incurable sores on innocent tongues,
> My friend, you would not tell with such high zest
> To children ardent for some desperate glory,
> The old Lie: Dulce et Decorum est
> Pro patria mori.

Owen was killed in action in 1918, a victim of the old lie: Sweet and proper it is to die for the homeland. But these voices of truth were heard only years later because of Canadian wartime censorship of telegraph messages and newspapers.

Meanwhile, the Imperial Munitions Board plan worked; within two years the Imperial Munitions Board was the biggest business in

Canada with 250,000 employees. By April 1916 Consolidated was producing a modest twenty to fifty tons a day of zinc; not a heavy output, the *Trail News* conceded, but "mighty important to Canada at this particular time." Industrialists in the neutral United States were also turning splendid profits by selling arms and supplies to any buyer; a Montana smelter was now also refining superior ore with a successful electrolytic zinc process. Consolidated soon had a sales office in Montreal, and contracts not only with the Imperial Munitions Board but with allies including Britain, Russia and Japan.

Workers were expected to back the war financially as well as philosophically. Consolidated employees contributed to the Canadian Patriotic Fund, a national charity to support soldiers' families. The company docked each man's pay cheque for the fund; contribution was not voluntary. Many workers gladly supported the war — many men enlisted, and reservists from the Italian army went to serve their country of birth — but in any case challenging Consolidated management over any such issue seemed a certain way to get fired.

Selwyn Blaylock gave a substantial one hundred dollars to the gun fund and was president of the Win-the-War Club, but his personal commitment went beyond charitable donations. In October 1916 he accepted a captain's commission in the Reserve Militia, Trail Company; he had been a lieutenant in the unit for about ten years. Francis Morin, president of Trail's Conservative Association and a political colleague of James Schofield, was a major. The reserve company was disbanded months before the armistice, in February 1918. This information comes, rather puzzlingly, not from regular Canadian army records but from Canadian military intelligence files. Through 1917 and into 1918, whether or not Consolidated employees knew it, the assistant general manager was Captain Blaylock.

The war had an escalating effect on Trail smeltermen. Wages rose slightly, but wartime inflation swallowed any advances and cut deeply into their modest standard of living. Already there were signs that the situation would worsen after the war, as union representative Helena Gutteridge illustrated in a January 1916 *Federationist* story.

> An example of patriotism was recently displayed by a local employer of labour, who very kindly discharged from his employment a man who was receiving $75 a month, taking on in his place a returned soldier at $40 a month. All in the name of patriotism.

Women suddenly played a more visible role during the war. They worked in public service and manufacturing — the *Trail News* couldn't resist a coy quip that female munitions workers were "no new stunt" since lots of girls were used to having arms around them—and ran family farms and businesses singlehandedly. Now their contribution might gain official recognition. In August 1916 the British Columbia government announced it would put not only prohibition (largely a women's concern because of alcohol's social devastation) but women's suffrage to referendum. Women would have a vote provincially if the referendum passed at the provincial election on September 14.

Trail was in Ymir riding. Candidates put up their hundred dollars and stepped forward one at a time. James Schofield, one of Trail's "big four," a real estate and insurance agent, Conservative MPP since 1908, would defend his seat. The Liberal hopeful was mining engineer Michael Sullivan, an assistant superintendent at Consolidated. The Socialist candidate would be a smelterman, Albert Goodwin.

Ginger Goodwin was working at the smelter by May 1916 after his notably short stint as a mule driver at Coal Creek and, as usual, threw himself into organizing for the Socialist Party of Canada. Trail socialists met on May 13 to discuss the advisability of organizing, according to the *Western Clarion*. "Com. Goodwin in a short talk emphasized the necessity of education and clear propaganda showing the falsity of attempting organization without a realization of the Class Struggle etc. He was followed by J. D. Vincent, an Italian comrade who briefly explained the Marxian theory of 'Surplus Value,' explaining how profit was made." The party had gained local interest and support in Rossland's February provincial byelection when the indefatigable candidate Wallis Lefeaux had drawn good crowds. Listeners particularly liked his claim, said the *Rossland Miner*, that socialism's role was not to condemn anybody or anything, but to explain and criticize. This view diverged sharply from Sam Guthrie's view in 1913, when the young UMWA local president in Ladysmith said, "the SP of C is not a very kindly or tolerant organization," adding that the party objected strenuously to reform. Lefeaux captured only 44 of 690 votes, however, losing to the Conservative minister of mines. Could the relatively unknown Goodwin do any better?

Trail's Socialist Party local placed a *News* ad announcing their unanimous nomination of Goodwin, who was "a Miner by trade, but for several years [sic] has been employed at the Smelter." His campaign program would be "no compromise" and "no political trading."

"That the interests of the workers, and that of the capitalists cannot be harmonized, it is essential that the workers of Trail constituency support both financially and at the Polls SOCIALIST CANDIDATE MR. ALBERT GOODWIN. Rally to the greatest cause that ever was, which means ultimately Economic Freedom."

Ginger Goodwin ran an energetic campaign. At Premier William Bowser's late July political forum attended by seven hundred people—more than a third of Trail's two thousand eligible voters—Goodwin "started right in to attack both parties.... He spoke clearly and forcefully and did not mince his words. In his opinion the Conservatives fattened on the surplus, and he wished to know why they did not pass a compensation act that would be of benefit to the workingman while he was alive, rather than after he was dead or injured. Their only hope lay in the theories of the Socialists, he asserted, and appealed to the audience to vote that way."

The audience heckled him, the *News* said, good-naturedly.

Trail idled through a slow summer. Doukhobors sold strawberries for fifty cents a pail. A dentist set up business in Trail, ending the need to travel to Rossland or Spokane for dental work. Crowsnest coal miners accepted a wage settlement, ending slack work at the smelter. The 131st New Westminster Battalion at the smelter barracks expected to be relieved soon. A smelter worker died on the hill, crushed against a column by a crane in a noisy work area. Charlie Chaplin appeared in the film *The Fireman* at the Star Theatre; next door, Fisher's Cafe remained open night and day to cater to off-shift smeltermen. Speculation abounded that Pancho Villa's revolution (like other Central American conflicts, too tempting for the United States to resist) was Kaiser Wilhelm's plot to engage the United States in a local imbroglio instead of the European war. The *News* placed a tongue-in-cheek ad: "Lost, strayed or stolen: one war in Mexico. Finder will please communicate with the White House."

Goodwin continued his campaign in the July issue of the *Clarion* with an article titled "Salvation" and signed "Ginger." Perhaps he was on short rations when he wrote imaginatively of "the inevitable economic law which gives to those who own (but do not produce) all the luxury and enjoyment that society has at its command. The abundance of wealth is displayed before the workers' eyes in such forms as bouquets and pageants, with monkey dinners and blackbird pies (chorus girls encased in baked dough) and other similar debaucheries to satisfy the insatiate appetite of the class that rules..."

He ended, "As the condition of the workers becomes more unbearable, the call for education and knowledge must of necessity increase, that the galling chains of wage slavery, with their accompanying evil effects of misery and want, insanity and crime, may give place to a society where slavery is no more, and happiness and joy, peace and plenty, be at the disposal of all. This will mean 'Social Salvation.'"

The Liberals also drew a large turnout to their meeting in mid-

August, but Schofield was missing. Sullivan spoke first, the *News* reported.

"Albert Goodwin, Socialist, then took the stage, and in his usual clear-cut manner, expressed his opinion of both the old parties and their tactics and methods. . . . He invited anyone who wished to see present conditions continue, to vote for the Liberals and all that they represented, which he considered much the same as the Conservative as far as the workingman is concerned. From Nova Scotia to British Columbia, he stated, the record of the Liberals was anything but favourable to labour."

Ginger Goodwin held his own political meeting on August 22, inviting his two opponents and a prohibitionist minister to speak. James McKinnon, of Trail's metalliferous miners' union, also spoke in the socialist candidate's support; he doubtless won approval from the generally anti-union weekly paper by defending it against earlier attacks by Reverend Black. Goodwin spoke for more than an hour "expounding the doctrines from his standpoint." The next Saturday he left to take his campaign through the Salmo district. This tour may have drawn rural hostility for his labour socialist views; two weeks later when the Liberal and Conservative candidates were already trumpeting their victories, Ginger said only that he was "certain of the best of it here in Trail anyway."

"Each of the three candidates in Trail riding are out to save the country—from the other fellows—and they are telling the electors and any who may attend the meetings how they will do it," the *News* commented wryly. From across the border the *Republic Journal*, bemused, wrote "Judging by BC papers both [main] parties are composed of hoboes, horse thieves, murderers, bank wreckers and ex-convicts. Elections in BC are held any old time," every week or every five years "depending how much there is to boodle."

The Liberal *Victoria Times* savaged the Trail socialist candidate in late August, but the *Rossland Miner*—which affectionately if bafflingly called him Sam Goodwin—came to the defence of "the socialists in the province who would dare to set forth their views regarding the socialist teachings. . . . Reference is made in the article to the speech of Albert Goodwin, the bright young Socialist candidate for the Trail riding.

"The *Times* says:—'Albert Goodwin is a young man, full of the vague and irrational sort of half-baked thinking which passes muster for reason.'

"Recently the *Vancouver Sun*, in a report made reference to the socialist candidate at Fernie as follows: 'In a near falsetto voice he reeled off yards of the usual twaddle and economic fallacies of his type of speaker.'" It's not clear whether the writer meant the local candidate or Goodwin.

Meanwhile, the *Vancouver World* was already predicting a Conservative win in Ymir riding.

August gave way to a hot September, with temperatures up to 100°F, in time for Trail's Labour Day celebration. Rossland streets emptied as residents packed special trains for the twelve-mile trip down the hill from the mining town to the smelter town. There were brass bands and baseball games and union speakers. "Sam Goodwin, Socialist candidate for the riding, then spoke briefly regarding the relation between socialism and labour," the *Miner* said, and stressed the value of organization to the workers.

"Women and socialism," a topic neither of the other Trail candidates had targeted despite the suffrage referendum, was the advertised title of Ginger Goodwin's last speech three days before election day. "This branch of study has been given some consideration by the speaker, and an interesting address will be delivered. Everyone is cordially invited . . . " Neither local newspapers nor the covering dailies saw fit to report his message, which may reflect the importance they placed on women's issues; certainly they appeared more anxious about beer and spirits running dry after a prohibition bill. Contemporary writing, however, suggests some of the concerns.

"Equal pay for equal work is an absolute necessity for the protection of both men and women workers," wrote Helena Gutteridge in her January 1916 *Federationist* story. Britain's compulsory military service would soon influence Canada; it had already inserted the thin edge of the wedge by asking employers to encourage male workers to enlist and replace them with capable young women.

"This action of the military authorities, which has received the hearty endorsation of several employers already, now makes imperative the immediate enfranchisement of women, and more important still, their industrial organization, both in their own interests for their own protection, and in the interests of labour as a whole, both organized and unorganized.

" . . . The cry is going out for women to do their share in the saving of the Empire.

"The women as usual are responding, but because of their lack of knowledge of economics, and a desire called patriotism, to serve their country, there is great danger that they will accept the honour and glory of so doing in part payment for services rendered, instead of hard cash to the same amount as that paid to the men, whom they have replaced."

Cheap labour, whether women or returned soldiers, was tempting some employers in the name of patriotism, she warned (see page 102, above).

The *Federationist* had expressed concern about women in the workplace as early as 1912, after a cost of living study revealed that even the most frugal working woman could not live decently on the wages generally paid. Some employers urged single women to bridge their financial shortfall by seeking male companionship, thus actively encouraging prostitution. At the same time, hypocritically, they would dismiss a young woman who lapsed from the demanded chastity. As for uncounted domestic servants raped by employers and then dismissed for immorality, this set a vicious double standard of simultaneous degradation and punishment. Neither law nor custom prevented this evil.

A socialist system, Goodwin may have argued, would empower women politically and economically and organize them for workplace security against harassment and arbitrary dismissal. Also, it would prevent them from being used, or threatened, as a cheap labour force to replace union men. It can be no accident that many of Ginger Goodwin's closest friends, especially in Cumberland, were women: homemakers, schoolgirls, grandmothers, workers, organizers. Not only did he enjoy their company at dances or socials, he recognized women's importance. Women, knowing this, would play a key role in his survival through the summer of 1918 — until a woman helped bring his death.

As election day approached, Britain announced that "shirkers" evading compulsory military service would be hunted down. Germany was already imprisoning and even executing socialists who opposed the war. Yet many people were now expecting the war to end in 1917, and Britain was planning "almost socialistic" post-war reforms to prevent poverty and limit wealth. Social barriers had already weakened somewhat as different classes worked together at the front and at home. Canada, bathed in its colonial Edwardian afterglow, was making no such plans yet. It was a fertile field for socialists.

War and the spectre of conscription were on all minds in September 1916. Prime Minister Borden had promised from the start that only Canadian volunteers would fight, that Canada would never adopt conscription, yet in mid-August he had announced compulsory registration for young men as a new aid in identifying workers, recruiting soldiers and taking note of slackers. Ginger Goodwin was later widely remembered as an outspoken opponent of both war and compulsory service or contribution. Yet from the time of the provincial election not one line survives to prove that his campaign was anti-war, anti-conscription.

Censorship did not become official policy until the order-in-councils of April and May 1918, almost two years later, but well before then newspapers were expected to apply a patriotic kind of self-censorship. Most did. Those that didn't either voluntarily mothballed their presses as the *Ledger* did in Fernie or, as the *BC Federationist* did, eventually fell silent after arrests and legal proceedings by Canada's official censor. It was acutely dangerous, in a climate of patriotic hysteria, to speak against the war as Goodwin did. To report it was merely untoward.

On September 14, Brewster's Liberal party swept British Columbia. Conservative James Schofield again won Ymir riding with 558 votes of a total 1,275. Albert Goodwin, Socialist Party of Canada, took 254 votes. Of these 214 were in Trail itself, as he predicted, from a total of 770; Schofield only took 237 votes in Trail, coming second to Sullivan with 319, apparently winning largely on the strength of his rural vote. Voters also approved both prohibition and the vote for women.

"In the Ymir riding," the *Clarion* reported, "a clean and vigorous fight was put up by Com. Goodwin who, for the first time, entered a campaign as the representative of the SP of C. This was the first election that other than a labour fakir was placed in this riding on behalf of the party, and much credit is due Com. Goodwin for the manner in which he conducted the fight. Mention must also be made of Com. Zanoni who proved of great assistance among the foreign speaking element of the Trail workers."

Defeat though this might have appeared on the surface, it reflected strong support for an anti-war labour socialist candidate in a wartime election. In fact, it launched the short trajectory of Ginger Goodwin's meteoric career.

Red

Trail's smeltermen discovered a strong speaker and experienced organizer in their ranks. Anyone who could coax a strong socialist vote from a longstanding Tory riding was a clear asset.

Albert Goodwin was elected secretary of the Trail Mill & Smeltermen's Union, Western Federation of Miners Local 105, on 18 December 1916. Six weeks later Goodwin and the local's executive board member J.A. McKinnon—his scrutineer and backer in the September 1916 election—were the local's delegates to the British Columbia Federation of Labour convention in the East Kootenays railway town of Revelstoke. Only months earlier at a Trail convention, Western Federation of Miners locals had reaffiliated with the federation; after several lean years this threw them back into the mainstream of the province's trade union and social reform movement. The organization's guidance and encouragement would be important within the year.

Flexing its new strength at this seventh annual convention, the federation wrestled with pressing concerns. The *Federationist* reported delegates "were alive to the new and wider responsibilities to be inherited by labour as an outcome of the present war." Without the bickering that had soured earlier conventions they took on the universal eight-hour day, the cost of living, a planned provincial workers' compensation act, and possible entry into provincial politics as a British Columbia Federation of Labour party (outgoing federation president J.H. McVety said the Socialist Party of Canada was no

longer a factor in the political life of the province despite the correctness of its platform). Above all, they discussed compulsory registration for military service.

Registration, Prime Minister Borden reassured a December 1916
meeting of British Columbia Federation of Labour representatives,
would merely assess available manpower and supply labour to necessary industries; no worker would be asked to move about the country
or accept a lower wage. Still, men were required by law to answer the
questions on the cards they were receiving by mail. But what use
would the National Service Commission make of the information it
gathered? "The government has not come to a decision," Borden said,
but refused to guarantee that registration would not lead to conscription.

Conscription was purely a philosophical issue for most of the
federation's executives, however, since most were over the age of
military service. Of the few who could be drafted, one of the most
outspoken was Ginger Goodwin.

Sounding increasingly like a pacifist gathering instead of a labour
gathering, the convention condemned compulsory donations to the
Red Cross and Canadian Patriotic Fund; instead the government
should provide for soldiers and their families rather than leaving this
to charity. It passed a vote of non-confidence in the federal government. It resolved — in response to a Winnipeg board of trade demand
for the arrest of two MPPs who opposed registration — to support and
aid the defence of any member of the working class charged with
treason.

Ginger Goodwin kept a low profile except to thank the *Federationist* for producing a worthy labour paper under adverse conditions. He made a favourable impression, however. In a mood to elect
left-wing executive officers, the convention chose his old friend Joe
Naylor president by acclamation, and voted Goodwin vice-president
for the West Kootenays.

Back in Trail, Ginger Goodwin settled into his duties as financial
secretary for the Trail Mill & Smeltermen's Union, Western Federation of Miners. Local 105's offices were at the labour hall downtown
on Cedar Avenue. His letters reveal his skirmishes with his perennial
enemies, English grammar and syntax, and the additional scourge of
typing. His first letter to Consolidated, less than three weeks after his
return from the Revelstoke convention, was a sharply-worded warning to the assistant general manager about men working longer than
eight hours in two areas. It was a direct violation of the law, he said,
and if it were not attended to immediately the union would take legal
action.

"There is a penalty imposed upon those that do not comply with the law, but we feel that you should have the opportunity to remedy the grievance before taking the case any further." Goodwin signed in his rounded legible hand, joining both names with one pen stroke.

His union letterhead still listed the previous president and secretary, their names scratched out. Lacking the check-off system, the union collected dues with difficulty and probably could spare no cash for printing. Not until June did the letterhead show Goodwin as financial secretary, and it didn't list the president at all; he apparently had stepped down. By late October 1917 the letterhead had changed again. It identified the union as the International Union of Mine Mill and Smelter Workers, Local 105. The federation had reorganized and changed its name but newspapers, among others, continued to use both names.

Selwyn Blaylock was none too pleased by this letter, his reply shows. The union's previous secretary had taken a mild and conciliatory tone and, it would soon become clear, had failed to challenge Blaylock adequately in negotiations. Goodwin was another matter.

"Prior to the receipt of your letter of the 27th February, the matter of some men working more than eight hours on the Converters had been corrected," Blaylock wrote; his letter was neatly typed by a secretary and signed with a flourish of vaunting capitals. Despite his reprimanding tone, he took care to explain the smelter's position: he had been unaware of similar violations in the copper refinery, but would see that the spirit as well as the letter of the law was upheld. It was difficult, he said, to arrange the copper pours precisely within a shift.

"We are running our Copper Department more for the convenience of the workmen both at Rossland and here, and the providing of munitions, than for any profit to ourselves; in fact it is no secret that the entire operation of the Smelter is not profitable. I think the men understand this.

"If any of our workmen notice any such irregularity in the future, I hope that it will be brought to our attention in a courteous way, and not be accompanied by a threat of prosecution in the Courts, before it is found out whether or not we are unwilling to observe the law." This was clearly a slap at, in his view, the union secretary's insolence. Battle was joined.

Solid organizing and rapid power gain characterized Ginger Goodwin's year-and-a-half sojourn in Trail. Soon he was not only secretary of the International Union of Mine Mill and Smelter Workers Local 105, but president of its District 6. In that capacity on 2 April 1917 he and fellow district officers approached Consolidated's managing director James Warren. They asked for a check-off of union dues and an across-the-board pay increase of fifty cents per day (between twelve and fifteen percent, depending on wages) for all smelter workers. Inflation rose an estimated twelve to eighteen percent in 1917. They pointed out that an existing agreement made by the previous union secretary specified no time limit. This was the crux of the dispute.

Even before the meeting and letter, the 30 March *Federationist* reported that District 6 was taking a strike vote on the matter, and warned workers away from Trail where they might find themselves jobless or, worse, hired to scab. Consolidated controlled most mining and smelting operations in the Kootenay and Boundary country, the story said, and all of its properties were running full blast. Other Kootenays plants paid about seventy-five cents a day more than the smelter.

Plain astonishment was Warren's first reaction. He wrote to J.D. McNiven, the federal government's fair wage officer, "Labour seems to have completely lost its head..."

Warren then wrote to Goodwin as secretary of the Trail local union, refusing to recognize that District 6 had any role in the matter. He said Consolidated had notified employees in May 1916 that the agreement was for the duration of the war, thus binding the union. But the Western Federation of Miners in Denver hadn't ratified any such agreement, the smeltermen's local countered. Goodwin replied that Warren's letter had been to McNiven, not the union, and in no way bound the union. "... I am instructed to notify you that there is no agreement between this union and the Consolidated Co., been drawn up." The district officers didn't budge from their position.

Warren eventually softened enough to offer a sliding-scale war bonus on April 28. The dues check-off was out of the question, though; he knew it would fund the union's future efforts. "Apparently restricting the financial well being of the unions was a higher priority than denying wage increases," Stanley Scott wrote. "Although neither side could claim victory, neither side had lost face."

"... The industrial situation in the Southern Kootenay interior mining centres, where strikes and lockouts have been in vogue for some time, is becoming somewhat clarified," said a May 18 *Federationist* story, adding that the agreements were with various local unions and not the district organization. Even in Vancouver observers seemed well aware of this drive for recognition, not only of the locals but of an umbrella organization. Joe Naylor wrote in the same issue — looking either back to the quiescent Wobblies or forward to Canada's One Big Union — that the only solution was industrial unionism.

Goodwin celebrated his pyrrhic victory three days later by leading Trail's May Day parade on horseback. He or someone else chose just the right mount for a slight and perhaps slightly vain red-haired man; in a surviving black-and-white photo the small neatly-made horse looks a reddish light bay. Its rider is smiling like a cat in a creamery, as the proverb has it, faintly but with distinct satisfaction. In a society still acutely aware that gentlemen rode and common folk walked, the sight could have startled anyone who hadn't known Ginger Goodwin as a mule driver. Karl Coe showed me the newspaper clipping and said, "I don't know, it seemed funny to me him being on a horse."

Joe Naylor, "the rough diamond," spent his May Day regaling a Nanaimo celebration with tales of the kaisers of Cumberland and their Prussian tactics. Wartime anti-German language in labour circles embodied a special irony. "Patriotic" — pro-war — Canadians such as the Winnipeg board of trade regularly denounced anti-war, anti-conscription socialists and trade unionists as German sympathizers or even German agents. Police files from the period also bulge with venomous letters, signed and unsigned, reviling fellow citizens as pro-German. Many smack of settling old scores, of personal pique carried into the public arena, rather than serious accusation. In Canada this was becoming a war of spite, vendetta, and voluntary or paid informers.

Few still believed Borden would keep his 1914 promise not to introduce conscription. Anti-conscription public meetings were held by labour, socialist and religious groups. In Vancouver meetings also protested the Canadian Patriotic Fund, not only compulsory contributions by workers but cavalier treatment for those who needed its financial aid. Most were widows or wives or mothers of soldiers. The *Federationist* demanded in April, "Why should women have to line up like convicts and be asked questions that no one has a right to know?"

The Military Service Act, announced 18 May 1917 after Borden's tour of European trench warfare, surprised few Canadians. It would draw on the information gathered by the registration campaign to enforce compulsory conscription. Reaction to the new act hit the British Columbia labour community in shock waves. As British Columbia Federation of Labour president, Joe Naylor wrote a scathing front-page editorial in the *Federationist* castigating idle and useless flag-waving patriots and supporting the workers as useful members of human society. The federation's secretary-treasurer wrote that Christ was a passive resister, true to his convictions to the death. Helena Gutteridge wrote that she couldn't find one good argument for conscription.

The anti-conscription outcry would remain at this pitch of intensity with a campaign of protests and meetings which met mixed success. An attempt to hold a meeting in Victoria fell through because no owner of a suitable hall would rent it for an anti-conscription gathering; one even refunded the federation's deposit.

Ginger Goodwin meanwhile was on the ascendant, increasingly a force to reckon with in the Kootenays. Backed by other union officers, he was steadily forcing the region's major employer to rethink its relationship with labour. Did he really believe he'd have the last word against powerful Consolidated Mining and Smelting, the CPR and the Imperial Munitions Board? At this stage his intent was clearly to parlay one minor, ambivalent exchange into a greater victory. Through the summer and fall of 1917 he levered the local union and the union district from a fragile toehold to a piton grip on the unscaled face of Consolidated.

Increasingly, he was becoming a man others noticed and remembered. His personal life in Trail remains little known. His name is missing from Trail's soccer roster during his stay. A stranger in a largely transient town, he was probably working too hard for the football and fishing and Saturday night dances he had enjoyed in Cumberland. By now he may also have been too unwell for strenuous activity. Apparently he lived alone, unlike fellow organizer Dick Marshall who raised eyebrows by living with a woman. Consolidated clerk Andrew Waldie remembered that Goodwin, a sick man, kept to himself and "didn't interfere with anybody apart from union affairs."

Ginger Goodwin lived in the Meakin Hotel on Cedar Avenue, just down from the union offices. Verandahs around three sides gave the three-storey wooden building an old-fashioned countrified air even in the centre of Trail. Mrs. Hurley ran the hotel dining room where Goodwin, like Andrew Waldie who rented a room nearby, took three meals a day.

"His teeth were like spikes of rusty barbed wire," Waldie told Buddy de Vito.

This interview was extraordinary, since Waldie interrupted himself several times to avoid saying something indiscreet. To reproduce one passage verbatim: "And after he was shot and killed on the orders of. . . Mrs. Hurley who knew him very well told me that she had never known him to eat a decent meal in all the time he stayed there, because he was not capable of eating a decent meal. He had stomach trouble. But that man was deliberately shot. . . . I wouldn't want to discuss it any further. But I knew Red Goodwin very, very well."

Waldie knew Goodwin mainly from his union work and their

shared mealtimes, but as a trusted company clerk he had access to confidential documents. Before the year's end some of these would shock him.

Mike Landucci, working in one of Trail's Italian groceries, saw a different side of the organizer he knew as Al Goodwin. "He was a nice fellow. I worked in the store, and of course I was indoctrinated that the customer is always right. You don't answer back, you're polite at all times. That was the way I had to conduct myself. And I got the same kind of treatment back."

He didn't know Goodwin well. "A small town, you know them to see them, hello how are you, and so on and so forth. He was not robust at all, rather inclined to be frail. Reddish complexion, auburn hair."

"He was an agitator," Landucci added, "the company would say."

Summer 1917 passed with minor complaints about some men working more than eight hours and others having their wages cut. Goodwin wrote Blaylock, more mildly than in his aggressive first letter, "The Union feels that it does not want to interfere with any plan that you may have for efficiency, but they want the wages that they are entitled to for the work they are rendering.... That is all we are asking for and nothing more. Hoping that you will give us a square deal, and trusting that you will favor us with an early reply..." Blaylock replied curtly that he must continue in his position that Goodwin should either leave the matter entirely to Consolidated, or else they should go over it thoroughly together to arrange a scale.

Local 105 helped to plan a company store which Consolidated had long wanted and the union had previously opposed. Now wartime inflation was rising steeply, and the company offered competitive prices. "... The men are anxious that the store be started as soon as possible," Goodwin wrote. "They don't want to be held up any longer is the cry of the men and all concerned."

Goodwill apparently smoothed these exchanges. But Ginger Goodwin hadn't abandoned his watchfulness over company abuses, and in August the summer's mannerly dealings began to evaporate. The kid gloves had been off for months; soon no one could pretend otherwise.

In late August Goodwin once again pressed Consolidated on an eight-hour day for carpenters, who were refusing to work Sundays. The company locked out the carpenters but, after a meeting with a committee of Goodwin and the carpenters' representatives, agreed to concessions. These showed a willingness to compromise—up to a point. Blaylock's letter ended somewhat ominously that if an agreement were reached and the men returned to work within three days, "there will be no discrimination against them." He left the alternative unspoken; no worker in 1917 needed to be told about firings and blacklists. As the widespread kickback system testified, most lived in fear of arbitrary dismissal.

The Rossland miners' union indeed wrote, cap in hand, to Warren only days later to ask that dismissed employees be reinstated. Warren answered blithely, "... I can assure you that there has not been, and never will be any discrimination against our employees by reason of any labour activities..." He blamed the interrupted coke supply (a veiled cut at striking Crowsnest Pass coal miners) for operations not working to capacity, and hoped that soon the company could rehire "all of our former employees who are able and willing to do a day's work for a day's pay."

Anti-conscription sentiment was still at fever pitch on the *Federationist's* front pages, as was criticism of the munitions industry. "Enforced military service is the complete and final denial of human freedom," an August 3 story commented. "What does Canada owe Europe? This may be answered in one word. Nothing!" The same issue presented a British Columbia Federation of Labour request for the federal government to take over the hated compulsory Canadian Patriotic Fund and for federation members to refuse further support to the fund after 1 December 1917. All protests were unavailing. On 29 August 1917 the Military Service Act became law.

A month later the British Columbia Federation of Labour held a special Labour Day convention in Vancouver to discuss its political role in the expected federal election, and the ongoing issue of conscription. The gathering voted overwhelmingly to "down tools" in a province-wide general strike over the first unwilling conscript. The debate was explosive even within the generally anti-conscription federation. Joe Naylor "urged the delegates to exercise tolerance, and to give everyone a free opportunity to express his views, no matter how much they might disagree with them." The federation knew this was a test of its mettle: "Organized labour is to be tried in the fire."

Ginger Goodwin, attending from Trail, said conscription meant life or death to the workers but still might not be put into practice. The Borden government deserved some credit if it could fool workers so easily, he said. The *Federationist* reported "If the war ended tomorrow he did not believe it would make any difference to the real interests of the workers. He believed there was a great force of opinion against conscription, and that the idea of striking and otherwise opposing it was not confined to Quebec by a long shot. He had, he said, been requested to become a socialist candidate in several constituencies, and if he took the platform in that capacity he would do all in his power to prove to the workers that the war was none of their business." He also told the convention that the Socialist Party of Canada "was uncompromising" about co-operating with candidates the British Columbia Federation of Labour itself fielded, since not all would necessarily be anti-conscription.

Ginger Goodwin's outspoken challenges to Canada's war participation, and the Military Service Act in particular, did not go unnoticed. His poor health would doubtless exempt him from military duty, but he spoke out for others. Why? Courage is certainly one explanation. Perhaps he also believed a Canadian commitment to free speech would protect him. Perhaps he thought—with some justification—the authorities simply didn't listen to labour, or he was quicker-witted and more ethically justified than the privileged elite who made up any country's "master class." Perhaps he believed the government, military and police fraternity were strong and resilient enough to take criticism in a constructive spirit. His intentions, it would turn out, were better than his judgment.

Around the same time the Vancouver Trades and Labour Council agreed to endorse a Trail smeltermen's union proposal that the provincial government make someone "from the ranks of labour" the next deputy minister of labour. The smeltermen recommended their own union secretary, Albert Goodwin. The Vancouver council hesitated— a recent recommendation for the new Workmen's Compensation Board had been rudely rebuffed—but ended by endorsing the idea.

Soon after, the *Federationist* erroneously reported that Ginger Goodwin and Joe Naylor might stand as British Columbia Federation of Labour candidates in a federal election. This embarrassed Goodwin, who wrote to the editor saying that he would run only for the Socialist Party of Canada. "Please insert this in the paper and it will help to clear up the atmosphere." The notoriously hard-line party may well have rushed to chastise him for this lapse.

Ginger Goodwin was steadily attracting attention and honours. He was West Kootenays vice-president of the British Columbia Federation of Labour, financial secretary of the International Union of Mine Mill and Smelter Workers local, president of the union's District 6, an eagerly sought socialist candidate, and now a nominee for the high provincial office of deputy minister of labour. This was an appointed, not elected, position; the successful candidate would report to the minister of the newly created provincial department of labour. More significantly by far, he had come one step closer to Joe Naylor's and apparently his own philosophy of industrial unionism. Company divide-and-conquer tactics were best foiled by gathering all trades in a given industry under one representation umbrella. Nearly two years before the industrial One Big Union came into existence, Goodwin managed a similar effect by helping to create the Trail Trades and Labour Council and becoming its first president.

In October, single-minded in his fight for the eight-hour day for all smelter workers, he again took on Consolidated. Now, in the all-inclusive Trail Trades and Labour Council, he had an effective lever to move the recalcitrant company. The council secretary wrote to Selwyn Blaylock asking for a universal eight-hour day at the smelter by 1 November 1917.

Blaylock would have none of industrial unionism in any guise. He wrote back, "As all our agreements re wages, hours, etc. have been made with the Trail Mill and Smeltermen's Union representing all classes of labour in the plant, all questions relating to any changes desired in these matters should be brought up through that organization." But the smeltermen's union represented only some of the company's workers. Others—including carpenters, machinists, pipefitters and plumbers—belonged to their own unions and were in no way bound by an agreement with the International Union of Mine Mill and Smelter Workers. Despite another bullheaded exchange of letters restating the case, both sides knew this well.

Goodwin and Blaylock had each made a first move in a winner-take-all game. In personal terms the minister's son and the coal miner's son were closely matched for patient and canny negotiation— all things being equal. A contest like this—between a powerful and profitable CPR company with government support and Allied war contracts, and a penniless labour council with the ink barely dry on its letterhead—was anything but equal. Goodwin was supremely confident, or monumentally rash, to take the risk.

Now they were face to face. Vociferously anti-war, anti-munitions, anti-conscription socialist Albert Goodwin was armed with moral certainty, dubious grammar, poor health and a rhetorical gift for swaying a crowd. Selwyn Blaylock—Captain Blaylock of the Militia Reserves, listed in military intelligence files, president of the Win-the-War League—was armed with moral certainty, intellectual brilliance, physical well-being, the confidence of a privileged upbringing, government contracts, and the pitiless Allied military machine.

Albert "Ginger" Goodwin paused in his pit clothes on a Cumberland porch in 1911. PHOTO COURTESY OF CUMBERLAND MUSEUM.

Ginger Goodwin played inside right forward for the championship Number Five Thistles mine team in 1911. Arthur Boothman played inside left forward. At back right are Chas Walker, and Peg and Meg Westfield.
PHOTO COURTESY OF CUMBERLAND MUSEUM.

An enamelled *CNP* for Crow's Nest Pass adorns the front of Ginger Goodwin's soccer medal, and the back is inscribed *Albert Goodwin*. He probably won it during his 1915–1916 stint at Coal Creek.

Number Five mine, described by one mule driver as "a mud hole," lay about half a mile from the centre of Cumberland. BRITISH COLUMBIA ARCHIVES AND RECORDS SERVICE PHOTO HP81812.

Number Four mine, famous for its clean-burning anthracite steam coal, partly underlay Comox Lake. Its roads were often awash in seepage water. PHOTO COURTESY OF CUMBERLAND MUSEUM.

An occasion for a pithead photograph: a multiracial 1912 Number Five shift broke a mine record for tons of coal loaded. PHOTO COURTESY OF CUMBERLAND MUSEUM.

Cumberland's local union 2299 of the United Mine Workers of America, chartered in 1911, lost the backing of its international union after the collapse of the Big Strike in 1912–14. PHOTO COURTESY OF CUMBERLAND MUSEUM.

Joseph Naylor, "the rough diamond," was Ginger Goodwin's closest friend. His labour and socialist activities brought him jail sentences, blacklisting and lifelong police surveillance. PHOTO COURTESY OF CUMBERLAND MUSEUM.

Union Camp in 1888 sprang up almost overnight among the tall stumps with rows of identical miners' cottages. Down camp, many of the houses still stand. BRITISH COLUMBIA ARCHIVES AND RECORDS SERVICE PHOTO HP11672.

Cumberland in its pre-1914 heyday was a hustling city of false fronts, boardwalks and pervasive mud. One old-timer called it "a wild west town." BRITISH COLUMBIA ARCHIVES AND RECORES SERVICE PHOTO HP41763.

Cumberland Chinatown once housed an estimated 3,000 residents among its dogleg streets, and was considered North America's third largest Chinatown after San Francisco and Vancouver. BRITISH COLUMBIA ARCHIVES AND RECORDS SERVICE PHOTO HP41770.

The Bucket of Blood saloon on Dunsmuir Avenue was usually more decorous than its unofficial name suggested. A handful of saloons and bootleggers prospered in early Cumberland. Miners drank mainly beer "to lay the coal dust." PHOTO COURTESY OF CUMBERLAND MUSEUM.

John Brown, miner and entrepreneur, prospected for gold in the Cumberland and Comox Lake areas for more than half a century. PHOTO COURTESY OF CUMBERLAND MUSEUM.

Campbell Brothers survived lean times during the Big Strike despite thousands of dollars in unpaid credit, but never reopened after two devastating fires in the early 1930s. Black Campbell is at far right. PHOTO COURTESY OF CUMBERLAND MUSEUM.

The Crow's Nest Pass Coal Company operated several mines and pithead works at Coal Creek, near Fernie. The townsite is visible beyond. BRITISH COLUMBIA ARCHIVES AND RECORDS SERVICE PHOTO HP62098.

Smelter Hill dominated the city of Trail in 1915. PHOTO COURTESY OF
TRAIL CITY ARCHIVES; BRITISH COLUMBIA ARCHIVES AND RECORDS
SERVICE PHOTO HP91431.

Trail's "big four" at the turn of the century, left to right, James Byers,
Noble Binns and William Devitt. Front, James Schofield. PHOTO
COURTESY OF TRAIL CITY ARCHIVES.

Consolidated Mining and Smelting Company executives R.W. Diamond and Selwyn Blaylock during the 1930s. PHOTO COURTESY OF TRAIL CITY ARCHIVES.

Ginger Goodwin led Trail's May Day parade on horseback in 1917. With him are Kootenays officers of the Western Federation of Miners. PHOTO COURTESY OF PACIFIC TRIBUNE.

A mass meeting in Trail's baseball park drew hundreds of smelter workers to vote on the November 1917 Consolidated strike. PHOTO COURTESY OF TRAIL CITY ARCHIVES.

Provincial Constable Robert Rushford with Jessie, Nava and Peter on the porch of their Penrith Avenue house in Cumberland. PHOTO COURTESY OF CUMBERLAND MUSEUM AND MRS. LOUVAIN BROVENLOW.

Ginger Goodwin and his fellow fugitives lived in several cabins at the head of Comox Lake, including one said to belong to trapper Tommy Anderson. PHOTO COURTESY OF HAROLD BANKS AND RUTH MASTERS.

Cumberland families spent idyllic summer holidays in tents or cabins at Comox Lake. PHOTO COURTESY OF CUMBERLAND MUSEUM.

Cumberlanders knew trapper Tommy Anderson as Scabby Anderson for his role in the shooting of Ginger Goodwin. PHOTO COURTESY OF BETTY FISHER AND RUTH MASTERS.

Albert Stephenson, right, was Provincial Constable in Cumberland during the Big Strike and Chief Constable of Namaimo at the time of the Goodwin manhunt. PHOTO COURTESY OF KAMLOOPS MUSEUM ASSOCIATION; BRITISH COLUMBIA PROVINCIAL ARCHIVES AND RECORDS SERVICE PHOTO HP23663.

Dan Campbell in his sixties, about fifteen years after he shot Ginger Goodwin. PHOTO COURTESY OF MRS. EVA HARRIS.

The Cruikshank River, still a good trout stream, flows through mountain wilderness into the head of Comox Lake.

"A mile of people:" the end of Ginger Goodwin's funeral procession was leaving Cumberland when the first marchers were arriving at the cemetery. Karl Coe, 13, was the boy leaning against the telephone pole.
PHOTO COURTESY OF CUMBERLAND MUSEUM.

LEST WE FORGET

GINGER GOODWIN

SHOT JULY 26TH

1918

A WORKERS FRIEND

Ginger Goodwin lay in an unmarked grave for about twenty years. When Cumberland miners finally gained recognition for the UMWA in the late 1930's, they remembered their organizer, "a worker's friend," and gave him an unusual headstone. PHOTO COURTESY OF CUMBERLAND MUSEUM.

A passionate and eloquent speaker, Ginger Goodwin addressed a
Kootenays audience about a year before his death. PHOTO COURTESY OF
CANADIAN UNION OF MINE, MILL AND SMELTER WORKERS; PUBLIC
ARCHIVES OF CANADA PHOTO C46568.

Azure tusk

Conscription was now law, for some men at least. Friends in high places could help; in October 1917 James Warren sent his workers a circular promising Consolidated would assist able-bodied men of military age to apply for exemption.

Noble Binns was outraged when he heard about James Warren's circular at a meeting in Nelson. Several Trail board of trade members were in attendance — including president Binns and Selwyn Blaylock — and Blaylock was first asked if the circular indeed existed. He slid the question over to his friend, who as police magistrate was a member of the exemption tribunal.

"Being a magistrate he had to look a little severe sometimes, not easy to approach," said Mike Landucci. He admired Noble Binns, for whom he had translated in court many times; the magistrate had been kind and encouraging to the young boy.

"Noble Binns was a man who never spoke to anybody," Andrew Waldie recalled. "He always barked at them. Bark, bark, bark, bark."

Binns did not mince words on this occasion. He knew of no authority that permitted Consolidated to issue such a circular, he said, and guaranteed that the provisions of the Military Service Act would be carried out with fairness to the company and the men. Personally he didn't consider the circular worth the paper it was printed on. Certainly men could apply for exemption from military service, and the tribunal would decide each case separately and individually on its own merits.

Conscripts were desperately needed. The United States had entered the war after discovering that Germany had indeed been busily fomenting a Mexican invasion, but no troops had yet seen combat. Britain was short of men even with conscription, almost bankrupt and unable to afford Canadian munitions. Prime Minister Borden had promised the Allied high command a hundred thousand soldiers. Volunteers were down to a trickle now that the enthusiastic and unemployed were already overseas, and the men had to come from somewhere — chiefly from Canadian industry. Employers were as vexed over this as their workers. Who would run the factories and businesses? Men between twenty and thirty-four, either single or widowed without children as of July 1917, were to present themselves to a medical examiner by November 10. Appearance was compulsory. Failure to report could result in immediate military service or five years' hard labour.

Four categories divided conscripts according to physical fitness. Category A men would be fit for service in an overseas fighting unit. Category B men would be fit for service in the Army Medical Corps, Forestry Battalion (like the units logging Scottish forests) or another non-combat service. Category C men would be fit for service only in Canada. Category D men would be unfit for military service of any nature. Application forms for exemption were available at the post office; applicants would be notified by mail when and where the exemption board would consider their claim. Exemption rapidly became currency in the workplace; one man seeking a clerk's position advertised in the newspaper that he was both experienced and exempt from military service.

Trail men had to travel to Nelson for medical examination. This was a case of the tail wagging the dog, the *Trail News* complained, since more men lived in Trail than Nelson. "Applicants hereabouts must lose a shift for the pleasure of appearing before the doctor." This added injury to insult in an already thoroughly unpopular program. The military took the hint and formed a Trail medical board, to begin sitting on November 1.

Ginger Goodwin was unmarried and thirty years old, square in the middle of the eligible age group, but his health was poor. His teeth were decayed to the gums in places, his ulcer prevented him from eating properly and his lung disease — pneumoconiosis or tuberculosis — was obvious to a casual observer. He was thin, even gaunt, and tended to walk stooped. He wouldn't survive a fortnight on hardtack and bully beef even in otherwise healthy conditions, which scarcely described the war's morass of Belgian mud and shrieking artillery barrages. Obviously he would be exempted.

Joe Naylor didn't trust the exemption system — in truth, didn't trust any government guarantee — as he told the British Columbia Federation of Labour's Labour Day convention. The *Federationist* reported, "He referred to the strikes of the munition workers in Britain and declared that the promises of the Borden government with respect to exemptions were not reliable."

A shocking blow fell in October when the Socialist Party of Canada, a group he had loyally sustained for seven years, expelled Ginger Goodwin. No member could seek office under an existing government, the charter stated, and Goodwin had allowed his colleagues and supporters to put forward his name for appointed provincial deputy minister of labour. The Dominion executive committee voted unanimously to expel him, according to the *Clarion*, for the reason "That any individual attempting to enter political life as a lackey of the present political parties is unfit to hold membership in the SP of C. That the action of A. Goodwin in allowing his name to be used as a candidate for Deputy Minister of Labor in BC, and his acceptance of the candidature by the absence of any public repudiation placed him in the position above stated."

The same issue notes two letters received from Goodwin, but not published. Over the next eight months he continued to send money for *Clarion* subscriptions he had sold and to write letters; the socialist party paper continued to file his letters unpublished. He remained loyal. The party remained inflexible, if opportunistic. Not until his death did the *Clarion* again take much note of the expelled comrade.

This ejection must have hurt and annoyed him, not least because of what it revealed about the party. The Socialist Party of Canada, never especially broad-minded or forbearing, seemed to be steadily narrowing its range of tolerance. Did he wonder if his ejection was due partly to his growing popularity? The stern, politically correct party would have little warmth for any man or woman who inspired a cult of personality. He mentioned neither his expulsion nor his reaction in a long October 29 letter which the *Federationist* printed in its November 2 issue under the heading *"Ginger" Goodwin's Size-up*.

"Despite the oratorical gabfests of these politicians that are booming their guns for a win-the-war policy, and that Canada will have to yield her every effort, it is plain to be seen that their cry is in harmony with the dominant interests of the Dominion . . ."

"It is essential to the manufacturing interests of this country to see to it that there is to be money for the sale of the wares that are necessary to keep up the war," he wrote. ". . . the workers of the old land have been weaned of their paltry savings in return for war bonds so that the industrial operation of the munitions plants could be kept going, and the profits flow into the war-mongers' pockets."

England, now in financial crisis, was purchasing United States munitions in return for substantial war loans (Canada and the United States, among others, today still make "tied aid" a condition of technological assistance to developing nations). This arrangement would soon affect all classes in Canada, Goodwin warned, and especially working people.

"War is simply a part of the process of capitalism, and it needs money in the carrying out of the exchange of the commodities essential to its prosecution," Goodwin wrote. "The old saying that 'you pay to learn' is evidently correct, whether it be with lives or money. The Morgans, Rockefellers, Rothschilds and other big financial interests are playing the game and it is they that will reap the victory, no matter how the war ends. It will be the law of the concentration of capital into fewer hands strangling the life out of the smaller capitalists in the process of creating a smaller number, but more powerful master class, than was before. Whether the capitalist system can survive this cataclysm remains to be seen. It is the hope of the writer that capitalism will fang itself to death, and out of its carcass spring the life of the new age with its blossoms of economic freedom, happiness and joy for the world's workers."

The next day, having aired his views on munitions and war profits, Ginger Goodwin as local union secretary wrote another letter to Selwyn Blaylock. Its tone was as uncompromising and pugnacious as Consolidated's recent refusals to discuss the eight-hour day. This time the difference was instead over the Canadian Patriotic Fund, detested both as an abuse of citizens compelled to contribute and of women forced by circumstance to request it.

"I am instructed to inform you that if the patriotic money is taken out of the mens' envelopes on next pay day, the men will refuse to work the following day. If you can assure the union that it will not be deducted any more it will avoid any stoppage in the operation of the Smelter." Rather than mailing the letter, Goodwin and a committee handed it in person to the assistant general manager.

Blaylock replied the same day in unusually reasonable and co-operative terms. He acceded to the request—perhaps in part because it had come from the smeltermen's union alone and not the Trail Trades and Labour Council, a blanket organization with undertones of industrial unionism—and offered not only one but two possible ways of carrying it out. Individual workers could instruct the company to stop deducting patriotic funds from their pay cheques, or any ten men could request a general meeting of the smeltermen to deal with the question. The meeting could have the war fund committee deduct contributions through the bank instead of the smelter, "in which case the Company would have nothing to do with any deductions on this account."

"I am instructing all foremen that men may not be fired because they will not subscribe to the Patriotic Fund. While the company has no right to force men to subscribe to the Patriotic Funds, I feel that this is a matter for each individual to decide for himself, which he may do without fear of molestation in his work," wrote Blaylock in tones of benevolent moderation.

Exasperation had caught up with him the next day when he wrote to the fund secretary, "it is impossible to convince the men that they will not be fired for failing to subscribe to the Patriotic Fund..."

The secretary, a former smeltermen's union officer, obediently called a meeting. That Saturday night, about eighty-five smeltermen decided to make contributions through the bank. At the meeting, Selwyn Blaylock energetically explained the company's position and its corporate donation of one thousand dollars a month. He was on the defensive, having heard insinuations that Consolidated was turning a profit on the contributions. The fund had cost only $6.40 to administer for three years, he said, and interest at six percent was accruing on the contributions. He was there to hear any man say otherwise, and would proceed to knock him down.

This angry threat demonstrated how painfully the accusation had struck a nerve. Patriotism was a matter of the greatest pride and gravity to those who "supported the war effort" in 1917; no one disparaged it with impunity. While Blaylock didn't name his accuser, the identity took little guesswork. The man who had recently railed against war profits and munitions manufacturers, who had recently demanded that Consolidated remove itself from the process of gathering patriotic money, was Albert Goodwin. Their dealings were taking on a tone of vitriolic personal enmity. Goodwin's slurs on munitions profiteers were scarcely veiled, and even ten years after the war Blaylock made caustic reference to wartime slackers and red agitators. In November 1917 few could guess that this private animosity might have tragic public consequences.

Over the Canadian patriotic fund, Ginger Goodwin had won another round with Consolidated—though at the cost of heightened hostility—and another step toward real improvements in smelter work. Labour's usually precarious position was now slightly less vulnerable because of the demand for war-related products. But when the war eventually ended, women's fragile toehold in the workplace and a flood of returning soldiers would threaten any headway in wages, hours or working conditions. Many people expected British Columbia to introduce eight-hour-day legislation soon, but what if the war ended first? Any further gains, labour needed to make right now. In early November 1917 Goodwin, as president of the Trail Trades and Labour Council, sent Consolidated yet another demand for a universal eight-hour day. This time there was a twenty-four-hour ultimatum: either all workers got the shorter day immediately, or all workers would down tools. Saying the company had an agreement with the smeltermen's union and couldn't deal with another organization, Selwyn Blaylock refused.

"Strike on at Trail. Advise all men to keep away," was the telegram Ginger Goodwin sent to the *Federationist*. He had called for the strike on November 10, the day he registered under the Military Service Act as required by law; he had already presented himself for examination to the Trail medical board sitting in Dolan Hall. Predictably, given his deteriorating health, he was placed in Category D as unfit for military service of any nature. The Military Service Act, however, still required that a man apply for exemption in any category; it was not automatically granted.

On Thursday, November 15, about fifteen hundred workers failed to report for work at the smelter. The strikers included about a thousand smeltermen and another two hundred of other trades, all members of the Trail Trades and Labour Council. Three days earlier council members had voted 352 to 42 in favour of walking out, the *Trail News* reported, and it was the first time the Consolidated works had been idle in twenty years. The company's first reaction was to reassign its office workers as labourers.

"They wanted me to go out and unload cars of coal and coke and ore," Andrew Waldie remembered. "And I said, 'No. The strike is between the crew and management and I belong to staff, and I'm not going to get involved.'"

A mass meeting at the ball park that morning drew about a thousand workers. Blaylock, securing permission to address them, read aloud his correspondence with the union and offered that the company arbitrate the dispute and abide by the decision—if the men would return to work. This clearly partisan offer the strikers declined. Ginger Goodwin addressed another meeting the next morning in the Star Theatre and, knowing where the strength of the union lay, Dick Marshall (Italian in origin, he'd taken an English name during his boxing career) followed in Italian. Meetings—of workers, managers, businessmen, various levels of government—would be Trail's major excitement for the next few weeks.

"Union discussion was prominent, very prominent. At home around the table, it was a boarding house with a dozen or so, somebody would start the discussion and then pretty soon they'd get a little heated, and mother would tell them, 'No more, out!'" Mike Landucci recalled.

Ginger Goodwin "was always a salesman, trying to put it across, pointing it out. He wasn't wrong. Conditions were such that most of the men just came home in their dirty work clothes and there'd be all their muck at home. There weren't washrooms. A lot of the benefits really came from demanding them, and putting up a bit of a fight."

Consolidated's insistence that it had an agreement with all workers affected was "the chief bone of contention that is up now before the two parties," said a strike committee press statement, "and the stand of the company is that they want the men to go back to work as they have violated an agreement.

"The representatives of the Mill & Smeltermen's Union have several times told the management of the smelter, that they (Smeltermen's Union) would take up the question of signing an agreement with the Consolidated Mining & Smelting Company. This the company would not consider up to the time of the shutdown . . .

"If that [agreement] is the only argument that can be advanced at this time, it is a very weak one, and it could not be adopted by the most impartial observer . . . "

It is difficult to imagine, in fact, how Consolidated could reasonably argue that an open-ended contract signed with a thousand smeltermen should apply for the duration of the war to another 450 mechanics, pipefitters, carpenters and so on, who had signed no agreement of any kind.

Selwyn Blaylock wrote November 23 to the *Trail News* complaining about its accuracy the week before, and took the opportunity to say that the smelter was shutting down operations completely; it would take several weeks before production could resume. Everyone, he added, should realize the seriousness of the situation.

News travelled quickly, and reactions were almost as rapid. The Kootenays' associated boards of trade sent telegrams to the provincial mines minister and to Prime Minister Borden: "If prompt settlement is not consummated means complete demoralization of the mining industry and business generally. Would suggest thorough investigation smelter and grievance of men immediately."

The British Columbia mines minister replied that his premier had telegraphed Ottawa "emphasizing gravity of problem and urging that because of extreme seriousness of the situation that immediate action is imperative." The province also offered assistance in reaching a speedy settlement.

This was a far cry from the provincial government's indifference to the Vancouver Island coal miners' strike in 1912, but there was good cause. The *Trail News*, probably with information from Consolidated, estimated that the strike adversely affected 150 mines, 25 to 30 of them in the United States, and about twenty thousand men. Of these, five thousand were directly thrown out of work.

Within days James McNiven, the federal fair wage officer, arrived from Vancouver. The Trail board of trade held a special meeting, inviting McNiven and the strike committee, and formed its own committee to approach Consolidated. Members of other trade boards arrived from across the Kootenays. No one took this strike lightly.

Consolidated immediately cancelled its orders of ore from the Kootenays and the northwestern United States, its shipments of coke and coal from the Crowsnest, and its other supplies from all over North America. The strike would affect thousands of workers involved in extracting and producing all these materials, plus their communities. It wouldn't necessarily have a disastrous effect, however, on Consolidated Mining and Smelting.

Ginger Goodwin and the members of the Trail strike committee may or may not have known of two pivotal events, though ironically Ginger's letter to the *Federationist* two weeks earlier had tangentially touched on one: Consolidated claimed to have essentially just finished filling its last metals contract for the Imperial Munitions Board. With Britain all but bankrupt and buying United States munitions to curry her new ally's favour and business, she was no longer buying Canadian arms and ammunition. Orders would now drop off dramatically. Zinc prices had already plunged from a 1916 average of 22.12 cents per pound to a 1917 average of 14.5 cents per pound; lead sales were slow and prices were also threatening to slide. Consolidated expected to scramble for any order at any price just to stay in production, and soon would lay off nearly one-third of its employees. A strike, while not strictly welcome, could provide a ready-made excuse.

This was no secret. It is difficult to imagine that the strike committee overlooked a letter from Consolidated to ore shippers reprinted on page one of October 12's *Trail News*. A reduction in the Imperial Munitions Board's shrapnel program, the letter said, meant drastic cuts in the lead market. Shippers could only send lead with limited zinc content while Consolidated worked away at its stockpile. "We need not say that we regret that we are compelled to take this step, but the Munitions Board find themselves unable to give us sufficient assurances to warrant our taking all the ores offered..."

Possibly Cominco was creating a smokescreen to forestall an expected strike, or possibly the union officials believed it was.

A second crucial development also resulted from the United States' entry into the war. Charles Moyer, president of the International Union of Mine Mill and Smelter Workers in Denver, had only days earlier issued a manifesto asking affiliated members not to strike for the duration of the war. In support of the war effort, local unions should find other ways out of their difficulties.

As a result, the Trail Trades and Labour Council not only faced lukewarm opposition from Consolidated to its strike, it faced the possibility of lukewarm support from its own international union. Instead of a live grenade thrown into the war business, the strike threatened to be a dud. But not entirely. Even a small spark was sufficient to ignite the volatile wartime atmosphere compounded of pride, fear, suspicion, jealousy, racism and greed, and smiled upon as patriotism.

If Ginger Goodwin, the acknowledged leader of this strike, did know of these two developments he was taking an enormous gamble at long-shot odds. Against the chance of forcing change before the war ended, he was staking the strength and credibility of his local and district union, his trades council and his provincial labour federation. He was staking the lives of more than fifteen hundred men, and his own life.

Ginger Goodwin, who was in the "unfit for service" Category D, appealed November 23 for exemption under the Military Service Act on grounds of ill-health and infirmity; this would mean a medical board re-examination. The Trail exemption board was now questioning applicants in the offices of the British Columbia Provincial Police. Noble Binns headed the board, aided by a Rossland man and an army lieutenant. By mid-November an estimated five hundred men had applied. Of the 125 heard so far the board had refused exemption to 30, just under one-quarter.

An uproar was in full cry on the coast, meanwhile. An unnamed source at the *Daily Colonist* in Victoria had transmitted frightening stories to Vancouver and elsewhere that the Trail strike had begun with a bonfire of Victory Loan literature, the strikers were refusing to register for examination or apply to the exemption board and the walkout was purely a protest against the Military Service Act. The *Vancouver Province* ran the story under a five-deck headline which claimed, in part, "Flatly Refuse to Obey Law at Trail" and "Terms of Military Service Act Flagrantly Disobeyed by 1,500 Smeltermen."

Trail, stung in its patriotic pride, counterattacked in force. The city immediately launched a lawsuit against the *Province*, threatened the *Colonist* with another, and demanded to know the source of this "gross libel" and "unwarranted slur cast on the workingmen of Trail and on this city generally." Board of trade president Noble Binns flung another telegram at the papers and the premier. "The demands of the men were solely for the inauguration of a universal eight-hour day at the smelter. The exemption tribunal is now sitting daily in Trail, and men are presenting themselves as fast as the tribunal can handle them, no reports having been received of men coming under Class A failing to register." He added that Trail's annual contribution of sixty thous-and dollars to war funds, lower only than Victoria's and Vancouver's, spoke for its support of the war.

Nevertheless, the Trail strike had implications for Canadian muni-tions manufacturing, now producing arms mainly for the Canadian armed forces. This brought Ginger Goodwin to the attention of the BC Provincial Police. A fast and furious exchange of code telegrams and letters now ensued between West Kootenays chief constable John T. Black, located at Nelson since 1910, and provincial police super-intendent Colin S. Campbell in Victoria. Black had previous ex-perience with strikes, and possibly with Albert Goodwin. He had been seconded, apparently for special duty, in 1913 and 1914 to Union Bay and Cumberland for the better part of the Big Strike. Union Bay had only secondary significance during the coal strike. It was a port of entry for Cumberland and the scene of an attempted dynamiting of a Canadian Collieries railway trestle. Had this succeeded, it would have prevented coal shipments from leaving Cumberland, thus stop-ping instead of merely diminishing mine output. Strikers were blamed for the dynamiting; they parried that any explosives they placed would have ignited properly. Was John Black sent in as a special agent to investigate? If so, he never solved the case, and soon returned to Nelson.

Colin Campbell had been superintendent since 1911, having worked his way up from constable at New Westminster in 1897. This was also the year that Daniel Campbell, probably no relation, joined the British Columbia Provincial Police in Esquimalt. Their careers took remarkably different paths. Daniel Campbell was cashiered within a decade after an extortion case. Colin Campbell advanced steadily, and his work record portrays a man of integrity. In 1912, under pressure from Conservative Party officials to hire a Penticton man as a provin-cial constable, Campbell resisted successfully. This did not necessarily please his superiors, nor did his rulebook correctness in dealing with military police in late 1917. On administrative grounds, he deflected several requests from Captain Tweedale, assistant provost marshal for Military District 11. Both Campbell and his successor suggested military police were too willing to bend the law to capture defaulters or deserters under the Military Service Act. Not so the British Columbia Provincial Police.

Campbell nevertheless kept a close watch on wartime political dissidents. In September 1917 he issued a bulletin warning his constables that gangs of industrial union Wobblies in Montana planned to enter Canada to burn crops and destroy property. It was an anxious time. In November 1917 the Russian Revolution was in full swing; Tsar Nicholas had been deposed months earlier, and the Bolsheviki were now seizing power. Terrible Canadian casualties at Passchendaele and elsewhere made a supply of Canadian men especially crucial, and British Columbia's labour socialists had made no secret of their anti-conscription, anti-munitions stance. Now the Trail strike, with its implications for both conscription and arms manufacture, had been provoked by one of the most voluble of the labour socialists, Albert Goodwin.

"Alchemy renal supple conservative tusk apologue charcoal," was the text of Superintendent Campbell's first telegram to Chief Black on November 16, a day after the strike began. Decoded, it read, "Advise regarding strike conditions Trail and cause."

Black wired back that the strike was most orderly, and demanded only a universal eight-hour day. He followed with a letter giving more detail, and added that Consolidated had started putting out all fires in different smelting and refining departments. Since these would take days or even weeks to fully resume, the decision indicated tacit acceptance of a long strike.

A few days later Campbell sent copies to his superior, provincial deputy attorney general A.M. Johnson, and told Black to keep him informed "in regard to any labour troubles or trouble that may arise in connection with conscription." This communication, via unmarked brown envelope or clandestine whisper, undoubtedly gave rise to the *Daily Colonist's* claim that the strike was a Military Service Act protest.

"Restrained hopingly toothed unconstitutional methodism assigned azure tusk . . ." The superintendent's next telegram ordered Black, "Reported here that trouble may arise at Trail on account strike. If necessary go to Trail investigate and report answer."

"Reported here" may well have represented nothing more substantial than the irresponsible *Colonist* story, a classic case of much ado about nothing. Or was it? After all, Ginger Goodwin and other labour socialists believed — like the Russian Bolsheviki — in the outright overthrow of the capitalist system. They were pacifist toward other workers, but not toward government and capital.

"The really big thing they talk about in whispers and don't print in newspapers is the fear of revolution right here at home—unless the high cost of living is knocked down quickly," the *Federationist* had in July quoted N.D. Cochran of Chicago, and made its own editorial comment: "Those who are so very anxious to bring the present war to an end may as well preserve themselves with calm and pickle their disturbed souls with patience. This delightful little ruling class scrimmage will be brought to an end in due time, and the force that will call the tune will be REVOLUTION. Slavery, with its horrible and disgusting phantasmagoria of robbery, rapine and slaughter, is destined to go. The red flag of human brotherhood may even now be seen upon the outer battlements. There will soon be a fine assortment of thrones, crowns, and sceptres available to the junk man of oblivion."

Such commentary outraged governments and their law enforcement bodies.

Campbell continued through the next week anxiously wiring Black about possible Military Service Act trouble at Trail; Black replied reassuringly that Trail police chief Downs and constable Williams saw no cause for concern. Deputy Attorney General Johnson, however, was not convinced. December 6, 1917, in the midst of British Columbia's most potentially volatile wartime strike, he replaced Colin Campbell as provincial police superintendent. In what may have been a demotion, Campbell was made warden of Oakalla Prison where he spent the remainder of his career.

William McMynn, another long-serving provincial policeman, was the new superintendent. If the provincial government or military district thought he would be easier to manage, they were wrong. Two days after his appointment he circulated a bulletin saying, "In regard to the enforcement of the Military Service Act, I beg to say that while anxious to assist the Military Authorities as far as possible, still the same care is necessary in obtaining evidence, or arresting a man without a warrant under this act as is required under any other act in the Criminal Code."

Little love was lost, apparently, between military police and the provincial force. This prickly relationship would continue throughout the war not only with the main body of military police and intelligence officers but with the less clearly defined Dominion Police.

After the early excitement, the strike settled into an inevitable round of meetings and picket lines and committees. McNiven reported that neither side was willing to make concessions, though he, and the Trail and Kootenays boards of trade, offered to mediate. Consolidated refused. Another federal officer, W.H. Armstrong, arrived from Calgary to investigate.

"Here we are with the mining industry and the smelter in the list of non-producers while there is the crying demand that metals and munitions are very badly needed," said a November 25 union press statement in the *Federationist*; like the earlier release it bore Ginger Goodwin's characteristic turn of phrase. "It looks as if the officials of the government are powerless to act against the wishes of the Consolidated Mining and Smelting company." Combative as usual, he called the government "tools for the big corporations."

On November 26, Ginger Goodwin was called to appear before the Trail exemption board, which heard his application for exemption because of lung disease, and rejected it. The smeltermen immediately held a mass meeting at the Star Theatre and protested the rejection as an attempt to "put Goodwin in Class 'A'" and dispose of him "by fair means or foul."

"As a result of the strike here, certain influences are at work to force Mr. Goodwin into military service, without any attempt to consider the circumstances. Mr. Goodwin, on his own behalf, filed a claim for exemption, on the ground of being physically unfit, a condition in which he has been for several years," said a press release. Despite this he had been assigned to Category D as only temporarily unfit.

" . . . The condition of which Goodwin complains is evident to those not even following the medical profession. This shanghaiing procedure will show to what lengths some people will go to accomplish their ends. . . . Seeing that Goodwin's claim is being entirely ignored on the presentation of his own case, the members of the various local unions of Trail, knowing the value of this man's services, are prosecuting a claim for his exemption in the interests and welfare of more than 1,000 men. . . . it means a great deal to the general interest of a large number of men, if their officials are railroaded to the trenches. . . "

The smeltermen applied on Goodwin's behalf to the exemption board, arguing that labour officials, like employers, should be eligible for exemption because of their service to industry. Their appeal went nowhere.

Ginger Goodwin, for the first and perhaps last time, graced the social notes by appearing in the *Trail News*'s "In and Around Trail" column on December 7: "Albert Goodwin, secretary of Trail Mine, Mill and Smelter Workers' Union, No. 105, and president of Trail Trades and Labour Council, left on a trip to the coast last week." Did he go to seek advice from the British Columbia Federation of Labour, or to offer it? Although he decided not to run in the December 17 federal election, friends later remembered that he spoke on behalf of other candidates.

Less amusingly, as agreed in the January 1917 convention, the British Columbia Federation of Labour inconclusively discussed a general strike. Steam engineer Duncan Kerr of Pitt Lake had refused to register for military service and had been arrested and sentenced to two years imprisonment. He was labour's first unwilling conscript.

In Trail, the exemption board by December 14 had considered 252 applications in eighteen sessions. Of 156 Category A applications, they disallowed 93 from Rossland and Trail. The remainder were given exemptions ranging from one to six months. They heard 29 requests in Category B, 34 in Category C and 2 in Category D. One of these two was Ginger Goodwin's.

The smelter strike meanwhile dragged into its fourth, then its fifth, week. Trail was attracting a stream of would-be conciliators. On December 10 the royal consular agent for Italy at Winnipeg, J. Barattiere di S. Pietro, arrived to spend the week talking with the smelter's many Italian workers about the strike and the war. He addressed a large group at the Colombo Lodge, but failed to convince his fellow-countrymen to return to work.

Ginger Goodwin and the strike committee, in a December 11 press release, predicted the strike would end soon but not necessarily before Christmas. Large employers now recognized an eight-hour day made workers more alert, contented and able to concentrate, the release claimed in a somewhat aggrieved tone. "There is something wrong when the workers have got to strike to increase the efficiency of themselves for the benefit of the employer, yet that is what the trouble at Trail really means to both parties."

Workers and businessmen were starting to tighten their belts by mid-December. The Star Theatre had lowered its prices for the second time and was presenting little or no musical accompaniment to its silent films. It was cold, Christmas was just around the corner, larders were bare, and even "the king's beef" wasn't available as a last resort; it was the worst season in years for deer hunting.

Mike Landucci saw the hardship in the grocery store. "I was of an age when I couldn't even conceive what the hell it could do or couldn't do. But I knew a lot of the customers, the wives would complain that there was no revenue coming in."

Soon inevitably the strike also brought Goodwin to the notice of Canadian military intelligence. Captain Tweedale in Victoria and the commanding officer of the 107th Regiment, on guard duty at Trail smelter, both wrote to Superintendent McMynn and to an unnamed intelligence officer. No copy of their correspondence is now publicly available, but it had immediate impact. Constable Black prepared to dispatch six special policemen with special badges, handcuffs and batons to Trail.

Others arrived first. The strike committee had earlier sent a telegram to the smeltermen's international union, asking it to endorse the Trail Trades and Labour Council strike. The idea backfired. Instead the new president of District 6, Marcus Martin, arrived with international board members William Davidson and Alfred Borsden, both delegated to investigate by president Charles Moyer in Denver. Davidson asked to address a December 16 meeting at the Star Theatre and, in a less than democratic gesture, was refused. The *Trail News* said, "He is understood to have decided views on the subject."

Borsden and Davidson wrote a letter to the smeltermen's local that night, saying, "We find that the Trail Trades and Labour Council had no authority under the laws of the American Federation of Labour, or those of our own international, either to carry on negotiations with the Consolidated company . . . or to call a strike."

The strike had forced thousands of miners out of work throughout the Kootenays, "causing undue hardship upon the members of our organization in those camps." Borsden and Davidson declared the strike unlawful and the company fair.

The smeltermen decided December 20 to return to work under their old conditions the next day. Ginger Goodwin got in touch with the smelter management, which agreed to open the works. Six special provincial constables, on their way to Trail from various Kootenays points the morning of December 20, climbed back on their trains the next day. Whatever trouble they had anticipated was defused by the strike's collapse.

"At a mass meeting of the various unions on the 20th," Ginger Goodwin wrote December 24 in a release to the *Federationist*, "the strike committee related the circumstances and conditions of the strike situation, pointing out that it would be folly to continue the strike any further as the obstacles were increasing that the men had to fight against, and without funds to keep it up, that to do so would be very indiscreet, entailing unnecessary hardship for the men involved in the strike."

The smelter workers had lost thirty-six days' wages, and the *News* estimated Trail merchants had lost about $216,000 in potential sales. Consolidated took men back as they were needed. Furnaces, roasters, converters and other equipment which had gone cold a month earlier would take some time to resume full operation. Workers would have to dig out the frozen furnaces before restarting them. One lead furnace was operating by December 28, and the copper and zinc plants would soon follow. With zinc and lead prices down and Imperial Munitions Board lead orders much reduced, however, production would be down from pre-strike levels. Consolidated planned to hire back one thousand to twelve hundred of its former fifteen hundred workers. The result, Goodwin wrote in his *Federationist* release, was a company blacklist.

"There is a number of men that will not be taken back by the appearance of things, men who had the conviction to fight for the cause of the eight-hour day, and who at the time of writing have got it from good authority that they are not wanted any more at the smelter.

"Those that are taken back have to sign a pledge to be of good behavior for the duration of the war (Why not for life?). . . . the men being driven by the lash of hunger to do that which is of interest to their employers."

Was there a blacklist, or did Consolidated simply need fewer workers because of a market slump? Andrew Waldie, working in the Consolidated offices, was shocked by the truth.

"I do know for a fact that there was a blacklist, because I had a brother there by the name of Adam who worked up at Highland Mine at Ainsworth. I saw a blacklist with my brother Adam's name on it," Waldie said. His brother took the only way out for many blacklisted workers, and enlisted. "Adam was killed overseas in the 1914 to 1918 war."

If Goodwin had gambled on international union's support, he had badly misjudged or mistimed his throw. The international was now supporting the war — especially war industry — and placed the interests of five thousand or more miners ahead of fifteen hundred smelter employees in an unsanctioned work stoppage. It also reacted to the labour council as a threat, exactly as orthodox trade unions would soon react to radical industrial unions. So hostile were the United Mine Workers in 1919–20 to the One Big Union, for example, that the federal government willingly backed the United States-based miners' union (which it had fought with militia and special police for years) against the Canadian industrial union. The Trail strike was in effect the first round of the struggle between two kinds of unionism in British Columbia. Also, the smeltermen's international union may have decided it was time to slap down an independent-minded and ambitious young organizer, Albert Goodwin.

Bleak prospects faced the former strikers and strike committee, but especially Ginger Goodwin. Six months earlier he'd been riding high in every sense — leading the May Day parade on horseback, an officer of a handful of labour organizations, a valued organizer for the

Socialist Party of Canada. No longer. The local union and trades council were out of money and probably out of favour with now impoverished and jobless smelter workers. Goodwin had been publicly disciplined by the Internation Union of Mine Mill and Smelter Workers. The Socialist Party of Canada had cast him out. As a final irony, at the end of December the provincial government appointed as its new deputy minister of labour (for which the smeltermen had proposed Goodwin) James McNiven, a former typographer's union member and the federal fair wage officer assigned to the Trail strike. Now Ginger Goodwin faced a conscription to which he objected on philosophical and pragmatic grounds. Given his lung disease and ulcers, military service would probably—even well outside bullet range—cause his death.

Box 312

"To let a case of this kind go by would be losing the chance of testing others that will inevitably crop up," Ginger Goodwin wrote from deep in the entrails of the Military Service Act appeals process, "and the more publicity the case gets the better for those that are not interested in the waging of the fight for the capitalist imperialism."

Conscription during World War One may stand for all time as Canada's most detested government program, bar none. It provoked riots and deaths in Quebec and protests across the country. It opened a gulf of bitterness between anglophone and francophone Canadians. It tapped a distrust of government that still runs deep and broad. Of 401,882 Canadian men who registered for armed service under the Military Service Act, 380,510 appealed for exemption.

Ginger Goodwin took his appeal as far as the legal procedure permitted. He believed in the supremacy of justice, despite his radical labour socialism, and insisted that his Trail strike be law-abiding and orderly. Until the day when he ultimately failed to report for military duty, nothing suggests that he once broke Canadian law.

Appeals under the Military Service Act were lengthy and complex. To recap the chronology: As the law demanded Goodwin took his medical examination at Nelson on October 24, and registered for service on November 10—the last day he could legally do so, also the day he called the Trail strike—and was placed in Category D. This category was first set aside for men "unfit for military service of any

Box 312   137

nature," but within months military representatives were describing it as "the classification of potential A men."

Next he went before the Nelson appeal tribunal November 23, and claimed exemption on grounds of ill-health and infirmity. This claim was disallowed. Then he again went before the Nelson medical board November 27, apparently to support his second appeal, which was to Tribunal 8 sitting in Trail under Judge Brown. The tribunal dismissed this appeal and refused exemption on January 15, 1918. His third appeal was to the central appeals judge in Ottawa, Lyman Duff of the Supreme Court of Canada, scheduled for hearing March 27. He had to appear before a medical board yet again to support this appeal. Not only did the medical board reject his appeal on March 7, it lifted his Category D status. The tribunal reclassified Albert Goodwin as Category A, "fit for service in an overseas fighting unit."

Why?

The exemption procedure was, according to historian Desmond Morton, unpredictable and arbitrary. Local worthies—often businessmen or civic officials—and army officers who made up the exemption tribunals across Canada inevitably brought their own philosophies to a subjective task. W.R. Braden of Rossland and a Lieutenant Curtin served on Trail's exemption tribunal, which was headed by local merchant and magistrate Noble Binns.

Noble Binns impressed people with his severity and curtness. His businesses had prospered in Trail since the turn of the century, affording him a comfortable lifestyle. His undertaking business prompted one retired smelterman to joke that if Noble Binns didn't get you one way when you were alive, he'd get you another way once you died. He had specifically promised fairness in his handling of exemptions under the Military Service Act, yet he must have found spring 1918—in fact, the whole period since late October 1917—a difficult and troubling time.

First, even before the exemption board began sitting, Binns' authority and even-handedness were undermined by the general manager of Consolidated Mining and Smelting. James Warren's circular promising to back workers' exemption bids was a slap in the face; it implied that Consolidated—so overwhelmingly powerful in the Kootenays—called the shots even with the Military Service Act, and could arrange to exempt whomever it chose. This almost obligated Binns to apply special severity to any smelter-related exemption requests.

Next Binns was wounded in his civic pride by scare stories from the coast that Trail's smelter strike was an anti-conscription protest. The *Colonist's* charges required him to defend an unwashed, semi-literate, largely foreign rabble whom he saw most often in the prisoner's dock, pleading to a distasteful array of crimes and misdemeanours.

Finally, the strike had cost Trail's businesses, Binns' furniture and undertaking enterprises among them, an estimated 216,000 dollars in lost income.

Noble Binns, given these circumstances, could be forgiven for hyper-sensitivity over the question of exemptions. But another factor was also at work, the complex matter of personal friendship. Noble Binns and Selwyn Blaylock had known each other nearly twenty years. Together they served on Trail's board of trade, the Trail Fruit Fair Association and various patriotic organizations. Even friends like MPP James Schofield and former Trail and Rossland policeman Bill Devitt weren't as close. "Blay" prided himself on a hard-won friendly relationship with his workers; the workers had recently showed themselves unworthy of his trust by calling the first major strike at Consolidated in twenty years. Now Binns had an exemption application from the emigrant, johnny-come-lately agitator who had recently cost Blay money, pride and peace of mind. The door had scarcely slammed on the British Columbia Provincial Police offices, where the tribunal was held, before Goodwin's comrades identified the man responsible for his downfall.

"It was the head of the Consolidated outfit in Trail. . . that is where the finger pointed and a whole lot of people had the conclusion that that is how Goodwin came to be called back for re-examination — and now from 4F he was classified 1A," said William Pritchard of Vancouver.

"They used the draft as a way to get him away from Consolidated Mining and Smelting Company. Blaylock was the company man up there. These were the people who got him. I learned all about it from Joe Naylor," said Jack Horbury of Cumberland.

"Ginger was a frail guy. And when he showed certain anti-war activities, Ginger was forthwith put in Class 1," said Dave Rees, then of the Crowsnest Pass.

"They wanted to get rid of him, I guess. They drafted him first and turned him down because he was unfit, and that's when he organized the smelter. They drafted him again and found him A1. They said he had TB," said Peter Cameron of Cumberland.

Selwyn Blaylock asked the Trail exemption tribunal to reclassify Ginger Goodwin as fit for overseas combat: this rumour still circulates energetically today. Some swore that Blaylock actually wrote a letter to that effect. If so (it seems doubtful that anyone would commit such a request to paper) no one admits to having seen it. But why would a brilliant metallurgist rising steadily through a first-rank

Box 312   139

corporation, sportsman, amateur horticulturist, arts patron, owner of a splendid native stone mansion amidst sweeping gardens, loved by his friends, a friend to his workers, be said to have blood on his hands?

Consolidated executive R.W. Diamond wrote of Blaylock's "absorbing interest in employee relations and in employee security. Certainly his advanced thinking in that regard made him a pioneer in that field, particularly in the mining industry. His efforts resulted in the adoption, in the early years, of splendid medical and hospital protection for Company employees, in Company loans for house construction, and in group insurance and non-contributory pension plans." At his superior's 1945 retirement party in Montreal, Diamond said, "He is a man with great imagination, initiative, courage and determination. He is a man with a big heart, fine judgment and broad vision — a man who inspires confidence and loyalty in all with whom he associates."

Newspaper and magazine profiles through the 1920s and 1930s praised Blay's modesty, fair play, generosity and deep commitment to his workers' well-being. An employee who said he had once been "a Red — an agitator" was quoted as saying smelter conditions were "as near to the socialist ideal as he could hope for in this world." By the time of Blaylock's retirement it took an entire page to list his memberships, community service awards and honourary degrees.

Selwyn Blaylock was somewhat intractable during the 1917 strike, one might conclude, but the experience had taught him to be a model employer.

Contrary indications seep up through the adulation, however, largely from former employees who were not interviewed in the shadow of the smelter chimneys by national publications. Some admired him, but saw his flaws.

"He sat up there like he was a small god. He was a big man, he was a great big frog in a little puddle," said Mike Landucci. "He was more on the good side than the bad. He wasn't a bad fellow at all. I liked him. But people were frightened of him, your whole life depended on him. If you got fired, what in the hell was your family going to do?"

Blaylock was a "Simon Pure," self-righteously shocked by other men's drinking or gambling or womanizing, said Landucci, who was once nearly fired for challenging his boss's interference in his workers' personal lives. Asked for information about an alleged Italian bootlegger, Landucci told Blaylock he'd come to interpret for the man, not to inform. Blaylock warned him, "One more incident and you're gone."

One employee was given twenty-four hours to leave Trail after

Selwyn Blaylock learned he was having an affair with a married women. Another contract worker was fired for drinking up his pay cheque while his children went to school hungry and thinly dressed for cold weather. Yet another was fired for bootlegging from his house, Landucci remembered. "What the man did in his home was his own damn business. It was none of Blaylock's business. But I couldn't get myself involved in it or I'd get fired over it."

"The man was very, very reasonable," said Andrew Waldie. "Like everybody else he had his grudges, he had a grudge against this man and a grudge against that man."

Blaylock's grudges were apparently reserved for ingrates who failed to appreciate his paternalistic goodwill toward the workers—as long as they respectfully toed the line. In 1917 the smeltermen's union secretary, after months of insolent challenges, had required that Blaylock be rescued from a gridlocked strike by an American union president disciplining an upstart local organizer. Blaylock's strike victory had won him little glory and cost him self-respect, and the fault was Ginger Goodwin's. This made him the natural target for a grudge.

How intense were Blaylock's grudges? Intense enough, it seems, to long outlive their recipients. An entire generation after the 1917 smelter strike, amid the obsequious praises of its business pages, the *Vancouver Sun* reported in 1938 that a union had charged Selwyn Blaylock with intimidation. He was accused of trying to prevent an employee from joining the International Union of Mine, Mill and Smelter Workers.

The Second World War seemed to revive his earlier attitudes. In 1941 Blaylock told a Vancouver Board of Trade luncheon that all Canadians should be conscripted for armed service or industrial duty to serve Canada's war effort. "Every day's delay will emphasize the injustice of depending on voluntary enlistment, which takes the best men to war and leaves the yellows, the reds and the pinks at home." He accused workers of using the war as a lever to gain concessions, causing unrest, and complained of "the labour agitators, many of whom are of alien or foreign nationality."

Selwyn Blaylock may have convinced himself and his peers that he was a workers' friend, but he failed to convince the workers. When organizer Barney McGuire saw him on behalf of the union in the late 1930s, Blaylock left the union men standing in front of his desk and sat looking out the window with his back to the room.

Les Walker told an interviewer that workers were cynical about Blaylock's egalitarian gestures. "Men appointed to the workmen's committee promptly quit work, that is they came to work each day

Box 312 141

and punched in the clock but they never put their working clothes on."

Committee appointees always advanced at Consolidated, except for one chairman. Others had always consulted the boss before each meeting about what should and shouldn't be discussed. Walker said, "He called the meeting to order and Blaylock came huffing and puffing in at the last few minutes, mentioned that the chairman usually came and discussed things with him, and he said, 'Mr. Blaylock, for your information I consider you just another member of the committee and I'm not discussing anything privately with you.' That guy didn't go anywhere after his term as chairman was finished."

An unusually credible voice on Selwyn Blaylock's role in Goodwin's life was that of Andrew Waldie, who worked in the smelter office. But Waldie, even in 1979, was stopping himself short of telling an interviewer anything incriminating.

On one occasion Waldie was less reticent. In 1975 he told an interviewer, "As it happened, Blaylock today is held more or less responsible for having martyred that man by way of a grudge for having called the strike. He was a man in a high position here and he pulled strings and he got anybody re-examined that he wanted."

Rumour proves only the existence of rumour. Where there's smoke there's fire — sometimes — but sometimes there's only smoke. Perhaps Selwyn Blaylock's later words and actions embody guilt or self-justification, perhaps not. We will probably never know with certainty whether he deliberately had a troublesome adversary, despite lung disease and ulcers and ruined teeth, put in the way of bullet fire.

The Ottawa hearing on March 27 would be Ginger Goodwin's last resort. Major McKay, chief public representative at Vancouver, later described this sequence in a *Trail News* story; labour organizer William Pritchard also said Ginger saw yet another medical board in Vancouver. Military authorities today claim the pertinent files were destroyed years ago, so only newspaper accounts remain. Ginger asked labour friends in District 6 to back his final claim. They sent resolutions to the central appeal judge on his behalf, but how whole-hearted were their attempts? District 6 officials, including president Marcus Martin, only a few weeks earlier thwarted Goodwin's Trail strike on the orders of his pro-war American international president. In the interim, Martin also openly opposed Goodwin on British Columbia Federation of Labour policies.

Ginger Goodwin also wrote March 14, from Cumberland, to ask the support of the Trades and Labour Council of Vancouver. Keenly aware of the propaganda effect and the potential to make this a test case, he asked them to hurry. The letter had an anxious, abject quality—Goodwin virtually begged for support, calling himself a humble slave—as though he held out scant hope for this last appeal.

"My claim is that of being an official of the labour movement and doing some useful function to the interests of the wage-earners," he wrote; labour might sway the judge by protesting strongly enough against the conscription of its officials. "This letter is addressed to those that feel interested in the position of a slave fighting for what liberty the system will permit him to get out of it and I can assure you that any assistance that can be rendered will be appreciated by this humble slave . . ."

Making no mention now of ill-health as a basis for his exemption, he signed himself "Fraternally for Socialism, Albert Goodwin."

His last appeal was before the court when Ginger Goodwin prepared to leave Trail for the last time, betrayed by his own international union, afraid for his life. But he knew his plans. In his correspondence with Military Service Act officials, he didn't give his address as the smeltermen's union at PO Box 26, Trail, or the Trail Trades and Labour Council at Drawer 2, Trail. He gave his mailing address as PO Box 312, Cumberland, Vancouver Island. The address belonged not to Joe Naylor (his was PO Box 415) but to Local 70 of the Socialist Party of Canada. In the short term at least Ginger Goodwin was planning to go to Cumberland, to go home.

First he had personal business, possibly in Trail but probably in Vancouver, that he'd been putting off for years. Perhaps the ads in the *Federationist* had given him the idea. "Why do you fear to visit a dentist? You know that your teeth need attention and that their condition is gradually becoming worse. Still you delay going to a dentist. Is not this fact due to your idea of the old-fashioned dentist and the thought that a dentist's chair means pain?" Dr. Grady on Hastings Street offered the painless anocain infiltration method of dentistry. For the dollar-fifty price of the best evening seat at D.W. Griffiths' new film extravaganza *Intolerance*, a sufferer could have porcelain or silver fillings. For two dollars he could have gold fillings. For five dollars per tooth he could have gold crowns.

"Ginger, he had a gold tooth," Johnny Marocchi remembered years later. A police description specified "some gold filled teeth in upper row shewing," and an inquest jury would later hear that he had "three gold crowned teeth with gold bridging and some amalgam filled and crowned grinders." Andrew Waldie remembered Red Goodwin's teeth like little pieces of rusted barbed wire, badly decayed, in Trail. Sometime between his union activities in Trail and his flight to the Comox Lake bush, he put at least thirty dollars into gold crowns, porcelain fillings and bridgework. It represented a fortnight's pay

Box 312 143

after deductions for a 1917 smelterman. Goodwin's work history from 1906 to 1916 had been an obstacle course of strikes, blacklists and sickness; his Trail stint as smeltermen's union secretary may have been the first steady pay cheque he'd seen in years. If so, he put it to good use.

Ginger Goodwin wanted desperately not to die but, with pneumoconiosis or tuberculosis, saw his death every time he looked in a shaving mirror. More than other men, perhaps, he wanted to avoid bullets and septic teeth and sickness. When first news of the deadly influenza reached Western Canada, he was quick to protect himself as well as anyone then could. Mike Landucci remembered him coming into the grocery store.

"As far as I know he was single. . . . He came up there one day and he wanted a pound of garlic. Holy Christmas, I looked at him and said, You running a boarding house or something? No, he said, I read in the paper where garlic will keep the flu away. And believe it or not, we sold more damn garlic over that. One of those things. And he'd take one, and take the skin off it, and put it in his mouth like you would a jellybean."

The theory was that the garlic kept other people, and their germs, at a distance during the devastating epidemic which killed so many. It must have worked, Landucci said. "He never got the flu."

Cash on hand may have been the chief reason Ginger Goodwin had his dental work at this time, but not necessarily the only reason. If his last appeal failed and he found himself in the hated military uniform, he would need good teeth to deal with army food. But if his last appeal failed, he still had an alternative. Thousands of young men ordered to report in the "first call" on January 3, 1918 simply failed to appear. Desertion, evasion, default, resistance, whatever the government wanted to call it, to many seemed a good solution to the detested Military Service Act.

Some draft evaders lay low at home. Some left for remote areas; an informer reported to police that a flotilla of handliners' boats upcoast could belong to defaulters. Some left the country. The United States was no longer a safe haven, as it had been briefly for fleeing enemy alien Alvo von Alvensleben in 1914, since it had now joined the Allied war effort. But there were also thoroughly inaccessible Canadian wilderness areas—where one could poach for dinner, enjoy the sunshine, even pan a little gold—and convenient boltholes like revolutionary Mexico. Good teeth and good health were a prudent precaution for any of these choices.

In Vancouver, the British Columbia Federation of Labour held its eighth annual convention the last week of January. Oriental immigration, conscription, returned soldiers and the federation's political party were the convention's pressing concerns. President Joe Naylor was there, ready to bluntly speak his mind on the year's doings. West Kootenays vice-president Ginger Goodwin attended with his fellow strike organizer Dick Marshall. So did the District 6 president who'd taken part in bringing down the smelter strike, Marcus Martin. It promised to be an animated convention.

Vancouver was full of returned soldiers. A few had satisfactorily resumed the work they'd left on enlisting but many others were unemployed — some had enlisted because they were unemployed, like the blacklisted coal miners on Vancouver Island — or hired at wages which sounded generous by pre-war, pre-inflation standards but were now impossible to live on. Provincial and federal governments did little to ease the returned men's and women's re-entry into Canadian life. A great bitterness separated those who had gone overseas and those who had stayed, especially those in the labour movement. The Great War Veterans Association was particularly vocal; secretary A.E. Lees and president David Laughnan tended to see labour men and women as competitors in the workplace, and thus enemies. Quick to address the social ills of the day, the British Columbia Federation of Labour realized it must deal with this problem for everyone's sake.

Joe Naylor opened the convention by expressing his disappointment in labour's progress in British Columbia and described the six-day gathering "as not being revolutionary, but reformative." This may have been a premature assessment, as it turned out, since the gathering was pivotal to later developments.

Ginger Goodwin kept to the background until Tuesday afternoon when he agreed to join a five-man committee to deal with returned soldiers, with coal miner W.A. Sherman of the Crowsnest Pass, to give it province-wide representation. On his suggestion, the committee met with veterans' groups. Later in the week, after meeting with Lees and Laughnan, the committee reported "The returned soldiers admitted that they were conscious they were subject to exploitation. This was an evidence that Labour and the returned soldiers could get together." The joint recommendations included a federation-veterans advisory board, attention to exploitation of disabled or pensioned soldiers being offered reduced wages, and creation of farm operations to hire veterans. It seemed the two groups had found common ground; by August 1918 it would seem distinctly otherwise.

On Wednesday afternoon the convention grew livelier. "Vice-president Goodwin then took the chair," according to the *Federationist*, "and President Naylor opposed the formation of a political party suggestion, calling attention to the Socialist party being in the field,

Box 312 145

as well as other parties comprising labouring men, and saying that these would oppose the Labour party."

The federation's six political candidates—in the likely ridings of Vancouver South, Burrard, Nanaimo, Victoria, East Kootenays and West Kootenays, where Ginger Goodwin had in 1916 raised interest in a labour vote—had not taken one seat.

Ignoring Naylor's advice, the convention took a roll-call on the question, "Are you in favor of a working class political organization?" Ayes numbered eighty-two, abstentions or absences fifteen. The eleven nays included Naylor, Goodwin, Marshall, Sherman and future MPP Ernest Winch of Vancouver. It was the first major dissent within the federation, but not the last. Harmony and co-operation had marked the 1917 convention; a deep rift between "nay" socialists and "aye" non-socialists would mark this one. The next few days crackled with differences of opinion.

The election of officers was Thursday afternoon. For the president's position, "President Naylor's name was suggested, but the president said he would refuse, and stated his reasons. His main reason was that he believed the union movement had been a failure in this crisis, particularly the American Federation of Labour." The British Columbia Federation of Labour, despite past disappointments and differences with the Canadian Labour Congress, had no affiliation with this body. It was an angry slap at an American Federation of Labour union's self-interested shutdown of a Canadian smelter strike. Another who declined nomination for federation president— angry, fed up, and probably already planning his disappearance from public view—was Ginger Goodwin.

Neither man stood for any office, in fact, and Joe Naylor's concluding remarks were uncompromising. Wages had risen in 1917, he said, but costs had risen further. The newly created minister and deputy minister of labour were a doubtful aid to labour. But it was conscription that drew his sarcasm. "Conscription has been placed upon us by the powers that be, without any real opposition from organized labour—owing, no doubt, to the patriotic spirit existing amongst our membership and officials, but mainly through our unorganized position, and in the beginning to the apathy of all concerned."

Naylor was a perennial Cassandra crying out unpleasant and unwelcome truths. In January 1918 he seemingly went unheard, as did an adopted but minor resolution from two Vancouver Island coal miners that craft unions should be abolished in favour of industrial unions. Other voices expressed cautious optimism about world events, citing working class gains in Russia and Britain although Lenin was already thundering about false socialists, "who mouth sugared phrases of Marxism, which prostitute its spirit. Men who are revisionist in tactics while talking revolutionary jargon." Lenin's reprisals and industrial unionism would emerge as the true shape of the future.

So would Naylor's cynicism. The Military Service Act, for example, was all he feared and worse. Ginger Goodwin's case was rapidly revealing exemption as a farce, at least for those whom the government or its friends saw as troublemakers. Conscription was so unpopular that conscripts were not given rifles until they reached Europe, perhaps as a precaution against armed mutiny.

Ginger Goodwin, meanwhile, doggedly pursued his case through the central appeals court. District 6 wrote on his behalf; the Vancouver trades and labour council decided not to. Lyman Duff heard the case on March 27; before he could bring down judgment, any doubts about sending this applicant to the front stumbled over a sweeping government decision. A huge majority of Canadian men wanted to avoid military service, and Prime Minister Borden couldn't meet his commitment to beleaguered England. On April 12 the government cancelled all exemptions. On April 15 Duff rejected Albert Goodwin's appeal.

A letter went immediately to PO Box 312, Cumberland, ordering Private Goodwin, serial number 270432, to report for military service at Number 2 Depot Battalion, Victoria, on May 2. The letter waited in Cumberland's two-storey brick post office long enough to be declared undelivered. Goodwin neither accepted the letter nor reported for duty. As of May 2 he was legally a defaulter, a draft evader or — according to military authorities — a deserter.

Pneumonia was one reason for his failure to appear, whatever his other reasons. Early in 1918 he had suffered a bout of the lung ailment, the *District Ledger* in Fernie later reported. Pneumonia resulted not only from poor diet and living conditions; in the case of a visibly sick young man afflicted by the ultimately fatal pneumoconiosis or even more deadly tuberculosis, it could indicate death would soon follow. How ill was Ginger Goodwin? Most friends and acquaintances recognized that he suffered from some lung disease, though they differed on the diagnosis; it was sufficiently advanced to be noticeable. Pneumonia, even if it didn't herald the terminal stages of a more serious sickness, certainly was no indicator of improving health.

Ginger Goodwin stayed with friends in Cumberland through the spring of 1918. Other draft evaders were not particularly cautious — had they known the number of pseudonymous letters informing the police of their probable whereabouts, they might have been more circumspect — and he probably took only the most obvious precautions. The newspapers were full of post-war plans; everyone knew

Box 312   147

the war and conscription would soon be forgotten. He needed only to lie low for a month or two until the military lost interest. He stayed with socialists Meg and Peg Westfield, possibly with Ole Oleson in Minto and the Clark family and the Williamson family in Cumberland.

Donetta Rallison remembered seeing him at the Westfield house. "I had the feeling that he was hiding out. We'd go there and he would come down from upstairs."

Perhaps Goodwin felt some ambivalence about his chances of surviving the war one way or another. Although he failed ultimately to avoid police trackers, he took some precautions to remain beyond the government's reach. A *Vancouver World* reporter would remember months later that Goodwin told a labour meeting that he expected the authorities would "get him."

Bob Rushford, an old friend, had gone back to work in the mines after his 1915 return from France as Cumberland's first casualty and first war hero. In May 1916 he'd become a special constable and game warden, but he lost that position in April 1918 when the British Columbia Provincial Police reorganized. A few days later he started work as Cumberland's full-time provincial police constable. His salary of eighty dollars a month was far from princely for a couple with a young family, but friends remember that his children were always well dressed. Nava, the oldest girl, didn't even wear hand-me-downs. In wartime Cumberland, where wages were losing ground to inflation, this was noteworthy.

In Victoria, Rushford's superior officer was stubbornly proving a stickler for rules under pressure from the military authorities. All provincial constables were expected to routinely keep a sharp watch for draft evaders. Increasingly they were also specifically ordered out for manhunts and arrests, although Superintendent McMynn would send them only if Military District 11 agreed to pay all costs, regardless of the venture's outcome. In June 1918 Constable Rushford had his orders: search out and arrest draft evaders in your jurisdiction.

Instead, he warned Ginger Goodwin to get out of sight. Rushford didn't want to be responsible for the arrest and imprisonment of his old friend.

"That's when they decided, let's get the hell out of here, to hell with it. Up the lake they went," Karl Coe said.

Ginger Goodwin, Ed Hunden, Jimmy Randall, Dave Aitken, Fred Taylor, Andrew Aitken, Ernie Court, and Bill and Arthur Boothman were among the young men who spent part of the summer of 1918 in the remote mountainous country west of Comox Lake. They came and went, four or five or six hiding at one time. Arthur Boothman had been seriously ill just before the Big Strike—had lost his soccer season to sickness, the *Cumberland Islander* reported—and Karl Coe confirmed this. "Neither one of the Boothmans were much better than Ginger for health."

None of them was willing to do military service, and that put them in the mainstream of Canadian sentiment at the time. Almost 95 percent of the men who registered under the Military Service Act applied for exemption. Even after the April cancellation of exemptions, and the revocation even of farmers' exemptions a month later, conscription added only 124,588 men to the Canadian Expeditionary Force. Of these only 24,132 reached France before the end of the war. Meanwhile the Borden government had ridden roughshod over Quebec alienation, industry's needs, workers' rights, the predicament of farmers, and the highest ethical, religious and philosophical principles of hundreds of thousands of Canadians. One of these was Ginger Goodwin.

"He wouldn't go to war," Chuna Tobacco said in a 1975 interview. "He didn't want to fight. He didn't believe in it. Him and a few more fellows all got together and they just went up there, and they hid in the mountains."

Perseverance Trail

Anyone who had a boat, or a friend with a boat, travelled Comox Lake by water. The easy way to reach the far western end in 1918 was by power boat, although wind and waves even in summer could make the trip miserable. The hard way was to hike overland across Perseverance Creek and roughly parallel to the southeast shore on the Perseverance Trail. This and other trails carried on west through a desolate field of snow peaks, glaciers and year-round snowfields, over the Comox Gap and the Alberni Draw, to Port Alberni on the west coast of Vancouver Island. The country was wild and mountainous, little frequented by Indian bands from either coast of the island, and always overhung with a glamour of danger. Tales of the Sasquatch in this region were concocted by Vancouver journalist Cecil Scott to aid a ski lodge owner — he also named Forbidden Plateau — in the 1930s, yet the country was remote and mysterious enough to make the story halfway credible.

Challenging to travel on foot, the terrain was mostly too difficult for horses. Rock slides and wild streams broke the tangled and steep hillsides which folded on westward and northward out of sight. No rivers or creeks were navigable for any distance. Hiking cross-country was a sweaty, jarring up-and-down struggle over broken rock, through clawing undergrowth and fallen trees. A few trails from the days of ox-team logging in virgin forest had long since grown over, and railway logging had yet to penetrate the mature second growth. Truck logging was still decades in the future. The only trails were creased through the bush, nearly impassable in places, by wild animals and a few humans who pursued them. Only the hardiest hunters and fishermen penetrated this fastness, and most of them stayed near the lakes and larger rivers. Between upper Comox Lake and the open Pacific miles to the west, from the outskirts of Victoria north to Queen Charlotte Sound, the island's mountainous spine offered a natural haven for those eager to avoid prying eyes. Scores, perhaps hundreds, of young men hid in the island's wilderness areas in 1918 to avoid military service.

"A lot of the boys went overseas, they joined up later on, but at that time there was a lot of what we would call conscientious objectors, and they went up the lake," Chuna Tobacco said in 1975. "Ginger Goodwin, he was one of them, mind there was a few more around. I think they're all dead now. And he went up the lake. He wouldn't go to war."

The summer of 1918 was unusually hot. As Cumberland people had been doing for thirty years, many families retreated to beach cabins and tents. A fresh breeze usually blew off the long curved lake, and one could always cool off by plunging in for a swim. The Cumberland area, six miles in from tidewater, was always colder in winter and hotter in summer than seaside communities like Courtenay and Comox and Royston. The moderating offshore winds rarely stirred so far inland and uphill, but dwindled among the sunny meadows of Minto.

"We camped every summer at Comox Lake. The road went from Cumberland to the lake, and there were cabins there to the right," Josephine Bryden told an interviewer. "Almost every weekend we would spend at the lake. We lived like millionaires, but we didn't realize it."

A number of cabins clustered near the bottom, eastern, end of the lake nearest to Cumberland and not far from Number Four mine headworks; others were accessible only by boat along the north and south shores, or at the far western end beyond Cruikshank Creek around Survey Bay. A few hunters, trappers and prospectors had cabins even further southwest into the wilderness around the chain of three Little Lakes.

Ginger Goodwin and a handful of other young men—four, or five, or six as they came and went—retreated to the Little Lakes where they stayed in several cabins. Ginger's friend Pete Galeazzi "the baker" from Cumberland let them stay in his cabin near the lake when they came down from deep in the back country. Another cabin was said to belong to John Brown, the prospector. Another may have belonged to trapper Tommy Anderson. The draft evaders took to the hills in late May or early June, too early for blackberries or huckleberries. Fish and game were out of season for another few months; anyway, these offered at best an undependable food source. The fugitives needed another food supply, and their Cumberland friends went to great lengths to provide it. Minto socialist farmers, former strikers, and Cumberland coal miners and merchants co-operated to prepare, marshal and deliver regular food shipments fifteen miles up Comox Lake and another few miles into the remote Little Lakes. Joe Naylor and the Campbell brothers were the chief organizers of this supply line, but various people made the deliveries.

"There's the big lake, you know, and the Little Lakes about two miles farther in. There's a trail there. I used to go up at two or three in the morning. Nobody saw me go," Sam Robertson said. His wife helped prepare the food. "My wife and Ginger were good friends, too."

Different friends provided what foods they could. Ed Williams recalled taking in "Mostly flour and sugar and stuff like that, and coffee.... No luxuries, just a maintenance sort of diet, I guess."

"The men thought they could live off the country," Jack Horbury said, "but they needed some pork and beans to be going along with." Fishermen would also leave them any extra food when they returned to Cumberland, Pansy Ellis remembered. "Anything which was left in the cabins, they always had a good supply. They had plenty of money in there, enough to see them through, anyhow, they all had a bit with them."

"My mother used to bake them home-made bread, and we had lots of butter because we had cows," Elsie Marocchi told an interviewer. "Mom used to make up boxes of food which she took up to Campbells' Store and Campbells sent it up to the men on certain nights, and the men would meet them up the lake and collect the food from them. People did everything they could to keep them well supplied with food. It was quite something those days, no fooling."

The Williamsons and Williamses, Sam Robertson and his wife, the Hundens and Aitkens, the Horburys and Ellises and Coes, were a few of the families that risked their own freedom to get food in to their hiding friends. As a rule they kept their children in the dark about their activities, but the women were a necessary link in the chain of supply. They owned the chickens, milked the cows, dug the vegetables, spared the last winter apples from the root cellars and baked the bread.

Winnie Williamson said her husband Harry "used to come to our house in the late evening, and I would be in bed. He would walk through the woods, he didn't want to let anyone know just where these people were. He would meet Joe Naylor, and they would go up to the lake, and I think it was McMillan or Williams who had the boat up there, and he would let them have his boat. Sometimes he would go along with them, and Harry and Joe had to do the rowing up the lake with the stuff. I think Harry used to get the stuff assembled. He would come to my dad's place, and he would take things from our garden, vegetables.

"We weren't supposed to know, of course, and we didn't know exactly where the men were. Actually Harry would not see the men. He used to leave the supplies at a certain place, and then they would come and pick them up. They would not have any contact with them or anything. They just left the stuff behind a log on a trail. I think Joe Naylor knew exactly where they were, and I think Harry knew too, but he didn't see them."

Chuna Tobacco's family stayed in a cabin at the bottom of the lake. "There was quite a few families that stayed at Comox Lake in boat houses, little houses, and they used to take food up to them at the top of the lake. There used to be a policeman, he used to patrol the beach all night trying to catch these people that were bringing this stuff up the lake."

Bob Rushford was in a cleft stick over patrolling Comox Lake for conscientious objectors. Three years earlier, Cumberland had welcomed the former coal miner home from Europe as its first casualty and war hero. The city had given him a cash gift and the British Columbia government had hired him as a game warden, later as a Provincial policeman. He and his wife Jessie had four small children and a pleasant wooden frame house on Penrith Street just down from the Catholic and Methodist churches. As a full-time Provincial constable, he could probably look forward to respected and secure employment for the rest of his working life. It was a considerable achievement for a man who only a few years earlier had arrived in Canada as a coal miner.

Also, Rushford's keen sense of duty had sent him to France with the Black Watch in 1914 although Cumberland friends advised him to ignore his call-up. As an ex-military man and now a law enforcer, he knew the importance of obeying orders and the cost of disobeying. Materially, he had everything to lose and nothing to gain if he refused orders. Like all Provincial policemen he had orders to locate and arrest draft evaders, and one of these was his close friend Ginger Goodwin.

"When Ginger Goodwin and the other one[s] took to the bush my father had to go in after them," Louvain Brovenlow wrote. "Now Ginger was a good friend of my father's. Dad says they were getting

the nod when to move on. My dad knew where the food was being left for them to pick up, and [would] in no way pick them up though he knew all the moves."

As the season wore on, the fugitives were more able to augment their Cumberland supplies by fishing, hunting and berrying. They caught trout in the lake and rivers, and they poached grouse, venison and bear. Ginger Goodwin borrowed Joe Naylor's .22 rifle and took his own fly-fishing rod. They had been in hiding for many weeks — no one alive now can say exactly how long — and their wilderness sojourn was becoming apparent.

Jack Horbury, then seven years old, was staying with his father in Jim Tobacco's cabin when they had unexpected company. ". . . Their clothes were all drab, not because they had drab clothes in those days, but from being in the woods so long. I think I saw Goodwin talking to my father, but my father never said anything to us. It was kind of strange to see a man just coming down the trail out of the woods."

Around June, Rushford started searching the area around Comox Lake for the draft evaders, though with no intention of making an arrest. It was soon common knowledge that he once encountered Ginger Goodwin and Fred Taylor, a man from the Nanaimo area, near their hiding place in the Little Lakes.

"When they first went up there they went into what they call Willemar Lake," Ed Williams said, "and there across the lake was a cabin which a trapper had built, and they were staying in that cabin. You couldn't get into it unless you had a boat, because you'd have had to walk all around the lake to get to it." Rushford and another officer arrived on the opposite shore of the lake and shouted across to the draft evaders to bring the boat over.

"They thought it was someone coming to visit them. That's what the guys used to do. There used to be a rock on the side of the lake, we called it the saddle. My dad and I used to go and camp and fish at night years ago, and the cabin was right across, it wasn't very far across," Williams said. The cabin lay just back from the lake near a big sand bar. "So this Fred Taylor, he comes across in the boat, they didn't know who it was though. They said this guy had a big beard on him, and he pulls across the lake, and when he seen who it was he turned to go back, and they started firing shots alongside of the boat. . . but he kept going."

Cumberland old-timers recounted this story as a great joke on Goodwin and Rushford alike — a mistaken identity crisis that should have ended in tragedy but instead created a Keystone Cops farce. Taylor flailed his oars all the way back across the lake and with his friends scrambled into the woods, while Rushford and the other policeman yelled futilely across the water, firing shots nowhere near the mark. The point was taken, however. It was time to move on, farther into the hills, beyond sight and ken of search parties. Just opposite the Willemar Lake cabin and the sandbar lay trails that led over Rough and Tumble Mountain and down the south fork to the north fork of Cruikshank River. The wild green river rises in alpine lakes northwest of Comox Lake, between Albert Edward Glacier and Whiskey Meadows and Paradise Meadows, and spumes down through Cruikshank Canyon to broaden into shallows near its gravel estuary on the lake.

"Anyway," Williams said, "they got out of there, and they come up over the mountain, they call in there the Fourth Mountain, there's a great big rock, I've been up there many the time, we used to hunt up there. The big rock came out and they had a shelter underneath there."

Pansy Ellis remembered that the big rock was also a cache. The fugitives left money and notes saying what they needed; Cumberland men left food and other supplies on the next trip. Another cache was a five-gallon tin pail everyone called the "post office." Here also money, requests and supplies were exchanged. As the police began searching and patrolling the lake more regularly, food deliveries became more difficult. Police parties intercepted and confiscated several shipments. The conscientious objectors got a message out to their friend Joe Horbury that they were short of food, said his son Jack.

"So he brought the message down to Joe Naylor and Jack Williams. . . . Joe Naylor wanted to take food over the mountain to them, but Jack Williams said, 'I'll get my uncle Sam Williams' boat,' and they went put-put-put up the middle of the lake at night with the food. It was Sam Williams' boat, but it was Jack Williams and Joe Naylor who went up in the put-put in the middle of the night, and they must have avoided the policemen."

Joe Naylor, Bob Rushford, all the Cumberland and Minto friends who organized the supply lines, appear to have taken the police searches very seriously. After all, draft evader Duncan Kerr was now serving a two-year prison sentence for ignoring Military Service Act requirements. The only person who sometimes acted as though he were beyond harm was Ginger Goodwin. He told Pansy Ellis that he thought the police had lost interest in the manhunt. "Ginger was always with these fellows. I always used to see him when I come up here. He was up there quite a while and any time I used to go up I used to see Ginger, and he used to come down. Aw, he said, I don't think you need worry much about us now, I think it's kinda gone stale."

Ginger was confident enough of his safety to make frequent forays

out from the Cruikshanks. Not only did he walk out of the woods to visit with families in their beach camps or cabins, he also ventured openly to Harry Williamson's Minto farm, about eighteen miles east in a populated area. Even less cautiously, he went right into Cumberland on Saturday nights.

"But Goodwin didn't show too good judgment," labour organizer Bill Pritchard said. "He was very popular with the girls and he'd come down into Cumberland out of that camp, Saturday nights to the dance."

Ginger liked to dance, danced well and was a sought-after partner, but there was more to it than that. He had a girlfriend.

"He was going with a girl and he was supposed to get married," Pansy Ellis said.

Jean Clark was her name, and her family ran one of the boarding houses on Penrith Avenue where Ginger Goodwin lived. Cumberland people remembered little else about her, for she left Cumberland and British Columbia with her family soon after 1918. To confuse things, two Clark or Clarke families kept boarders, informally at least, on Penrith Avenue at the time. Both had daughters named Jean. Andrew and Mary Clarke were renowned for their very Scottish New Year's Eve parties. All five children came home—sons Eck and Scotty who were coal miners, daughters Jean and Mary and Nell—for the singing of Auld Lang Syne and the arrival of the "first foot" or first dark-haired stranger through the door in the new year. The Clarkes were singularly hospitable, welcoming even Chinese guests to their home at a time when this was uncommon. Mary Clarke Fedichin told me that other regular guests were Joe Naylor—who belonged to Cumberland's Rabbie Burns Society although he was anything but Scottish—and Ginger Goodwin.

"I can remember them quite well. And they were great men, they really were," she said. While she was too young to remember incidents or appearances, "They were all friends of my dad, because my dad was a great union man too, he fought for his fellow man."

Jean Clarke McKinnon, the oldest sister, remembered Ginger well—but she was still a young girl in 1918. Ginger Goodwin's fiancée was a different Jean Clark, also Scots, the younger daughter of a coal miner.

Karl Coe alone was able to tell me where the other Clark family moved. "They moved out of here and went up to Alberta to a coal mine and run a boarding house there," he said. "Dad wanted to go to Alberta and try coal mining there, so we went in 1922 and stayed at Clark's boarding house," in the coal mining town of Brûlé, not far from Jasper.

But where did the Clarks, parents and children, go from Brûlé? No one in the small town, now without industry, remembers today. Perhaps the family wanted it that way, having lost a prospective son-in-law in tragic and clouded circumstances. In 1918, all that lay in the future. Everyone knew the war was nearly over, there was a new atmosphere of hope and recovery, and Ginger Goodwin was less concerned about sidestepping the police than stepping out with his fiancée.

One night Ginger turned up at the Horburys' cabin, Ben Horbury told an interviewer around 1975, for a memorable visit. His comments are worth quoting at length.

> One evening, this man come out of the woods to the cabin. I knew who he was because I had seen him around town a lot. He was an exceptional soccer player, football they called it then, or "fitball". . . and of course he was well known to us kids. And it was him, Ginger.
>
> We were sitting down to supper and of course my father got up and shook hands with him and asked him to sit down and eat. Incidentally, he cleaned us out of all our fresh bread. My mother had just finished a baking and we had two great big loaves of bread. So that was the first time I ever knew anything about Ginger. All through that time, whether my father was in contact with him or not, I don't know. He wouldn't have said anything anyway, but this time Ginger had come out in the open. Father just told us, "Now that's not to be talked about."
>
> All this time there was police on the lake continually. They would see father and I going up the lake—we were just in a sailboat—and they would come across with their power boat and stop us and check everything we had in the boat. All the grub and stuff and "How long are you staying up?" and this. When we were going down, they might spot us with glasses and come over and check on what we had then, too. Sometimes, we would just live on what fish we could catch. They didn't want people bringing food to Ginger and the boys.
>
> One thing I do remember was my father asking a question of them. Ginger and Boothman were both together, sitting on the beach talking. And I remember father asked them, "What are you going to do? Are you going to shoot back if they corner you?" They both said, "No, we're up here because we wanted to get away from war and we're

not going to start a private one of our own." They were pacifists, they didn't want to go to war, they didn't want to kill people. Well, the way they wanted it was that they would just give themselves up. If they were cornered, they would give themselves up.

A hot July that year was plagued with mosquitoes in the high country, and sleeping rough would have been miserable even for healthy young men on a pleasure outing. For Ginger Goodwin and the Boothman brothers, on the run and in poor health, it must have been a torment. For one other draft evader, it was worse still. Dave Aitken's brother Andrew reportedly "went out of his head" during a short stay up the lake, had to be taken out and died not long after. Physical discomfort, hunger and constant foot travel in rough terrain would be sufficient vexation. Add to that the primal terror of being hunted by increasingly dangerous and determined enemies—even easygoing, cheerful Ginger Goodwin would eventually feel the strain. Like the pernicious mosquitoes, the police parties grew larger, more frequent, more effective and more intent on their prey.

In July, the manhunts intensified. Several search parties—Provincial Police, Dominion Police and now special police sworn in for the purpose—combed the area. The Dominion Police, a military force responsible for wartime intelligence work, later became part of the RCMP. Bringing in the Dominion Police to help the Provincial Police was a major escalation, and represented an acknowledgment that this was a military matter and of sufficient importance to merit a full-scale intensive manhunt. Questioning any Cumberland people they encountered, they tried unsuccessfully to bar others from travelling on the lake, and searched even sailboats both coming and going.

No longer did good-natured Bob Rushford come in alone from Cumberland for a quick once-over, firing a few warning shots and turning a blind eye to save his fugitive friends from a hellish war. Now a police party walked overland all the way from Port Alberni on the west coast. In June 1911 this arduous thirty-two-mile trek over mountains and snowfields had taken Provincial constable Bert Stephenson, then stationed in Cumberland, twelve hours from Port Alberni to the top of the lake. Another posse occupied a shack at the bottom of Comox Lake, commandeering power boats whenever they needed to travel up the lake to Survey Bay, the Cruikshanks or the Little Lakes.

Jack Horbury's family was staying nearby for the summer. "There was kind of a ban on people going up the lake. The special policemen were staying right across the road from where we lived. It was a little two-by-four place, a garage actually. Some of the policemen were living there part time, living out of a can and dumping their ashes out the window," he said. "My father used to go up the lake every weekend. He said, 'No cops is going to keep me down.'"

Co-operation was scant and grudging from Cumberland people, who resented the outsiders' intrusion and did everything possible to protect their friends from arrest. Josephine Bryden said, "We children were told that if we were asked by the police about anyone taking food to people up the lake, we must say, 'I don't know.'"

Provincial Police, Dominion Police and mixed posses came away empty-handed, and their determination to find the draft evaders had by no means gone stale. Cabins, boats, gold prospectors, fishermen, people out picking blackberries all drew intense police scrutiny. The police in turn attracted intense curiosity from everyone else spending July 1918 at Comox Lake.

"Ginger had told me, I could have shot the whole damn works of them if I'd wanted to," Pansy Ellis said. "They heard this boat coming up and they were suspicious it was the cops coming in, so they beat it and they got away up in the hills, and the cops came in and they took everything in the cabin. They left them nothing to eat or anything."

A rumour now circulated in Cumberland that Ginger Goodwin and his companions had left their refuge, in fact had left the country; until the war ended they were hiding out in Mexico.

Mexico was not involved in the European war—apart from sheltering German agents trying in vain to provoke a diversionary war between Mexico and the United States—and was deep in Pancho Villa's peasant revolution. Mexico had no conscription, no internment of enemy aliens, no arrest of conscientious objectors and a less than vigilant police system. Draft evaders from the United States were already drifting south across the Rio Grande. And if Mexico got too hot, one could drift on south to Guatemala or Nicaragua or another Central American refuge.

Dollars were the passport. Fifty dollars, two or three weeks' pay in Canada, say, would probably provide basic food and shelter for months in Mexico. In late July—perhaps for the ongoing transactions at the tin-pail post office or another cache, perhaps with travel plans in mind, probably acting as banker for his companions—Ginger Goodwin wore a money belt containing $334.60. In 1990 currency this would be several thousand dollars.

Arresting the draft evaders was the manifest purpose of the police parties, and breaking the supply lines was the easiest way to accomplish this. Not only could they trace supplies to their destination, eventually they might wield starvation to flush the fugitives from their concealing wilderness.

Two remarkably different perceptions of that wilderness governed the search, however, at least until its final days. Military and Provincial Police officers, many born and raised in the domesticated landscapes of the British Isles or Eastern Canada, believed that civilization (or citification, since the Latin root word means city) lay in the placid countryside of Europe which these rude colonials had a cultural obligation to defend with armed service. They saw the densely forested heights around Comox Lake as a trackless waste, hostile to human survival. No one would willingly spend time there, they argued, for honest purposes. Anyone living there must therefore be a desperado.

The draft evaders and their friends, whatever their birthplaces, had severed such emotional ties. As the *Federationist* had suggested, "What does Canada owe Europe? This may be answered in one word. Nothing!" And instead of seeing the wilderness as a dangerous and terrifying unknown, they fled to it for succour and safety.

This philosophical divergence hindered the manhunt only temporarily. British military officers in North America for two centuries had resorted to native Indian scouts and trackers, but this wasn't Indian country. Military District 11 in Victoria, by now directly overseeing the operation, instead brought in other specialists: two trappers, one who knew every river and hillside of the search area where he maintained his traplines, and a special constable noted as a hunter and woodsman.

Blackberries

Daniel Campbell occasionally still accepted special assignments on police posses and manhunts. The stepson of long-serving Provincial policeman John Donald Campbell of Esquimalt near Victoria, he followed his father in this position until an awkward incident. In 1905, Myrtle Williams and Audrey Morton charged Dan Campbell with extorting thirty dollars from them. He had pulled them over for driving too fast in a hired buggy along the Gorge waterway, a favourite rendezvous for prostitutes with their customers, and demanded money on the spot. While the Provincial force was investigating their complaint, he tried to force the women either to change their testimony or to leave town. He was indiscreet; there were witnesses to both incidents. At the same time he also negotiated a cash advance equal to an entire month's salary from Victoria gun dealer John Collister. Learning that Campbell was being dismissed, Collister approached his sergeant; the Provincial Police made over to the gun dealer Campbell's last monthly pay cheque.

Apparently Campbell needed far more than the seventy dollars a month he earned as a constable. Over the next thirteen years he worked as a special constable—including a stint in the Crowsnest Pass town of Michel during the 1911 UMWA coal strike—and as a cooper and carpenter. Soon after his dismissal he was managing a hotel near Victoria. His Colwood Inn, about seven miles west of Victoria, was popular with the sporting crowd from the nearby racetrack. Around the time of the Goodwin manhunt, he sold his hotel and "watering hole" after more than a decade as manager and later owner. At forty-five, Campbell was known as a hunter, a woodsman and a gun fancier.

"When we went fishing at Shawnigan Lake—whenever I went with him we'd always get fish. Yes, he knew how to track game and where to find the fish," his grandson Newton Campbell told an interviewer. Campbell's Hill on the Malahat is said to be named for Dan Campbell who frequently hunted in the area.

"Dan Campbell was a crack shot. Oh, a deadly shot. And a fine, fine hunter. The Campbell family was all good hunters," said Eva Harris, his niece. She recalled his lessons on gun safety and responsibility. He would show the children a rifle, butt resting on a table and barrel pointing to the ceiling. "'This is the boss,' he'd say. 'This is the boss. When it's loaded, this gun is in charge. You're not.'"

Campbell claimed to have once served with the North-West Mounted Police. If so, it was under another name; an RCMP historian has been unable to find any record of a Daniel Campbell in the force's ranks. Cecil Clark, a British Columbia Provincial Police officer and later deputy commissioner, said some people regarded Campbell as the second-rate son of a highly-respected father. Despite special assignments, he never permanently rejoined the British Columbia Provincial Police. Wearing the badge of a special constable of the Dominion Police, Campbell was on duty at Comox Lake by early July patrolling for draft evaders and a deserter.

Dan Campbell was a natural choice for the manhunt. Not only was he a first-rate tracker and marksman, he was also familiar with police work. He may even have brought some patriotic enthusiasm to the task of hunting draft evaders, since his son Jock was serving on a naval destroyer hunting German submarines in the North Atlantic.

"He had a pleasant personality. Lots of personality. He was a joker," Newton Campbell said.

"Dan Campbell was a jolly person. He had a good personality. He was very good with kids, you know," Eva Harris remembered. "He was a happy man. I never saw him cranky or downcast. He was a joker. I just remember him as a big, tall man. He was happy-go-lucky. Always fooling with you."

But her father, a Provincial policeman, had little warmth for the husband of his wife's sister. "Uncle Dan was welcome in the house but it was a very cool reception. No, he didn't like Dan at all—but he was a policeman. I think it went back to that police situation where Dan was fired. Daddy wouldn't like that. He was a stickler, a real stickler."

Campbell made a lasting and unfavourable impression on Cumberland people.

"Some figured he was a bounty hunter," Harold Banks said, "who got paid for that work, and well paid for it."

"I think he was picked to do the shooting," Ed Williams said.

"Mac, we are here to get these men dead or alive," Dan Campbell told Peter McNiven when they met at Comox Lake on Friday, July 25. Earlier he'd told four Italians that if he met the evaders, he wouldn't be like Bob Rushford and fire over their heads.

"He was just a goddamn killer, that's what he was. A hit man," Karl Coe said. "He was a man that didn't live here, he was imported just for that one purpose. And he disappeared just as quick, too."

Four other policemen searched with Campbell through July, including the British Columbia Provincial Police chief constable from Nanaimo. Albert Stephenson, ten years younger than Campbell, had grown familiar with the area during his posting to Alberni in 1909 and to Cumberland from 1910 until April 1913. He served there for the first eight months of the Big Strike, and gave evidence in the 1913 trial of striking coal miner Richard Goodwin on charges (later dropped) of assault and intimidation against a strikebreaker. His duties made him aware of another striker and organizer, Ginger Goodwin.

Stephenson had recently exchanged letters about the Military Service Act and draft evaders with new provincial police superintendent William McMynn. Military officers were still asking provincial policemen to undertake searches and arrests at provincial expense. On February 2 McMynn ordered Stephenson to pursue draft evaders hiding in the Nanaimo Lakes area, and to "render every reasonable assistance you can to the military authorities . . . and your own expenses will be allowed and paid by the provincial government as in the prosecution of ordinary offences. All other assistance or costs must be provided and paid for by the military authorities, that is, the military authorities must pay all their own expenses." This point of contention appeared to cause continuous friction between Provincial Police and Dominion Police throughout the war.

Captain Tweedale, assistant provost marshal of Military District 11, got his own back in this funding dispute two weeks later. On February 16 he wrote to McMynn asking the superintendent to inform his staff that the military would disallow a number of their claims for reward money for the arrest of deserters and absentees under the Military Service Act; provincial and federal employees were not eligible. The reward at that time for turning in a draft evader was two to three days' pay for the average skilled labourer: ten dollars.

Stephenson was with the posse on Friday, July 26, when it burst into the Comox Lake cabin, called McDougall's cabin, where Pansy Ellis was staying.

"They had the gun on the three of us. They looked under the beds, and they looked all over, but they couldn't find no signs of. . . . so they looked around the cabin. It was a beautiful morning, and this morning they pulled out, I knew they were heading for the Little Lakes because Ginger and them had been in to the Little Lakes before. . . . I knew it was lucky for them guys that we didn't get in with them, because they'd have come in to the Little Lakes with us. Because we was going to go into the Little Lakes.

"I had to show my exemption card, I said, 'I've got my card in Cumberland,' I said, and [Campbell] said, 'You're under arrest, you're supposed to have your card with you.' So I says, 'That fella there knows me well.' Bert Stephenson, you see. 'No, I don't know you.' I said, 'You don't? Now listen, I'll tell you where you live.' But he made out that he didn't know me. So they came and we was up in the Italian's cabin there, me and my father-in-law and Joe Naylor, when in comes these five cops, two come inside with six-shooters, expecting Ginger was in there, and the other three stood outside with rifles. . . ."

He stood on the beach while the police pushed off across the lake in their boat. In the silent, sunny morning he could hear the birds singing. As they left, guide Tommy Anderson thought Ellis was waving to someone; the policemen's voices carried clearly across the water. When they returned, the trapper said he thought he'd forgotten his rifle. Ellis couldn't resist goading, "You're a dandy, going hunting for people, and forgetting your rifle." Again Campbell threatened to arrest Ellis for not having his exemption card, until another policeman intervened.

Campbell questioned other people at Comox Lake about the draft evaders. Camille Decoeur of Cumberland, who ironically was a barkeeper and hotelier as Campbell himself had been, later told a courtroom that he was at the lake around July 6 with his wife and baby. Campbell and another man wearing a red sweater asked Decoeur about the fishing and told him there were plenty of berries on a nearby trail. When Campbell asked if he knew anything about the draft evaders, Decoeur said he'd heard they were in Mexico. No, the special constable said, they'd been seen around the lake. One policeman had come within thirty feet of them. Campbell said, "If ever I get that close they will never get away."

Decoeur met Campbell again around July 20, and shook hands with him. The Cumberland hotelier had forgotten his registration card, but several policemen identified him and left him alone.

In late July 1918, the military and police were increasingly determined to locate Ginger Goodwin. Search parties ceaselessly travelled
the lake and the surrounding bush. It was almost as though they had
to meet a deadline.

Tommy Anderson and Dad Janes, both trappers, were part of the
search. Anderson had traplines and at least one cabin around the head
of Comox Lake and the Little Lakes, and lived part of the time at
Bevan, the small town that housed workers at Canadian Collieries'
Number Seven mine. Janes lived in Victoria, according to a note in
Bill Devitt's field notebook. Like Cecil "Cougar" Smith of Black Creek
between Courtenay and Campbell River, and "Cougar" Craig of
Craig's Crossing near Parksville, Dad Janes hunted cougars for their
government bounty. In early spring 1918 he'd bagged a fine panther
near Duncan, prompting one of many wartime anonymous informers
to complain to the provincial police that Janes wasn't serving in the
army, that he was reputed to be "nutty" and that he therefore shouldn't
hold a gun licence. Janes was apparently married, and therefore
exempt. He and Anderson may have joined the posse out of patriotic
fervour but, since neither apparently was a provincial or federal
employee, the reward of ten dollars may have provided a further
incentive.

Sam Robertson's explanation for their co-operation was simpler
still. Anderson guided the police "To make a name for himself, I
guess."

Other motives are more intriguing, if more obscure. One rumour
claimed that Anderson was angry at the draft evaders for using one
of his cabins and failing to replace provisions they used, as bush
protocol demands. If missing provisions were a factor, ironically, they
were just as likely removed by police searchers seeking to withhold
supplies from the fugitives. The second rumour had it that Tommy
Anderson was a strikebreaker during the Big Strike, and held a grudge
against former strikers and union organizers because of their open
hostility and contempt. Certainly the 1913 voters' list for Bevan shows
a Thomas Anderson, occupation miner. This in itself is not significant, since even striking union officers were listed through the Big
Strike as "miner" whether they were working or locked out.

"I think he was a scab," Cumberland's retired barber Peter Cameron
told me. "Must have been, because we used to call him Scabby
Anderson."

Many people remembered Tommy Anderson, whose other nickname was "Towse," not fondly.

"I remember that old bugger," Karl Coe said. "He was an old
trapper."

"The guide's name was Tommy Anderson. He was a trapper, and he was the guy who took them in and guided them to all these trails and traplines, see," said Pansy Ellis.

Ginger Goodwin's group and Anderson had a near meeting around midsummer, Ed Williams recounted. The draft evaders came across a still-smoking fire where someone had stopped to make a meal; later they decided it must have been Anderson's fire, and Anderson who in turn discovered their location.

This was the first in a sequence of mishaps that ultimately led the police search parties to the wild hills between the north and south forks of the Cruikshank River. Part of the misfortune was carelessness, perhaps Ginger Goodwin's own rash assumption that the police weren't searching very seriously.

Young men ignoring their military call-up were drifting in and out of hiding all over Vancouver Island, indeed all over Canada. The group of draft evaders at the top of Comox Lake was no exception. Most of Cumberland seemed to know about their existence, if not their exact whereabouts. As a result, newcomers regularly joined them and departed. In July 1918 Ginger Goodwin apparently had three companions: Fred Taylor from South Wellington near Nanaimo, Jimmy Randall, and his good friend Arthur Boothman. Then a fourth man joined them. His name was Ernie Court.

"And what upset things," Pansy Ellis said, "this here Ernie Court, he went in, he was called up, so he went back here to join with them, and his mother had this ranch here at Royston, took half a sack of potatoes, Dave Aitken took them in, he was in on it too, and the old woman told the police he was up the lake, which they were, they were looking for him, and somebody goes up and brings the son down, so then of course the son joined up, he had to, he was conscripted, and then she let the whole cat out of the bag. . . ."

Some say she did it from spite — if her son had to join the army, why should those others go free? — and some say from fright, under threat by the police. With the full weight of criminal and military law behind them, they were in a good position to threaten. This second mishap led the police to intensify their search in the Cruikshanks region.

The third mishap was clear carelessness. Fred Taylor, the man from the Nanaimo area, left a note at the "post office" bucket saying that he needed a new pair of high-topped shoes. Pansy Ellis and some companions brought the shoes in — almost certainly from the shelves of Campbell Brothers' store — along with a bottle of liquor and other supplies, and left them at one of the nearby cabins. Taylor had earlier been reckless in rowing across the lake toward an unknown man who turned out to be a policeman; now he recklessly tore the wrapping paper from his new boots and discarded it with his old boots in the undergrowth behind the cabin. The police had a paper trail to follow; Taylor might as well have left a map.

"This Taylor, we'd taken him up a pair of high-topped shoes for in the woods, and the paper and box and everything was there," Ellis said. "They didn't say nothing about the post office, so I don't know if they got into where we used to leave the notes under the tin can. A five-pound bucket." This gave the posse their break and, with the expert tracking skills of Anderson and Janes, all the information they needed. It was time to call in a superior officer of the Dominion Police for the final stages of a weeks-long, even months-long, wilderness manhunt.

Inspector William John Devitt of the Dominion Police was forty-nine years old, and had spent a lifetime in law enforcement. One of ten children of a poor gardener, he'd emigrated from Ireland at fifteen. Misrepresenting his age to enlist in the North-West Mounted Police in 1887 during the Riel Rebellion, he served under the legendary Colonel Sam Steele. Like the Irish gentry and those who emulated them, Devitt loved fine horses and large hunting dogs. In the North-West Mounted Police he broke broncos, his son Dennis Devitt said, and impressed even Southern Alberta Indians — famous horse breeders — with his superb horsemanship.

A horse was once his downfall. After saddle-breaking one splendid creature as his mount, his senior officer commandeered it for his own use. Devitt struck his officer in the face. Amazingly, he wasn't cashiered — but he did spend the next year riding solitary patrols along the Montana border until his tour of duty ended. He was later reinstated, but only with testimonial letters from friends including Senator James Lougheed, the famous grandfather of later Alberta premier Peter Lougheed. At forty-nine Devitt was less hot-tempered. He still stood tall and trim, cherished his gift as a dramatic storyteller, bred marvellous bloodhounds and wolfhounds and had a keen eye for horseflesh. He had a reputation for generosity, compassion to the unfortunate and honesty as straight as his back. Bill Devitt from 1896 to 1917 served as provincial constable, city clerk, tax assessor and police chief in the British Columbia interior towns of Trail, Nelson and Rossland. He was police chief in Rossland when the smelter workers were on strike in Trail, just twelve miles away. Long afterwards, in applying for a position, he wrote that he had commanded forty-five men in the Dominion Police. Undercover work was among his duties.

"I sent the Minister of Justice many hundreds of thousands of files on the agitators of the period," he wrote. "I have the endorsement of the Consolidated M & S Co Ltd [Mining and Smelting Company Limited] and The C.P.R."

Consolidated and its parent company were later grateful to Devitt, perhaps for his help in eliminating a troublesome labour organizer, perhaps for other undercover work.

Inspector Devitt joined the police posse at Comox Lake at first light on Saturday July 27, though he had been supervising various searches from Vancouver since March. He considered their quarry armed and dangerous; he told a courtroom later that he had telegrams on file stating that the deserter had said he would shoot any police officer who tried to draft him into the army. The description circulated to police officers portrayed the fugitive as a thoroughly undesirable member of society; apparently Albert Goodwin was socialistic, shifty-looking and Jewish. Anti-Semitism usually surged in Europe and North America whenever people wanted scapegoats; in 1918 Jews were being blamed for the Russian Revolution.

"Single man, was clean shaven on the 2nd May 1918; hair reddish brown, face wedge shaped rather than round, furtive glance, some gold filled teeth in upper row shewing, thin build, walks with slight stoop, complexion fair with freckles, weight about 145 lbs. accent English, Cockney, speech voluble and assertive, partial to wearing skull caps, socialistic," was the description entered into the court record. It also gave his height as five feet six and his chest measurement as thirty-three to thirty-six inches. He had blue eyes, three vaccination marks on his right arm and a small scar on the first finger of his left hand.

Campbell, Janes, Anderson and Lance-Corporal George Rowe—a former customs officer at Union Bay—were already at the lower end of the lake, and several other men were stationed at various other points. They travelled by motor boat west and south along the curving lake to Survey Bay at the far end, and climbed west into the Cruikshank area on an old survey trail.

Devitt sent the two trappers around the north side of Alone Mountain, as far as one can reconstruct their routes from later court evidence, while he and the two other policemen took the south side. They probably followed the south and west bank of the Cruikshank River. After about a mile they came to a large boulder and nearby found cooking utensils, a "take-down" rifle, a pair of miners' boots, a shake-making tool and items of clothing. They had located one of the draft evaders' caches, probably aided by information from the trappers' earlier reconnaissances.

Re-concealing these discoveries nearby, the posse ate lunch at around two in the afternoon, then continued following the trail of someone who had passed earlier. Deciding the fugitives were hiding in heavy undergrowth near the river, the police party split up. At 4:30 p.m. Devitt and Rowe climbed the steep hillside above the Cruik-shank, according to later courtroom testimony, while Campbell kept to a lower trail.

Early afternoon was the watershed: fugitives somewhere in the dense underbrush, police separately searching the river trail and mountain slopes. To this point, all the stories more or less fit together into a pattern. Many pieces are missing, and some are oddly shaped and leave unsettling gaps in the overall picture, but it's still possible to loosely reconstruct events. After this point, two main versions of the events of Saturday 27 July 1918 become impossible to fully reconcile.

Which path to follow? A wise writer would stop here, set aside the photocopies and notes and audio tapes, and send the reader on a two-part pilgrimage to the Cumberland Museum. First, Ruth Masters' crucial Ginger Goodwin album compiles the recollections of Goodwin's friends and Ruth's own thoughtful analysis. The old-timers' accounts illustrate some of the limitations of oral history— names not quite right, sequences of events foreshortened or unclear, partial knowledge— but are the best accounts we have. Second, the transcripts of the coroner's inquiry into the death of Albert Goodwin and the preliminary investigation into manslaughter charges against Daniel Campbell (also in the British Columbia Archives and Records Service in Victoria) present the account the government decided to have remain on the public record. These also have their limitations, not of imperfect memory but of the wartime politicization of the very substance of life and death.

Having read these important sources, or having consented to plunge onward into steadily deeper and more tangled undergrowth, a wise reader will throw away compass and map. Here we attempt a synthesis, breaking trail by dead reckoning.

"The draft evaders were camped in the meadow, and Tommy Anderson, the trapper, was supposed to have told the policemen, in fact he took them up on what we call the West Coast Mountain, where they could look down on the meadow," Jack Horbury said.

"I received information when I got to Cumberland where they might be located," Devitt said later.

The camp—a bark lean-to—and the cache at the big rock were known to the police. So were Pete Galeazzi's cabin at the upper end of Comox Lake, the Hundens' cabin on the Cruikshank and other camps like them. In one of these cabins a posse had recently found shotguns, ammunition and other items they decided belonged to the draft evaders. One was a bandanna with holes in it. This, they reasoned, must be a mask for travelling incognito in the bush. The fact that two of their quarry had respectively bright red hair and a bushy black beard, glaringly obvious features despite any mask, did not deter this speculation. In a decision which surely raises doubts about their story, the posse neglected to confiscate or even fully describe the shotguns in this supposed revolutionary arsenal. And no one later said what finally became of the rifle found at the big rock cache.

Ginger Goodwin, Arthur Boothman, Fred Taylor and Jimmy Randall were meanwhile enjoying a day's fishing on the river. The Cruikshank in this stretch was very much an island wilderness stream, green and eloquent among gravel bars, studded with pools where an occasional eddy or swirl indicated sizeable trout. A fine pale sand beach made a perfect camping spot among overhanging alders and cottonwoods. With the heat of high summer shimmering above the gravel bars, a late afternoon fisherman would welcome a stray breeze dawdling from the sun-dappled river into the shade of the trees. Even the persistent mosquitoes couldn't diminish the place's appeal.

A hundred or so yards back from this riverbank, the land rose steeply in cliffs or treacherous slopes of deadfalls and brambles. Trails traversed it, but some were so faint the few people who used them blazed trees to mark the way. As the shadows began to lengthen eastward across the murmuring river shallows, Boothman, Randall and Taylor walked the trail toward their camp. They carried Goodwin's prized fly-fishing rod and the day's catch of silver-flanked trout.

Ginger Goodwin stayed longer, Arthur Boothman later told friends, to pick blackberries upstream. At the height of a good season, plumped out by rain and sweetened by sun, they were thick and heavy on the tangled vines. Some friends later claimed he stayed to catch more fish or shoot grouse instead, though Arthur insisted he had no gun; apparently most people believed Ginger was the best woodsman and the main food provider in the group. His trail led across a forty-five-degree slope where each footfall sank into moss and fallen evergreen cones, and sunlight slanted long dust-ridden shafts among the mature second-growth cedars and firs and hemlocks. Sounds came clearly: the river murmuring below, birds singing in the tree canopy overhead, the close whine of mosquitoes, the wind gently shifting branches. As he came abreast of a deadfall log lying across two other logs uphill to his left, Goodwin's attention caught on something out of place. The metallic slide and click of a gun being cocked, perhaps, or the flare of filtered light on a police badge. The man who stood silent and alone in the shadows above was not a complete stranger. Dan Campbell was one of the policemen Goodwin could have shot from cover during the past month at the Little Lakes or around Survey Bay. He stood almost close enough to touch.

Ginger Goodwin raised his hands — putting them up in surrender, or making a reflex attempt to ward off destruction — in a gesture he would never complete. A single shot at point-blank range fired a soft-nosed hunting bullet, the kind banned in warfare by the Geneva Convention because of its terrible destructive capability, from a custom-made .30 Marlin rifle. The bullet ricocheted from Goodwin's left wrist into the left side of his neck, where it severed bone and nerve and life.

Ed Williams later said, "He was coming up this trail and there's a big log across the trail, and this policeman was behind it watching him coming, and jeez he must have been close to him, because he shot him right in the neck there, and there were powder marks on his neck.

"The way everybody figures, he was laying with the gun right on the log, and when Ginger seen him, I guess he swung around."

Bill Devitt's courtroom testimony confirmed that when he came upon Campbell, the special policeman was standing on a log. A drawing — sketched in pencil and later gone over in black ink — in the Dominion Police inspector's field notebook shows the relative position of three large fallen logs and the body. One dot of a medium blue ink on one of the sketched logs may indicate Campbell's position.

The ricochet bullet tore a gaping wound in his neck and destroyed part of his spine, leading some to claim he was shot in the back. The truth was sufficiently devastating: he was shot not from the front (as Campbell would claim) but from the side.

"He was absolutely ambushed as far as I am concerned," Karl Coe said. "The bullet went through his neck."

Harold Banks, the son of the Cumberland undertaker, confirmed this. "I went in and I saw the body and I looked at both wounds. I know exactly where they were and what I say is the truth," he said. "The bullet went into his neck and come out the back of his neck, it was long gone, blown to pieces by the time it came out.

"There were no marks on his body anywhere as far as I know or I saw, and I saw him stripped. And he had just these two bullet marks, one in his throat that come out the back of his neck and the other one across the top of the wrist here, and there were powder marks on the back of his wrist." Powder marks occur only with a shot fired from a distance of less than ten feet.

Five men at least heard the single shot. Devitt and Rowe, only about fifty yards away on a higher trail, heard Campbell shout, "Come!" The two Dominion Police officers started fighting their way down through the heavy underbrush toward the shout. It took them several minutes to get there.

Boothman was at the bark lean-to making supper and Randall and Taylor were nearby. He later told friends what happened.

"Then one fellow said, Hear that shot? So they went up, and here's Ginger laying dead, and them guys beat it, they got out of the road, see," said Ellis.

Boothman wondered for a moment who'd fired the shot, since Goodwin wasn't armed, but immediately guessed that the police posse had come across Ginger.

"He didn't have a gun with him. He was picking blackberries at the time. Arthur Boothman was back in their camp when he heard this shot. He went out to see what it was, and he seen the guy had shot him. That's what he told me. It looked like Goodwin was just putting his hands up," Cameron said. "I guess maybe the guy hollered at him."

The draft evaders at once fled into the deepest brush.

Bob Rushford, who earlier that summer had encountered and warned Goodwin, believed that a great wrong had been committed. His daughter Louvain Brovenlow wrote, "My dad [said] in no way was Ginger armed. My father had to arrest Campbell and take him to Victoria where he got off free claiming self-defence. My father spoke often about how terrible it was, how they handled it, shooting a defenceless man."

When Devitt and Rowe reached Campbell, he stood on a log pointing at a man on the ground. Goodwin lay face down on the hillside with Joe Naylor's .22 rifle in his hands. Little blood flowed; his heart had stopped instantly.

Campbell said, "I surrender to you, Inspector. I had to do it to save my life." Later Campbell would claim that Goodwin, suddenly confronting him face to face on the trail, raised his .22 at the policeman. Campbell raised his own gun and fired.

Inspector Devitt ordered the special constable to turn over his rifle. As they talked, Goodwin's body shuddered as the last muscles relaxed, and rolled downhill several feet. It stopped against a log, face up and lying slightly on its right side. There it remained from late Saturday afternoon until midday Tuesday.

Devitt told Rowe to make the .22 rifle safe by removing any bullets and putting it on safety. Rowe did so but, he later claimed, with some confusion about how many bullets the gun contained and how the safety worked. This alteration of material evidence drew questions in court; Devitt answered that with other draft evaders in the area, he didn't want to leave the rifle for them to find. Two facts make this claim puzzling. First, Goodwin's body was guarded more or less continuously while it remained at the shooting site. Second, the rifle the posse said they'd found at the big rock cache—was it Joe Naylor's .22 or, if not, why wasn't it identified in court?—was left hidden but unattended despite this concern about firearms falling into the wrong hands. In his on-site field notes, Devitt noted what he regarded as the significant features of the gun: it was a "take-down" rifle (many rifles could be separated into two main sections, stock and barrel, by removing one screw; most single-shot and automatic .22-calibre rifles had this capability) and it appeared to be in good condition. This was only one of dozens of contradictory or problematic aspects that diminish the general credibility of the courtroom testimony.

Devitt sent Campbell to Cumberland to fetch the undertaker, doctor and coroner. His intention was to bury Goodwin where he'd fallen, saying that the country was so rough he didn't believe they could remove the body.

"The police came to Dad and wanted him to go up and bury him in the bush," said Harold Banks, the undertaker's son. "It was these special police that were on this deal." Thomas Banks refused to go fifteen miles up Comox Lake into the wilderness to bury a man, essentially in secret. "He said that there was no way he would do that. Then they said, Well, they'd been to Courtenay to get the undertaker from Courtenay to go up, but he wouldn't have anything to do with it either."

Were the police trying to conceal something? The undertaker found the request strange, but held his tongue. "He wouldn't dare make any statement unless he was asked by the coroner." Harold Banks said, "There was a lot of trying to hide that deal, but it didn't pan out, though.

"It wouldn't have been legal, there's no doubt about that. It would have to have been somebody in quite high authority" who requested the wilderness burial.

But who would that have been? Someone higher in authority than Devitt, Stephenson or Campbell—military police inspector, provincial police chief constable and special policeman—each of whom seemed to control some element of the search in uneasy harmony with other agencies? Dan Campbell seems to have taken his orders direct from Military District 11 in Victoria (not from Bill Devitt, who couldn't say who swore Campbell in or what gun he carried), but no documentation survives to suggest the nature of those orders or their ultimate origin.

Cumberland coroner Joseph Shaw and Dr. Harrison Millard of

Courtenay travelled as far as the head of the lake by boat. There, noting the rough terrain, the coroner refused to attempt an inquest in the wilderness. The military police, crossed by this stubbornness, instructed Banks to have the body brought out for autopsy, inquest and burial. Meanwhile, Rowe and two other Dominion constables kept watch over Goodwin's body; Devitt withdrew to some cabins about a mile east to wait. Traditionally, the death watch was kept by friends. Ginger Goodwin's was kept by his killers.

No attempt was made, apparently, to locate the other three draft evaders. While Devitt claimed in court that he had no special orders regarding him, it was clear that Goodwin was the chief quarry. The inspector's field notebook contains brief descriptions of three other men: Boothman, Taylor and Randall. All three occupy one small page, and include only details of age, height, weight, complexion, colouring and unusual features. Goodwin's description, in contrast, was highly detailed and included mannerisms, personality and attitudes.

"Then everything went quiet all of a sudden," Ben Horbury said. "The police came down the lake, they got out of the boats and they left. I don't know if it was a full day later or not but that was when the word came out that Ginger had been shot and killed. And there was no more police went up after that. Just one man, that's all they were interested in."

"They could have shot the whole works of them," Pansy Ellis said, "because they'd all come over the same trail, but they was waiting for Ginger, see, and they shot Ginger and they left him lay."

"Ginger hadn't a chance," Sam Robertson said. "Boothman, they never even looked at him. It was Ginger they were after. He was a good man."

"Sure, that's all they were after," Peter Cameron said. "As soon as they shot him they just went away, they never bothered with Boothman and them."

Doll Williams agreed. "I don't think there's any doubt, they were out for that man, whatever way they could do it."

"They didn't want to capture Goodwin," said Roy Genge. "You can see, they shot him, they wanted to get rid of him."

The Dominion Police had no intention of arresting Goodwin, many in Cumberland believed and still believe; from the start, the authorities planned his death.

Weighing the different accounts, why would one believe the partisan voices of Goodwin's friends over the courtroom testimony of law enforcers? Why would one believe that Goodwin never aimed his gun at Dan Campbell, or even that he carried no gun? Why would one speculate that Naylor's rifle found its way from the ground where Goodwin dropped it, or even from a cache, into a dead man's hands with Campbell's help? Some friends — Bob Rushford, Joe Naylor and Dave Aitken among them — forfeited their own safety to speak out. Even discounting this as misguided conviction, the heaviest argument against the evidence is the evidence itself. Inaccurate, incomplete, self-contradicting, unclear and (perhaps most troubling in a country that takes unwarranted satisfaction in its justice system) scarcely challenged by coroner, judges and prosecutor: any untrained person could pick gaping holes in the official story. Casual study of the inquiry and preliminary investigation transcripts raises enough questions for a major judicial review. But the actions of the Dominion Police speak loudest.

Dan Campbell, alone at the time of the shooting, was demonstrably an unreliable witness. Whatever other virtues he may have had, he showed himself repeatedly to be a braggart and a liar. His former employer, the British Columbia Provincial Police, fired him as a criminal extortionist and blackmailer. While he continued to be called out for manhunts and posses, he was never again placed in a position where he could embarrass the force.

Perhaps most significant to credibility, the highest political stakes rode on the outcome of this wilderness adventure in a wartime climate of fear and confusion.

Why the great haste, no trouble or expense spared, to deal with Ginger Goodwin? The answer was starkly evident within days.

On August 1 1918, King George V issued a proclamation of conditional amnesty to all men evading the Military Service Act. It was published in newspapers across Canada. Men who had evaded the draft, deserted or gone absent without leave had until August 24 to turn themselves in. These men, the proclamation stated, "have misunderstood their duty or obligation, or have been misled by the advice of ill-disposed, disloyal or seditious persons." They would still have to join the armed forces, but they would face no criminal charges.

Did Special Constable Campbell or Inspector Devitt get special orders in late July? The Dominion Police surely knew in advance of this impending proclamation. Goodwin had shown his inclination over and over in the past nine months to pursue every legal avenue of appeal. Although he had never reported for duty, had never been formally inducted into the army, the military had arbitrarily assigned him the rank of private and the serial number of 270432. This allowed the Dominion Police to categorize him not as a mere draft evader or defaulter, but as a deserter. The disgraceful act of desertion excused almost any degree of force by military police; at the front, deserters were summarily executed by firing squad, often without court martial and capriciously.

Now, what if Goodwin decided to turn himself in, thwarting any attempt to remove the threat he posed to the government and its friends in industry? The police would have no excuse to hunt him. He couldn't be allowed to slip through their fingers. With little time to spare before the fateful proclamation, a bullet conveniently eliminated that possibility. Four days before the amnesty announcement, agents of the Crown shot and killed Ginger Goodwin.

Aftershocks

Darkness had fallen on the night of Tuesday, July 30 when the steady throb of a power boat signalled an awaited return.

Several of Goodwin's friends finally walked into the Cruikshanks that afternoon at Thomas Banks' request. In the summer heat they found the body seething with maggots; the stench of putrefaction was so overwhelming that they sewed their burden in canvas and carried it out on a pole, their faces covered with handkerchiefs. From Cruikshank estuary it travelled by boat down the lake, then by hearse to Cumberland. The police came out in two groups the same night, according to Bill Devitt's field notebook.

"There was three or four Italians who went in and packed the body out," Pansy Ellis said, "and that body had lain there for two or three days and his face was all riddled with maggots, and oh, what a mess he was in, so they brought him down here."

"We knew when they brought Goodwin's body down the lake," Josephine Bryden said. "Big John had this huge old tub of a boat with a very deep-sounding engine. I believe he was a driver for the mine, because they trucked coal in those days. Big John the Driver they called him. And they brought Goodwin's body down in Big John's boat in the middle of the night and I heard it."

"The *Ripple* was the boat they brought Goodwin down the lake in," Jack Horbury said. "I guess they sort of conscripted the boat."

By morning Goodwin's body lay in the Cumberland undertaker's parlour, and some of the children who had known Ginger stood silently around Big John's empty boat looking at the blood on the floorboards. Word travelled quickly.

Harrison Millard, a Courtenay doctor, examined the body Wednesday morning at the request of the Dominion Police and reported his findings that evening at a coroner's inquiry in Cumberland courthouse. Apart from conspicuous reliance on medical terms from Gray's *Anatomy*, anyone could have carried out the investigation. Millard measured the body, noted characteristics such as height and hair colour, traced the course and effects of Dan Campbell's .30-calibre bullet, and set aside clothing and personal items. Strangely, since Goodwin's state of health was the underlying issue, he did not open the body to examine Goodwin's physical condition.

"The surprise to me though was that they brought a Courtenay doctor up. What was the matter with our own two doctors in Cumberland?" Harold Banks said. "And they weren't called in, so there was something odd right there, there was something fishy there all right. Dr. Hicks and McNaughton would be dealing with the miners all the time."

The local doctors would be aware of Goodwin's 1915 hospitalization in Cumberland and perhaps of his other ailments. They might have let slip that the young man whom several military service tribunals insisted was Class A, fit for overseas combat, in fact suffered from stomach ulcers and a fatal lung disease. Their testimony might have suggested that drafting Albert Goodwin, as surely as setting an ambush for him, was an attempt at legal murder.

Dr. McNaughton did provide services for one unspecified 1918 inquest, however. According to the public accounts for British Columbia, he received payment of twenty-seven dollars; undertaker T.E. Banks received thirty dollars, and Constable Rushford three dollars. If this was the Goodwin inquest, why did Dr. McNaughton of Cumberland receive payment instead of Courtenay's Dr. Millard who performed the post mortem and provided courtroom testimony? This is yet another unexplained element.

Dr. Millard, either in ignorance or following the orders of a police force with extraordinary wartime powers, made only superficial observations.

"The body was that of a well nourished, well built man of about thirty years of age, five feet six inches in height and weighing approximately one hundred and fifty pounds," Millard told the coroner's inquiry; his statement to the preliminary investigation a week later was much the same.

There was post mortem staining on the back and but-
tocks and some slight rigor mortis. The body had been dead
some three or four days. On his left little finger was a ring
containing a red stone, and around his waist was a leather
belt containing a sum of money in bank bills, and some
silver. The hair on deceased's head was light colored and
fairly short; that on his face sandy of about two days
growth, with stubby sandy moustache. The mouth contained three gold crowned teeth with gold bridging and
some amalgam filled and crowned grinders (molars). On
his upper lip, half an inch above and to the outer left angle
of the mouth, was a small punctured wound half an inch
deep, and one-twelfth of an inch in diameter. . . . On the
outer surface of the left radius (forearm) two inches above
its lower extremity was a lacerated flesh wound extending
nearly to the bone half an inch wide and one and one half
inches long, crossing the forearm diagonally from without,
inwards and upwards. On the left side of the neck in the
anterior triangle, anterior to the sterno mastoid muscle is a
lacerated gun-shot wound sufficiently large to admit of two
fingers directed backwards and to the right. This wound
enlarges as it reaches the spinous processes and posterior
portions of the bodies of the third and fourth cervical
vertebrae. These structures are shattered with comminuted
fractures. The spinal cord is completely severed. On the
right shoulder, immediately beneath the skin. . . . I found
the flattened ragged greater portion of a bullet. . .

Talk ran wild in Cumberland. Ginger had been shot in the back,
people muttered. Campbell was a bounty hunter, and should be
lynched.

Piggy Brown, then a young boy living in Bevan, spent weekends
with his grandfather down in Jerusalem. One evening in late July 1918
he was standing near the railway water tower, where the Perseverance
Trail approached Cumberland. "I saw this policeman coming down.
You know they had, they wore those leather things [leg puttees] and
with a big hat and a pack on his back and his rifle on his back. And
lo and behold, that was the guy. Because there was only one way to
get up here, and there was a big cedar log across the swamp down
here just below the tank, to get up into the Perseverance Trail, and
then you could get back up into the lake. And that was the guy that
shot him, Ginger Goodwin."

Cumberland folklore claims that when Dan Campbell reached

town, he ordered a meal in a hotel dining room. The bush telegraph had preceded him. The waitress refused him service, ignoring his threats, as did every other eating place in town. But he was in danger of worse than an enforced fast. Cumberland was talking lynch party.

Bill Pritchard, labour organizer and editor of the Socialist Party of Canada's *Western Clarion*, arrived from Vancouver with other labour socialists. "I had one hell of a time in a back room talking to the Italians—you know, they were right steamed up—getting them to calm down and be quiet—don't start anything for God's sake. . . ."

"There was pretty close to a riot up there, the special police, they pulled out of Cumberland just as soon as they could after that happened," Harold Banks said. "They got the fellow they wanted, and they were probably too darn scared to go back in there looking for any more, because they'd have known what would happen, they'd have been the people who were getting shot, not the people who were in the woods."

Bob Rushford, the provincial constable who had warned Ginger Goodwin to stay out of sight of the Dominion Police for his own safety, now warned the Dominion Police to stay out of the sight of Goodwin's friends for their safety. He'd already arrested Dan Campbell and taken him in custody to Victoria to wait for the preliminary investigation into his manslaughter charges, but he feared for Devitt, Rowe and the other military policemen. Even before the shooting at the Cruikshanks, the Dominion Police were hated.

Why were they hated with such intensity? My father Arthur Mayse told me they had much the same reputation as the English Black and Tans military police during the Irish Rebellion of 1916 to 1922: misfits, ne'er-do-wells, remittance men, petty criminals who signed up to avoid prison, brutes with a disturbing taste for violence. It was a point of pride to his own father Amos Mayse that he had refused an officer's commission in the Black and Tans when he was too badly wounded by shrapnel at the great slaughter of the Somme to return to the front in 1916. When a former coal miner—with a broad Yorkshire voice, three years' schooling, and no other hope of self-betterment in the English class system—spurns an officer's commission in a military unit, it does not speak highly for the military unit. However many worthy men served in the Dominion Police, the force empowered to enforce the Military Services Act was widely held in contempt.

Now, worsening this unsavoury reputation, a Dominion constable had shot Ginger Goodwin.

"The miners in Cumberland were so incensed over it, it was a good thing for Campbell that he got out and disappeared when he did or he would have been either hung or shot. Somebody would have done it," Ben Horbury said.

"If anybody here had caught him, he would have got it sure as anything," Doll Williams said. "There was a vicious bunch of people here at that time."

"They took him away. They had to move him, oh yes," Sam Robertson laughed. "They would have shot him. . . . There were lots of rough-necks around there, they'd have got him, sure the guy would have been shot. He just disappeared, never came back, they never told us where he went, they'd better not have told, because he would have been shot. . . ."

Dan Campbell's reputation followed him back to Victoria and Colwood, where even today old-timers speak of him uneasily, as though he could still take revenge.

"He was a guy that nobody had very much good to say about. I won't say that he enjoyed the job, but he had no qualms about what he had to do — not much character to him, not much principle to him," Ben Swindell said. He never knew Campbell, but worked twenty years with men who did. "You kind of pick up the idea that Dan Campbell was somebody nobody wanted to say he was a friend of.

"He was the head roundup guy for conscription — you can guess he wasn't too popular."

Swindell said Campbell also pursued draft evaders in the Colwood area during the First World War. "He was a government torpedo man . . ."

"My people talked about him," Bromley Quinney said, adding rather cryptically, "nothing as bad as you hear."

The Dominion Police were also held responsible for a fire that swept from the Cruikshank River to the south fork of Cruikshank Creek.

"Of course as soon as they killed him they burned it, they burned all the woods around, so you couldn't find a trace of anything," Karl Coe said. His father Richard Coe took him up later to show him the place. "They burned up any evidence that might be found, I guess. I never did find out why they did it."

Cumberland people were at white heat with grief and anger, and they weren't alone. Ginger Goodwin had friends across British Columbia, many in the labour movement and political circles, and some as distant as Nova Scotia. Union locals in Northern Alberta who'd probably never known him recorded in their minutes their regret over the death of Bro. A. Goodwin. But most eloquent of all in their wrath, either over his shooting or over his draft evasion, were the newspapers.

"Strong feeling is expressed in the Cumberland district, and 'Ginger' 's friends, both on the Island and on the Mainland, are demanding the most searching investigation," The *British Columbia Fed-erationist* wrote on August 2. "The fact that a soft-nosed bullet, or dum-dum bullet was used, and which has been ruled out of 'civilized warfare' in Europe has caused widespread indignation, and especially in the Cumberland district, where Goodwin was very popular.

"Testimony regarding the bullet used caused considerable sensation at the coroner's inquest."

There Joe Naylor first raised the question of the bullet type. He also was the first to challenge Devitt's interference with the position of the body and the .22 rifle—Naylor's own rifle, lent to his friend for shooting small game—thus preventing independent investigation of which way the rifle was pointing when he died.

"From the path of the bullet, it is asserted that his head must have been turned away, and from this it is argued that he could not have been sighting his rifle at the officer," said the *Federationist* story.

Even the daily newspapers with their generally pro-industry, anti-labour bias had praised Goodwin in his recent public appearances, Bill Pritchard told a special meeting of the Vancouver Trades and Labour Council, and "stated that his delivery was a polished effort, and complimented him on his inoffensive language, which is a proof of the character of the man."

"Like all members of the executive of the Federation [of Labour], he fought against conscription. . . . Unlike most of the other officers of the Federation, Goodwin came under the first call under the Military Service Act," said the *Federationist*'s front page story. "He was well posted on the working class movement, an orator of no mean ability, and a gentleman in the best sense of the word: kindly hearted, earnest and sincere in his efforts to bring about a change in the system, which he knew so well was the cause of wars, and all the ills from which society suffers."

The *Western Clarion*, which had virtuously reported the Socialist Party of Canada's ejection of Ginger Goodwin a few months earlier, now published a front-page portrait in a black mourning border and lamented "The Killing of Comrade 'Ginger' Goodwin." For the first time since the Trail smelter strike, and often for the last time, Ginger Goodwin also made front-page news in commercial newspapers.

The *Cumberland Islander*, a generally anti-labour paper under the editorship of E.W. Bickle, merely reported the police version of the shooting.

Printers at the *Vancouver Sun* walked off the job, refusing to print an anti-Goodwin editorial, and printing instead a handbill defending their viewpoint and castigating their new management. John P. Mc-Connell, the paper's own founding editor, had characterized it as "the harlot of Canadian newspapers . . . the vehicle of lies piled on lies" in *JP's Weekly* of June 3, 1916.

The *Trail News* reported the shooting in more detail than most of the coast dailies, and produced a hostile editorial containing back-handed praise:

> Albert Goodwin a year ago was known to every resident of Trail and made no secret of his opposition to the Military Service Act. However, he was examined and placed in Category D—which means subject to further examination. Later he was reclassed in Category A, asked for exemption, was refused and appealed before Judge Brown, who again refused it and Mr. Justice Duff did the same. Goodwin was certified for service and failed to appear. Months later he was located in the wilds of Vancouver Island, and last week was shot and killed by the military police with a rifle in his hands while attempting to evade service—paying the penalty for armed resistance.
>
> Deceased had stated more than once that he would not serve, and he did not, but was shot by the police in self-defence while resisting arrest. He was an Englishman, a Socialist of pronounced type and has two brothers with the colors in France. There was no just reason why an exception should be made in his case, according to the laws laid down, by which we all must be governed.
>
> Goodwin deserves no sympathy nor do those who think as he does. Canada is at war and has called its young men to the colors. He was one of them, and his persistent evasion of his duty brought the natural consequence. Thousands have gone willingly and gladly and many have paid the price. Albert Goodwin paid it, not in the line of duty, but because he would not conform to what we are all subject to and threatened an officer. He was a bright man and could have made a name for himself.

Cries of righteous ire also arose from the pro-conscription "patriotic" camp.

"The ones who caused us the biggest stink was them that had been overseas and had just come back," Pansy Ellis said, referring especially to provincial and military policemen. "They was the ones who caused the big rumpus, they was the ones who went up in the air over Ginger and them being up there . . . "

An editorial in the *British Columbia Veteran's Weekly* of August 8 declared Goodwin, not Campbell, was the murderer, since his smelter strike had prolonged the war. A pseudonymous letter declared that Goodwin was "a coward who because he was afraid to fight for his country wanted the brave boys over in France to be cut off ammunition by calling a strike in the Trail smelter."

Had the writers known of the military's determination to railroad a sick man into the trajectory of German ammunition, they might have redirected their indignation. Even the veterans' paper showed loathing for the military police, which often harassed returned soldiers in the belief they were "skulkers" and "slackers."

In Vancouver, both supporters and opponents of conscription did more than raise their voices. The Trades and Labour Council and Metal Trades Council, in a black-bordered "in memoriam" notice in the August 2 *Federationist*, announced that all their members would "cease work for twenty-four hours commencing 12 o'clock noon, Friday, August 2nd, 1918, as a protest against the shooting of Brother A. Goodwin."

The subsequent work stoppage is generally recognized, despite its failure to shut down all industry and services, as Canada's first general strike.

A general strike had already been tentatively planned in support of striking post office workers. And talk had been buzzing around the British Columbia Federation of Labour for months of a general strike to protest the first unwilling conscript. Now a work stoppage would have more specific, and more tragic, grounds.

First the Vancouver streetcar drivers took their vehicles back to the car barns and went home; New Westminster and North Vancouver drivers followed their lead. The metal workers at Coughlan's shipyards downed tools, as did electrical workers, construction workers and other service workers across the city. All longshoremen walked off the job; so did all garment workers. Some union members remained at work, but transportation and services in the city were effectively halted.

"The soldiers raised hell in Vancouver about this," Jack Horbury said. "It was put in as Goodwin being a draft evader, but he wasn't the only draft evader, there were lots of them all up the island."

Returned veterans rallied enthusiastically to oppose the labour action, throwing themselves into an afternoon of vandalism and attempted murder. Several hundred of them — allegedly organized by city businessmen and women from upper-crust Shaughnessy—marched on the Labour Temple at the corner of Dunsmuir and Homer Streets. The returned soldiers broke in and demonstrated their intellectual refinement by throwing the Vancouver Trades and Labour Council's books and records out into the street.

Sighting Victor Midgeley, council secretary, at an upper-storey window, they surged upstairs to throw him out. Instead of falling to his death, he scrambled onto a second-storey ledge. When he managed to climb back inside, the soldiers attacked in another attempt to throw him out. His life was probably saved by the council's telephone operator, Frances Foxcroft, who barred the veterans' way to the window. The mob contented itself with beating Midgeley and George Thomas of the longshoreman's union, and forcing them to kiss the British flag to howls of "traitor," "skunk," "reptile" and "German."

Whipped into a frenzy by members of the Great War Veterans' Association, particularly by a Private Devereaux, the returned soldiers plunged into street violence and further vandalism. Now drunk, some of them tried to work on the docks or drive the streetcars, egged on by the Shaughnessy women. That day and evening they held strident anti-labour, anti-foreigner mass meetings, calling the labour movement Bolsheviki and un-British, and ejecting anyone in the audience who protested.

This was an intriguing contrast to the attitudes of the three hundred thousand allied troops who in 1918 were in Russia attempting to snuff out the nascent revolution. There, ". . . the soldiers mutinied," says Phillip Knightley in his book *The First Casualty*.

"The French, the Americans, the Canadians and the British all mutinied. Some shot their officers and surrendered to the Bolsheviks. Some raised red flags, sang revolutionary songs and refused to obey orders. So little of this appeared in print that not only was the newspaper reader at the time kept in ignorance of the role his countrymen were playing in the intervention, but a student today can find little reference to it in his country's history books."

The Vancouver soldiers showed special hostility to the Greek community although it had generously supported various war funds. The rationale was that Greek grocers and restaurateurs were "living on the fat of the land and piling up a big bank account" while "Canadians" earned $1.10 a day in the horrendous trenches.

The veterans crowned their day's achievements by yelling for the deportation of seven labour leaders, among them Midgeley, Thomas, Pritchard, Ernest Winch and Joe Naylor. Mayor Gale said, "The good citizens of this province should not tolerate any action that will carry on the propaganda of the Kaiser," and advised against further attacks on labour property or persons until it was absolutely necessary. Vancouver's three daily newspapers — the *World*, the *Province* and the *Sun* — reported this rabble-rousing with zealous approbation.

Labour leaders, one man told a mass meeting, "are just as bad as the man who got shot in the back or front — I hope both." There were catcalls that a soft-nosed bullet was too good for Goodwin, and that police should have used a machine gun.

A judge summed up the frightening emotional climate in dismissing charges against one union man who stated his opinions aloud. "Think yourself lucky to get away so easily. In times like these the wise man keeps his mouth closed and does not air his sentiments in a crowd." It was a long march from the smug Canadian assumption of fair play and free speech.

Fair play was not something Ginger Goodwin had expected, according to one minor aside in all this sound and fury. A *Vancouver World* story said, "Goodwin, however, was well known in labour circles here as an organizer and had told a labour meeting months ago that he expected the authorities would 'get him,' although it is hardly likely, unless it was even then his intention to die rather than be arrested and conscripted, that he meant or anticipated the actual denouement."

Cumberland mourned while Vancouver rioted.

"After Ginger was brought down the lake and went through the process of the government getting what they wanted to know about him, they took him to Clarke's house. He was buried from Clarke's house instead of a church or undertaker's office. They packed him right from there up to the top of the street and around and down right out of town," Karl Coe said, looking at his photograph of the funeral procession. "He was the only man who ever got carried on people's shoulders — that's the coffin they're carrying."

The funeral procession went up Penrith Avenue to the corner where several churches stood kitty-corner, then over to Dunsmuir Avenue and all the way down through the city centre. Karl Coe, then thirteen, watched from the sidelines. In the photograph of the funeral march, he's the boy in a cloth cap leaning against a telephone pole. Many others did march, including scores of visitors from the mainland, the Italians' West Cumberland Band and a good proportion of the city population. Most shops shut down, and the streets were empty. The mines nominally remained open, but most miners took the shift off to attend the funeral of "the worker's friend," their one-time union organizer. Leading the parade, and probably striking a fatal blow to his police career, was Ginger Goodwin's friend and Cumberland's war hero Constable Robert Rushford.

He wasn't the only veteran marching that day. "Ginger was shot in 1918. I was in the army then, and I come home for his funeral. Oh, it was a big shock, all that. And yet I had a uniform, but I went in it just the same," said Johnny Marocchi.

"I never saw the funeral because father, I guess, more or less wanted to keep us kids out of it and we didn't go into town and view it. But the casket was packed shoulder high right through Cumberland," Ben Horbury said. "When one bunch of men got too tired, another bunch went in. He was so highly thought of, you know. A man has to be highly thought of when he's accused of a crime and killed as a criminal and yet the whole town turns out for the funeral and he's packed shoulder high through the town."

The white coffin was piled high with flowers. When the procession reached the outskirts of town the pallbearers dropped it from shoulder height but still spelled each other off on the dirt road eastward. Past the brewery, past the road to Number Five pit where Ginger had worked before the Big Strike, past Slaughterhouse Road, through the marshy flats of the company farm where broken-down pit mules ended their days, they walked up and around a gentle hill.

At the crest, just where the road swings north toward the Japanese and Chinese cemeteries and on to Courtenay, any who looked back that sunny day would see smoke from Cumberland chimneys, and beyond, the Beaufort Range spanning the western horizon. A little snow would still cling in the high snowfields; eagle and raven would wheel above the smoky blue mountain wall glistening with slow glaciers.

Some perhaps looked back and thought, *I will lift up mine eyes unto the hills, whence cometh my help. My help cometh from the Lord, who made heaven and earth.* . . . Joe Naylor would not be one who thought so. Like his dead friend, he had little patience with parsons, and the only help that had come to Ginger Goodwin among those hills came not from heaven but from the common clay of friends: Minto farmers, merchants like the Campbells, coal miners who brought their own languages and customs to a new country steeped in old-world cruelty, socialists all the more determined to bring to birth a new world from the ashes of the old, their children, their wives and husbands, their friends. Cumberland people remember that when the head of Ginger Goodwin's funeral procession reached the cemetery, the last marchers still waited to leave town.

The funeral included "everybody in town practically. They called it a mile of people," Karl Coe remembered. "Everybody loved him, you know."

Ginger Goodwin's funeral was a great event in Cumberland, the greatest since the Big Strike. One could even argue that it was the first day of Cumberland's long slow decline to the present. People still remember, a few with grief and anger, all with wonder.

"I'll never forget Ginger," Sam Robertson said. "The day of the funeral, you couldn't go down the street. They came from all over, he was so well liked."

Mary Fedichin told me, "About all I can remember — I can't remember his looks or anything — but I know that we knew him quite well. And I can remember his funeral, because everybody took the day off, being a kid. They walked down the main street and it was solid all the way down, carrying his coffin."

No minister officiated, and the short ceremony was arranged by Local 70 of the Socialist Party of Canada. Joe Naylor, and Vancouver socialists W.W. Lefeaux and Bill Pritchard, spoke at the graveside. Not in the Catholic section, not in the Protestant section, but away in the unpopulated back quarter near the overhanging fir trees, the people of Cumberland buried Ginger Goodwin.

"On request of the chief of police the Dominion police were removed from the district prior to the funeral, that official stating that he would not be responsible for the results unless this was done," the *Federationist* reported, adding, "Goodwin now rests, free from those ills which had in life many times made his sojourn on this earth a burden."

"And it was very beautifully arranged and peaceful," Bill Pritchard remembered, "and as is the case with miners, in coming back from the cemetery which was four miles away at Happy Valley, you pass the brewery — and after there's a funeral the boss of the brewery is there to wait for the mourners coming back — and it's a hot day and they all go in the brewery and have a drink — that's how they remember him."

Funeral and wake were not the end of Cumberland's ordeal. Three young men, pacifists evading a hated war and pursued by a hated military police force, were still in desperate need. The friends who'd fed Boothman, Taylor and Randall all summer now outfitted them for escape.

"After Goodwin was shot, they brought the other men out of the woods to Cumberland and then to Campbell Brothers' basement," Elsie Marocchi remembered. "Campbells had the big store on the main street. There they shaved them all and cut their hair, and Campbell gave them all new clothes. It went on most of the Friday night after Goodwin was shot. My dad was one of the ones who were there helping to clean them up. Then people took them to different places. Some of the men went to Victoria, some to Vancouver, they spread around.

"... they thought it would be wise to bring the rest of the men down. So my dad and a number of other men went to Campbell Brothers' store, in the basement, and Campbell provided every one of those men with a suit, shoes and clothes because they left here at night. Nobody knew they were down, but of course they all had long beards and everything. So they brought them all down in Campbells' basement and had hair cuts and shaved them and dressed them up and then they were taken to Nanaimo. They were broken up, you see. You go this way, and you go that, so as nobody said, I seen so-and-so. I know my dad was away all night. They were getting these men ready to leave. They all left."

Harry Williamson got the three draft evaders to his family farm in Minto, then after dark led them down "the goat track" to tidewater at Royston. They boarded a boat—a local fishboat, one story said— which carried them overnight to Vancouver. There they split up to avoid pursuit, but no one bothered them again. Apparently the military police had what they wanted, once Ginger Goodwin was dead.

Rex versus Campbell

Joe Naylor was a thorn in the side of the Cumberland coroner. Not only did he view Goodwin's body at the undertaker's, taking notes and measurements of the injuries, he attended the inquest into the death on behalf of the dead man's family and friends. On top of that he was critical of the inquiry procedure. He commented on an earlier inquiry for the *British Columbia Federationist* in June 1917 after a Cumberland mine accident.

"As to the inquest, I have little to say, but to say the least it was disgusting," Naylor wrote a year before Ginger Goodwin's shooting. "In the first place, the jury consisted of five men out of the six that didn't know what was taking place, only that they were holding an inquiry over four dead bodies. They didn't know the first thing about a mine. I don't mean that they are to blame, but I do say that the system and custom of picking juries is rotten and should be altered. But then, are we not living under capitalism, and what do we expect it to do? Only look after Capital and the capitalist class. The jury, after deliberating for five long minutes brought in a verdict of accidental death . . ."

The inquest on the body of Ginger Goodwin took place the evening of Wednesday, July 31, just hours after it arrived from the head of Comox Lake and underwent Dr. Millard's perfunctory examination. Coroner Joseph Shaw and his jury viewed the body at Banks' Undertaking Parlors and then carried on in Cumberland courthouse. The body also received painstaking scrutiny and measurement from Joe

Naylor on behalf of Goodwin's family and friends. Naylor would put his keen observation to good use in the inquiry, to the discomfiture of the coroner and others, and ultimately to the detriment of his personal safety and freedom.

The coroner's jury consisted of six men. Charles Parnham was a Canadian Collieries mine overman and had been Cumberland's mayor two years earlier. The voters' list identified foreman Frank Dalby as a freight agent, Neil McFadyen as a teamster, John Fraser as a barber, and John White Cooke as a mine weighman, perhaps one of the "nincompoops, good-looking idiots and know nothings" complained of in the 1912 letter to the *United Mine Workers Journal* written by "A Driver in the Mud Hole." The coroner was a farmer in Union Camp. As Joe Naylor had complained a year earlier, these non-union jurymen owed their sustenance to capital—Canadian Collieries—and could achieve at best nervous neutrality to a labour socialist like Ginger Goodwin, dead or alive. And it was clear from the opening minutes that, whatever the stated intent of the coroner's inquiry, it was not Dan Campbell's act which was under investigation but Albert Goodwin's character.

Four other men played an official role in the evening inquest. Dan Campbell's lawyer was W.C. Moresby of Victoria. Cumberland lawyer P.P. Harrison represented Goodwin's friends, and Superintendent F.R. Murray, the same officer who had dismissed Campbell in 1905, observed for the British Columbia Provincial Police. A court stenographer arrived from Victoria. Four witnesses took the stand: Dr. Millard, Dominion Police Inspector Bill Devitt, Lance-Corporal George Rowe, and the Nanaimo provincial police chief Bert Stephenson. Stephenson had reached the site of the shooting three days after Goodwin's death. Dan Campbell took no part in the proceedings, which meant that the only man who truly knew what happened above Cruikshank River did not testify until the case reached a higher court. His statements there are not recorded.

Dr. Millard portrayed Goodwin as a fit young man in good health— "a well nourished, well built man of about thirty years of age, five feet six inches in height and weighing approximately one hundred and fifty pounds"—not a gaunt stooped man with lung disease and an ulcerated stomach. His height was easy enough to measure, though it was later given more accurately as five feet six and a half, but his weight was apparently arrived at by visual estimate. Since even the police description represented Goodwin as thin, 150 pounds sounds heavier than likely, especially after two or three months spent in the bush and constantly on the move. Was Millard familiar with the bloating effect in a body left unburied for four days in hot weather?

It would appear heavier and more solid, and would at best make a visual estimate difficult. Had he opened the body cavity, it would have released the bloating gases, and made possible the examination of stomach and lungs. For whatever reason, Millard failed to take this step. The doctor went on to describe the wounds, and under questioning speculated on their origins.

Bill Devitt, despite his role as a West Kootenays policeman during the 1916 election and the Trail smelter strike, said he had never met "the unfortunate deceased man." The coroner never questioned the logical inconsistencies: Devitt refused to move the body until the coroner saw it, but had Rowe move the gun; he had seen documentation of Campbell's swearing-in as a special constable but couldn't say when or where or by whom he was sworn in; he carried a military description of Goodwin, but had no special orders concerning this man; he said that his own instructions were to arrest Goodwin, but not whether he had instructed Campbell to that effect; he described Campbell as carrying a .32 Smith and Wesson pistol and not a rifle, but identified a .30 calibre Winchester rifle shell as coming from his Marlin gun; he described Joe Naylor's rifle as a high-powered automatic .22 (it was merely an automatic or repeating .22) in its owner's presence, then back-pedalled to say it wasn't. And there were still other contradictions.

Rowe's testimony portrays him as a less polished, but punctilious, man. Straightforward questions about his handling of the .22 rifle caused him intense discomfort. "With reference to the cartridges I want to explain clearly about these, and as far as my evidence is concerned it will be very clear; I am not afraid to hide anything... "

This surprising defensiveness seems quite unprovoked by any previous aspect of the inquest. But soon it appeared that he had cause to be anxious. At first he said, "I found it loaded, and I found it ready to go off; to press the trigger was all that was necessary."

Rowe described himself as "rather an admirer of rifles in general" but claimed unfamiliarity with Goodwin's rifle; he was uncertain about the function of the safety catch, the firing pin, the trigger and the magazine release mechanism. Rowe said that in attempting to make it safe he had sprayed all ten of the .22 cartridges out onto the ground. He could find only eight. How many made a full load? Without knowing the rifle model no one can say, but ten is a possibility.

Bert Stephenson told the inquest that three days later he found a box in Goodwin's shirt pocket containing eight cartridges, exactly the missing number. Could it be that Ginger Goodwin was carrying an unloaded gun into which someone hastily loaded two bullets once he was dead? If Rowe knew or guessed this, it could explain his nervous garrulity.

Coroner Shaw seemed mainly concerned that witnesses' descriptions be clear to the stenographer and, despite a tendency to lead the witnesses, asked few probing questions. Joe Naylor—clearly unwelcome at the inquest, judging by the coroner's responses—asked each witness for more detail or interpretation.

Naylor's questions reveal much about the shooting, and the inquest procedure. He asked Millard about the difference in size between bullet wounds made at first impact and on ricochet; the doctor said Campbell's bullet struck something else before it made the gaping hole in Goodwin's neck. He asked Devitt whether the bullet was steel-jacketed or a soft-nosed dum-dum; Devitt said he knew nothing about the bullet, although he had just identified a similar shell as a .30 Winchester central fire type. Naylor asked Rowe why Campbell, having surrendered to Devitt, travelled unguarded and alone down the lake to fetch the coroner and then back again; he also asked whether Campbell's bullet was steel-jacketed or soft-nosed. Rowe couldn't answer either question. Naylor asked Stephenson why Campbell was sent to bring him to the scene when others knew the way; the police chief said that Campbell remained in charge of the operation even though he was under arrest. Even these terse answers suggest a shockingly lax approach to the whole incident.

Far more alarming, the questions show Joe Naylor's suspicion that Campbell acted on secret "shoot on sight, shoot to kill" orders, used the deadliest possible bullet of a kind sold for killing large animals, shot Goodwin from the side and from ambush with no attempt to arrest or warn him, and was in no way governed by his own supposed surrender to Bill Devitt. Naylor told the *British Columbia Federationist* that he wanted to know why the police had removed the rifle from Goodwin's hands "so that independent investigation might be made of the exact position and whether Goodwin's gun was pointed at the officer."

The coroner's jury returned at 7:30 p.m., after half an hour's deliberation, with the conclusion that "Albert Goodwin evidently met his death by a bullet from a rifle in the hands of Constable Campbell who was trying to effect the arrest of the deceased Albert Goodwin, who was evading the Military Service Act." Despite the irregularities of both incident and inquest, the jury did not add any special recommendation or observation.

Several coast newspapers reported on the shooting and the inquest. Censorship had become law by order-in-council a few months earlier; coverage was thin, biased and monumentally inaccurate. Several points stand out, however. The *Daily Colonist's* first story, filed from Cumberland on July 30, a day before the inquest, quoted Robert Rushford on Campbell's actions: ". . . he suddenly encountered Goodwin in a heavily wooded section near the upper reaches of the lake.

"'Stick up your hands and come forward,' shouted the officer."

The story added that Goodwin appeared to comply but dropped his arms and levelled his rifle when he got closer, and "Campbell shot quickly from his hip in frontier fashion and Goodwin dropped with a bullet through his chest."

Significantly, this account changed hands while Goodwin's body still lay in the bush. Campbell had been sent out to bring coroner, undertaker and doctor back to the Cruikshanks for a wilderness examination and burial. He spoke freely. Clearly he didn't expect these men to refuse, or that anyone would learn he shot Goodwin, not in the chest, but in his raised arm and the side of the neck; not at five yards with a revolver but at point-blank range with a hunting rifle. The second *Colonist* story, filed from Cumberland the next day but also before the inquest, made an even stranger assertion. "Goodwin surrendered and showed every sign of accompanying the officer peaceably."

The Cumberland inquest and Victoria preliminary investigation would hear a significantly different version of this story, and Devitt's and Rowe's on-site field notes present yet another variation.

Bill Pritchard meanwhile told the *Vancouver Province* that his socialist colleagues intended to find Goodwin's body and establish how he died. They didn't believe Campbell's story. Goodwin was inoffensive, even timid, and an avowed pacifist.

Dr. Millard's testimony about the wounds made Campbell a liar in the inquest's first minutes the evening of Wednesday July 31. Devitt described how he found Goodwin fallen clutching his .22 with his trigger finger extended, after Campbell had been alone with the body for an undetermined period of time estimated at five to fifteen minutes. Rowe succeeded in confusing himself and everyone else about the condition of the rifle: loaded or unloaded, cocked or uncocked, two bullets or ten, safety on or off. Once the coroner's jury returned its finding, there was no more credence for Campbell's boasts about shooting from the hip, which he was soon retelling in an Esquimalt hotel. But were they lies? Or truth? A hybrid seems likeliest. A man who portrayed himself as an intrepid woodsman and crack shot was not going to boast of shooting a man with his hands raised in surrender barely an arm's length away. A detail added here, omitted there, and Dan Campbell was a hero after a few tellings. One of Coroner Shaw's few pertinent questions concerned the special constable's general sobriety, an odd question unless the man had a reputation for drinking; Devitt said he was sober at the time of the shooting. All in all, it seems increasingly unremarkable that Campbell never took the stand — not that he would normally be asked to testify in a lower court — during the inquest or the preliminary investigation. His statements could be used as evidence against him in a higher court, otherwise.

Once the newspapers had reported the inquest, once the official story was on record, coverage became more accurate though no less biased. The *Federationist* commented on August 23, "If the capitalist press in Vancouver had to publish the truth by accident, just once, the population of the city would die from shock."

Rex V Daniel Campbell, the preliminary investigation, took place a week later before judges William Northcott and Lewis Hall in a crowded Victoria courtroom. Cumberland people, military police, local labour movement and socialist representatives, returned soldiers and the press packed the public gallery. Once again the court's nemesis, apparently absent though accused of fomenting trouble, was Joe Naylor.

Millard, Devitt, Rowe and Stephenson — the four inquest witnesses — were the only men called by the crown to testify August 7. This time their evidence would be subtly different, on the whole more seamless and coherent, in thought-provoking ways.

Millard repeated his inquest testimony about the condition of Goodwin's body, but questioning drew out some additional responses. The doctor said he couldn't identify the wrist wound as a bullet wound, and he found none of the powder marks sixteen-year-old Harold Banks had noted in the undertaker's parlour. Powder marks indicate that a shot was fired from closer than ten feet. Crown prosecutor W.D. Carter asked how the doctor accounted for the absence of powder marks.

"I cannot say, the clothing was removed before I saw it, and it might be on account of the clothing being removed, the clothing might have rubbed it off," Millard answered.

Powder marks result from gunpowder being driven into the skin at point-blank range; washing will not remove them. Millard probably looked carefully for marks, as he claimed, and gave an honest account of his findings. His answer, however, speaks poorly for his knowledge of gunshot wounds and casts doubt on his assessment of Goodwin's shooting. His gaping and fatal neck wound certainly indicated the bullet's side entry on a ricochet course. Had it struck directly, the opening would have been smaller. Probably it ricocheted off Goodwin's left wrist, leaving powder marks on his shirt — but not as

Inspector Devitt and Campbell's lawyer W.C. Moresby wanted the court to believe. If Goodwin had been aiming a gun at the special constable directly in front of him, as claimed, the bullet would have ricocheted from his wrist into the front of his throat, not the side of his neck. Even space-age military technology hasn't yet devised a .30 calibre bullet that will travel in a right-angled turn.

Millard was also more cautious this time around about supposing Goodwin's position or stance from the location of his wounds. Moresby questioned him about Goodwin's hands—Devitt had claimed the right forefinger was extended as though ready to pull the trigger—and Millard said there would be no relaxation. Neither Carter nor anyone else asked: if someone placed a gun in the body's hands after death and arranged the hands suitably, would there have been relaxation? It was one of many important questions that went both unasked and unanswered.

Devitt's testimony likewise was an expansion on his inquest information, with minor variations. He described finding a gunny sack under a big rock during the early afternoon. It contained "a rifle, a frow for making shakes, a pair of miner's boots, two pairs of pants and some underclothing. We cached this in another place. . ."

All of it, or some of it? Where? Was it left there? What calibre and model was the rifle? And most important, since Devitt's excuse for moving Goodwin's .22 was to prevent it from falling into the draft evaders' hands, why was the rifle neither described nor brought in as evidence? Was it a .22 automatic rifle belonging to Joe Naylor, soon to find its way into a dead man's hands and thus be unavailable for use as a courtroom exhibit twice over? No one asked.

Another crucial item now mentioned for the first time was never produced or fully described in the Victoria courtroom. Devitt said that he had a description of Goodwin but no warrant (no warrant was needed for arrests under the sweeping Military Service Act) and no special instructions regarding Goodwin. But talk had been going around, he began. Carter objected; talk was not evidence. Devitt then said, "aside from outside evidence I had on file certain telegrams which stated that he would shoot any man that would attempt to draft him into the Army." Where were these damning telegrams? What was their detailed content? Who sent them, and to whom? No one asked.

Devitt then topped his catalogue of mysterious non-exhibits by identifying a sole double A shotgun shell for large game as being similar to those found among "a large number of rifles and ammunition" found in a cabin supposed to have been used by the draft evaders. These the newspapers gleefully seized upon as a desperadoes' arsenal intended for sinister use; if they existed, they were probably the cabin owner's hunting equipment, trustingly if unwisely left for use in hunting season. Devitt claimed the cartridges were in police possession. Neither guns nor ammunition became court exhibits. Why not? No one asked.

Rowe essentially repeated his earlier testimony about fumbling with the .22 rifle and losing eight bullets. Again he said that Campbell, whom he'd known for some time, seemed to show extreme feeling at what had happened. If anything more anxious in Victoria than in Cumberland, when asked about the position of Goodwin's trigger finger, Rowe answered evasively, "I could not say, I won't say because I cannot." Yet it was Rowe who supposedly removed the gun from Goodwin's hands. Exactly what emotion was Campbell showing? Why couldn't Rowe describe the position of Goodwin's hands? No one asked.

Stephenson was terse, offering no unnecessary information as though he wanted as little as possible to do with the case. He said that he knew Goodwin, who was socialistic but not offensive. Campbell's lawyer Moresby leaped in with an objection to this character evidence, saying that they were trying Campbell and not the dead man. Well he might object. The proceedings were by now much more an investigation of Goodwin than of Campbell—Moresby could be in trouble if anyone introduced character evidence about his own client. His objection was denied. It was one of the few indications that there were indeed judges on the bench, and that they were awake.

In Cumberland, Robert Rushford had decided three policemen and a doctor made for a one-sided hearing, and advised several other men who'd encountered Campbell at the lake to take the train down-island and testify voluntarily. Campbell's lawyer Moresby suggested that Rushford and Naylor had primed them to be false witnesses.

Some truth underlay this insinuation. Pansy Ellis told an interviewer years later that he was coached by Socialist Party of Canada lawyer W.W. Lefeaux in case he was called as a witness because of his early July encounter with the police posse. "I'll tell you what a lawyer is, boy, he tried to make up some of the damnedest, you know what I mean, the biggest lies. I said, 'Well, it's no use, I'm going to tell the honest truth, all I ever seen of it,' and then he come back again, 'Don't forget now.'"

Camille Decoeur, the Cumberland hotelier, took close questioning from Moresby about Rushford's and Naylor's role in getting him to Victoria. Perhaps Campbell's lawyer knew Decoeur's wife was a former employee of the Campbell Brothers, and possibly part of Cumberland's socialist and pacifist network that aided the draft evaders. It was unsuccessful as a smokescreen to obscure Decoeur's unwelcome evidence. Decoeur had chatted with Campbell in early July at the lake, exchanging information on berries and fishing. The special constable described Rushford's tragicomic encounter with the fugitives and said, "If ever I get that close they will never get away."

Goodwin's friend Peter McNiven also volunteered evidence. Ben Horbury said, "I remember the fellow living on the beach here, Pete McNiven, went to Victoria for the trial. He was a witness to the effect that this here Campbell what shot Ginger had told Pete: 'I won't be like Rushford (that was the previous policeman that went in) and just shoot over his head. If I confront him he'll be killed.' And when Campbell shot him, he claims that Ginger drew the gun on him, packing a .22. The bullet wound was right here and into his neck. That Campbell was hiding behind a tree, just waiting on the trail. But the trial said it was self-defence."

In court, according to the transcript, McNiven testified that Campbell told him, "Mac, we are here to get these men dead or alive."

As a friend McNiven was more, or less, than he seemed. Although he travelled to Victoria to testify that Dan Campbell planned extreme measures from the manhunt's outset, he takes a different role in Bill Devitt's field notes. One entry reads, "While at end of lake McNiven (Peter) told of Naylor and Robinson taking grub out and leaving Williamson in bush." Of course, he may have been an unwitting or unwilling informant rather than an informer.

Four other men, all Italian miners with limited English, testified that they had met Campbell when they were boating at the lake on July 7. All were there at the request of Robert Rushford. All had heard Campbell say, "This time we are going to get them, dead or alive," or "If it was me I would get him. . . . We are going to get him, dead or alive."

The hearing ended on that note late Wednesday, August 7.

Carter's argument throughout was that Campbell was following a "dead or alive" policy and had not attempted to warn Goodwin before firing. He asked for a jury trial, admitting that Goodwin was evading the law.

"But not every man who evades the law gets killed. Not every man is entitled to be killed," Carter was quoted in a *Daily Colonist* story. "In cases where death is involved it is imperative that there should be a thorough investigation. You would imagine when Campbell encountered Goodwin there would have been some conversation. That is just what I cannot explain."

Others could explain, however, if they chose. Bill Devitt wrote explicitly in his notebook, "Constable Campbell said, 'I had to do this to save my life. I asked this man to surrender and give me his rifle and he covered me with his rifle as though to shoot. In self-defence I had to shoot first.'" Rowe's notes in the same book told much the same story. "On getting up to [Campbell] he said take me in charge Inspector Devitt, but I could not help it. I told him to surrender but he covered me and to save my own life I had to pull." Neither man repeated Campbell's words in full in the inquest or preliminary investigation, leaving it to him to speak for himself in the higher court. Why did they keep silent? Did they disbelieve his story and seek to avoid perjuring themselves? This could explain Rowe's extreme nervousness and the contradictions presented by Devitt, an experienced and informed policeman.

Moresby asked the judges to dismiss the case, saying that Campbell as a special constable had the authority to arrest Goodwin. The *Vancouver World* quoted him as saying, "Why put this man to the expense of a trial when it is a foregone conclusion that no reasonable, fair-minded jury would convict him? As to the use of a soft-nosed bullet, Campbell would have been justified in using a bomb in self-defence."

Judges Northcott and Hall thought otherwise. On the morning of August 8, they said that since there was some doubt in the matter, they would send the case on. Northcott said, "I am sorry for Mr. Campbell, we will commit him to the Higher Court."

Campbell, through all these deliberations, had said nothing. He was already free on bail of ten thousand dollars, about ten years' pay at the time. Now he said only that he would give evidence and call witnesses before the higher court. The *Vancouver World* reported the next day, "Campbell retained his composure throughout the hearing, showing absolutely no signs of emotion."

Cecil Clark cast Dan Campbell in a different light when we talked. He said he had met Campbell only once, in the Provincial Police's Victoria headquarters. Between hearings, the special constable was waiting for a meeting with a Provincial senior officer. Clark, new to the force at the time, watched Campbell. He leaned against a hallway wall, lost in thought and seemingly anxious about the outcome of his case, turning and turning his broad-brimmed hat between his hands. He may have concealed his feelings in court, but here he appeared worried.

Campbell was to be tried for manslaughter before a grand jury at the fall assizes in Victoria on Tuesday, October 1. This would take place in camera, behind closed doors, and only the final decision would be known.

Mr. Justice Murphy handed the case to a twelve-man grand jury, which heard witnesses through Tuesday afternoon. The next morning the grand jury returned a decision of "no bill," in other words, the case would go no further. This process occupied less than four lines in the judge's bench book, and one line in the court calendar, which showed that Campbell entered no plea and received no verdict; Vancouver labour lawyer John Stanton in a private conversation described this situation as a kind of legal limbo. On Moresby's application, Dan Campbell walked from the courtroom a free man.

"It would be a deplorable thing," the *Vancouver World* quoted Murphy, "if a case like this were not investigated before a petit jury unless a reasonable man could say that it needed no further investigation.

"The facts must be so plain as to leave no question in the mind of a reasonable man that it was absolutely necessary for Campbell to kill Goodwin."

What made those facts so plain, after they had been so muddled in the Cumberland inquest and the Victoria preliminary investigation? Did Campbell or his lawyer merely reveal his orders from military intelligence and military police to act under the all-powerful Military Service Act? Did these include a "dead or alive" policy as the crown prosecutor W.C. Carter suggested? If so, they would operate under the deepest secrecy. In a slightly parallel situation, no one has ever been able to openly confirm that British military officers follow unwritten "shoot to kill" orders regarding the Irish Republican Army.

Joe Naylor was neither thorn nor nemesis to the fall assizes hearing of Campbell's case; he was too busy in the role of scapegoat. On the evening of August 14 he was arrested in Cumberland, amidst the first organizing drive for the United Mine Workers of America since the Big Strike. The union, the Socialist Party of Canada and other sympathetic organizations donated to his defence fund. The case was also a final blow to Robert Rushford, who was called as a witness and cross-examined closely about his own military service and beliefs. On October 1, as Dan Campbell's manslaughter case was being considered in Victoria, Naylor was in Nanaimo embroiled in his own court case. The charge of assisting draft evaders was as good a method as any for derailing a man who asked too many embarrassing questions about the shooting of his friend Ginger Goodwin. Only days after Campbell was discharged, Naylor's charges were dropped for want of evidence.

But the long-term damage was done, whatever the short-term outcome. Once those questions were on the record — even the obscure record of the coroner's inquest and the tangential record of the *British Columbia Federationist*'s news coverage — the fact that they remain unanswered stains our public right to information and justice.

Pulling pillars

U nderground coal miners drive tunnels to the furthest limit of the coal deposit. Then they work their way back out toward the portal, sometimes for years, digging and loading coal and sending it to the surface for sorting. By removing all the coal at once they would collapse the mine, so they leave coal pillars in place to support the roof. When as much coal as possible is extracted, it's time for the final stage.

To pull the pillars, miners place their explosive charges and leave the immediate area. Detonation is a throaty *crump*, a long shudder through miles of solid rock and coal, perhaps eventually a half-imagined breath of air arriving from the absolute darkness beyond the lamp's faint yellow sphere. A coal mine is never silent, never quite still, but now it seems like a living creature stirring in its sleep. The mine collapses pillar by pillar, level by level, all the way back to the main drift or shaft and ultimately all the way to the portal.

Quitting time at last. The miners emerge heavy-footed after a long shift, tools in hand, blinking as their lamps suddenly grow pale in the broader light. Another day, another shift, another meal on the table.

So with history. We explore out to the limits, extract what we can, and retreat toward our point of entry. But in dealing with history, we also try to make sense of our extraction. We try to understand not only fact, the serviceable fuel to create warmth and light but essence, the iridescent coal fossils compressed between the seams by relentless time, long lost from sight but shimmering again now in rediscovered daylight.

First, the fact. What happened in the lives of the people who drove the cross drifts of Ginger Goodwin's own short life?

Joe Naylor stayed in Cumberland, under intense police surveillance, for the rest of his life. At the time of Ginger Goodwin's death he was forty-six years old, still blacklisted by Canadian Collieries, barred from the trade he had practised since he was a Lancashire pit lad. His steadfast opposition to injustice in industry soon drew him into the thick of a new political and union movement. In March 1919, at a Calgary labour conference (under police surveillance, suggests an entry in Bill Devitt's notebook), he became one of the charter members of the One Big Union.

The OBU ignited the island coal towns, the Kootenays, the Crowsnest Pass, the coast logging camps and handliners' camps, the city sweatshops. It was Canada's most ambitious homegrown union, unlike the American-based IWW, and it was an industrial union rather than a trade union. It was an attempt to muster a broadbased representation of the kind Ginger Goodwin reached for when he called the Trail smelter strike, not in the name of a single union, but in the name of the trades council. In the brief heyday of internationalism after the Russian Revolution and World War One, the OBU was a radical promise of power to the powerless — right now.

"It was the OBU that wanted to enforce its demands by direct action rather than by parliamentary lobbying, because parliamentary lobbying often took too long, so they got nowhere," said Margaret Eggar. The OBU also helped organize the 1919 Winnipeg General Strike, which some have identified as the first blow of Canada's own stillborn revolution.

The Canadian government took one sharp look at the OBU and Winnipeg, and cracked down with uncharacteristic speed. Everything that made it nervous about radical labour socialists like Ginger Goodwin made it frantic about the OBU. The OBU clearly had potential strength on the political as well as the labour front. So anxious was the government to stop this industrial union movement in its tracks that it came out in support of conventional trade unions, including the United Mine Workers of America. The OBU's loss was ultimately the union movement's gain, since more progressive legislation came into being as a result. This was like the first tentative movement in a stalled glacier, ponderous and deeply fractured, that is still inching forward today. One of the men who nudged it forward was Joe Naylor.

Karl Coe talked with him often in those years. "Politics never come into it very often. He'd given up on the One Big Union, after he quit organizing. He just went to work and practically forgot everything. I don't know, really, why he quit. He come back and started to try to get a job then."

Like a number of other confirmed bachelors, Naylor moved out to the lower end of Comox Lake. He had two small cabins, one for sleeping and one for cooking and eating. He liked children, and they liked him. There was always a swarm around, including the boys and girls who delivered his milk and several newspapers. One of these was Cumberland's long-serving mayor Bronco Moncrief, whom he always greeted, "Hey, Canuck!"

Anyone was welcome in for breakfast stew, which the brave tried. Joe's culinary habits became eccentric; he left congealed bacon fat in his skillet on the stove shelf until he needed to fry something, and instead of cleaning out his stew pot he just kept adding a little of this or that. He fished the lake, and sang long-forgotten music hall ditties to Cumberland children. His beer came from Marocchi's by the quart bottle, and his bread was specially steamed for him in the way he believed was healthiest. He read and reflected and talked politics. With any who would tarry he debated social reform in the high tradition of Socrates and Plato, two Greek fellows that many Cumberlanders had never met. An eloquent and polished writer, undoubtedly self-taught in his rhetoric, his pen unfurled satire and dry wit and thundering oration with apparent ease. One could say he lived an idyllic bachelor's life, except that this was not his choice.

"Joe Naylor didn't have but the one love," Roy Genge's mother told him once as they made their delivery rounds in the milk wagon, "and she wouldn't have him in the end."

After her husband died Joe Naylor bought her a house, intending to marry her and share it, but she had other ideas. It was more complicated than that, of course. Her husband apparently committed suicide because she was seeing gentleman customers in the Belgian woman's fancy house; it's even tempting to think that's where Joe Naylor met her and fell in love. He wouldn't be the first man in that predicament. Her name doesn't really matter, after all these years, and Cumberland people develop a selective amnesia about such things. Though he enjoyed the irony of showing a few friends the deed to a house he never lived in, his pain was real.

His pain over the death of his friend Ginger Goodwin also took many years to fade, Karl Coe told me. "He felt very bad. He felt very bad. They were always together when Ginger came to town, you know, they were inseparable practically. That's why they always used to take me. I guess you could call them a Big Brother. Like this Big Brother stuff? That's the only way I ever could think about them."

Joe Naylor went every morning — day in, day out — to stand outside the manager's office at Number Four pit near Comox Lake in his own passive resistance to the company blacklist. Eventually, perhaps, the manager would tire of seeing Joe's burly shape and saturnine stare outside his door.

"It took him a long time to get a job in the mine after that," Karl Coe said. "He stuck out at the lake there for a couple of years or more before he got a job out there. Then he finally got one."

Naylor's name appears in police and military intelligence files as a dangerous agitator from the time of the Big Strike until his death. The Dominion Police and later the RCMP maintained an undercover agent in Cumberland for years, and Naylor was a main focus of their attention. Canadian Collieries (Dunsmuir) Limited blacklisted him for nearly ten years. Yet, level-headed and pacifist always, he told people what they needed was class consciousness and not class hatred.

In the late 1930s, when the United Mine Workers of America at last successfully organized the island coal mines for their last two decades in production, Naylor was again briefly active. The campaign work he left to a new generation of hotheads, and instead offered an occasional voice of experience. On one occasion, Cumberland miners allowed Canadian Collieries to roll back their wages.

"All the miners went up there, and they were yakking all day long, and they finally gave in and give him his eight percent cut," Karl Coe said. "That's when Joe Naylor got mad. He got up on that platform and he bawled them out. He says, 'I've never seen such a damned mess in my life. You guys, starving to death, and you give him eight percent. Oh, he gave them hell that day.'"

For many more years, once the company capitulated, he worked underground and later on the pithead picking table where he had probably started as a boy. It was a job reserved for the inexperienced, ill or disabled — hard work, but not as backbreaking as digging coal in the seams. By the 1940s he was approaching seventy, and a sick man. In 1946, at the age of seventy-four, he died of cancer.

Joe Naylor's significance has gone largely unnoticed, since he neither attracted nor nurtured star status; the cult of personality was anathema to early socialists. Joe was dark, stolid, silent until he stirred to lead the way, quick to hand control to others. This made him an effective organizer in the socialist ideal, but not a memorable historic figure. His friend and protégé Ginger Goodwin — bright-haired, mercurial, magnetic, a brief meteoric streak across the labour cosmos, soon pulled to earth — was everything he was not. Or perhaps we should consider that Joe Naylor was everything Ginger Goodwin was not. No wonder they were natural friends; their characters were so different as to be complementary. Ginger organized with considerable flair for a decade; Joe organized unobtrusively for four times as long. Who had the greater effect? There's no way to measure.

Ginger Goodwin gained enormous significance retrospectively from his manner of death. He has provided a rallying point, a cause célèbre, for the labour movement ever since.

Much of Naylor's own significance derives from his catalytic role in making this known. He perfectly demonstrated the citizen's right and obligation to dispute the official story. If Joe Naylor in his personal danger and grief had avoided asking hard questions—questions the authorities did not want to hear and would do anything to suppress—we would know only one side of Ginger Goodwin's story. After the shooting, Joe raised the first coherent, informed voice of challenge. The only immediate result was his own arrest. The extended result has been generation after generation of stubborn refusal to swallow lies and half-truths about a grave breach of justice.

Joe Naylor suffered no dramatic death on a hillside, and he drew no lamenting chorus of strangers. Yet when he died in grey old age, friends sat shifts by his bed in Cumberland Hospital keeping the timeless tradition of the death watch.

We can see Joe Naylor's life as a tragedy or a triumph. The visible remnant of his life and death is a grave marker smaller than a union card, a tin plate inscribed with his two names and two dates. A number of people and organizations have considered replacing it with something grander, but no one has done it. Joe Naylor wouldn't care much. As teacher, friend, organizer, leader, and unrelenting and incorruptible voice of our conscience, his legacy is without boundaries, a triumph.

Arthur Boothman returned to Cumberland after the war, working for Canadian Collieries and urging kids to play soccer. No local boy ever matched his prowess, though the company continued to hire star players for its semi-professional team. (Dave Turner, later named Canada's Athlete of the Half-Century, played briefly for Cumberland.) Never a talkative man, Arthur now became a silent one. He spoke when he had something to say, one friend said. Ginger Goodwin's death, and his own armed pursuit in the high country, left deep scars.

"Oh, I felt sorry for Arthur. Because Ginger got along with everybody. I don't understand it. There might be other things we don't know anything about, but I don't know what they could be," said his sister Gert Somerville, meaning that Goodwin's death seemed needless and without purpose. "He nearly died himself, he was so upset. He was up the lake, too, at the same time. My brother never spoke after that, hardly, to anybody about anything."

Arthur did speak with friends, including Pansy Ellis and Peter Cameron, over the years, telling them what happened that final afternoon above the Cruikshank River. He died before anyone thought to record his story at first hand.

"I am proud of them both. They had a lot more guts than many who went overseas," Gert Somerville told one interviewer, but refused to say much more at that time. (Fortunately, she changed her mind by the time we talked.) "The rest that I remember is between Arthur and Ginger and myself, and I am not going to tell you about it. I was married at the time and had small children in Cumberland, so I never knew all about it anyway."

Robert Rushford's police career effectively ended the summer day he fired warning shots over the head of a draft evader in the Little Lakes, but it limped on for a few more months. His infant daughter Ypres died during the great influenza epidemic at the end of World War One, and is buried in Cumberland cemetery. In August 1919 he and his wife Jessie took their remaining three children—Nava, Peter and Louvain—back to Scotland, where he worked for the post office.

"While serving in the post office my father was the first postman to be picked for picking up the Queen's mail at the London train at Perth and drive it up to Balmoral each time the King and Queen were in residence," wrote Louvain Brovenlow. This was a point of pride for the entire family, including Mrs. Brovenlow's own two children.

Eventually both of his legs had to be amputated, but he never complained. Robert and Jessie Rushford died within a short time of each other, both at ninety.

"He sure was a grand old man and everybody loved him. He was so good-natured, happy and content with his life, and my mother and him were in love as much when they died as the day they got married."

Karl Coe, at thirteen, was really too young to understand what had happened to his "big brother" Ginger Goodwin in 1918.

"I was so young during all the years I knew Ginger. I've learned more about him after he's gone. I was too young to even care, and I didn't realize what had happened to him for years. Oh, it really hurt after I found out what it was all about. I used to go out there and talk to Joe Naylor, day after day I used to go out there, because he was always by himself batching most of the time. And he'd start to tell me, or try to tell me, what was going on then."

Karl remained an active fly fisherman until he was nearly eighty, fishing the Puntledge and Tsolum and the wealth of mountain streams around Comox Lake. Occasionally he ventured as far north as Oyster River, where he traded fish tales with my father, mother and grandfather. He inherited Joe Naylor's fly rod, a fourteen-foot monster built for hauling salmon from river estuaries. Mostly he used Ginger's fishing rod, which Bill or Arthur Boothman brought down the mountain to him in the summer of 1918. The Wilkie rod was long by today's standards, but manageable for someone who could control the cast. Its action remains fluid and smooth even after seventy-odd years.

But Joe's .22 rifle, which Karl had shot many times on their expeditions, was lost forever. "I don't know who ever got it and where it went to. They'd probably take it to the police station and keep it for a while," he said. "Evidently he was out hunting grouse the same day and run into this guy Campbell. If he'd been fishing in the river he'd have that [rod] with him and so Campbell would have got that too, but he got the gun instead."

Karl Coe lived down camp in Cumberland with his wife Elsie until his death in 1986. Ginger's and Joe's fishing rods and reels are now on display in the Cumberland Museum.

Daniel Campbell never spoke with family members about the death of Albert Goodwin. He lived out his life in Esquimalt and Colwood, though he also had mineral investments in the Sooke area, working as a carpenter for various firms. He sold the Colwood Inn around the time of Ginger Goodwin's shooting, possibly after prohibition closed down most saloons and roadhouses.

After the manhunt and shooting and court proceedings, Dan Campbell lived an unsettled life for many years. Misfortune struck him time and again. Twice his house burned, destroying all of his possessions. In his later years his many different jobs included groundskeeper for his daughter's wealthy husband, and operating a Sooke resort and a Thetis Lake concession. He did various jobs at the Esquimalt dockyards where his father-in-law had been chief engineer. No job held him long.

A 1928 *Victoria Times* story referred to his police career. "Dan Campbell, known throughout this Island and up the coast as one of the most courageous posse leaders as a result of the years he spent in the Dominion police, when the search for desperadoes who had escaped to the wilds was, as a rule, turned over to him, has arrived in Victoria on a visit." By this time he was apparently living in the Sooke Road area of Colwood.

Tom McEwen, in his book *The Forge Glows Red*, writes of an incident in a Calgary hotel in the 1930s. Delegates to a Crowsnest Pass miners' union convention recognized a wheelchair-bound hotel resident, and told the proprietor that either that man left or they moved their convention.

"The hotel proprietor promptly wheeled him out on the sidewalk, after learning the identity of his guest—the provincial [sic] police Constable Campbell who shot and killed the miners' organizer Ginger Goodwin to death in the hills above Cumberland..." While it's possible that Dan Campbell visited or briefly lived in Calgary, it seems more likely that they evicted the wrong man.

Dan Campbell died in Victoria at the age of eighty in 1952. His occupation was listed as "retired carpenter."

Bill Devitt pursued his career in law enforcement for many years, serving as Burnaby's chief of police from 1919 to 1935. Vigorous and active always, he remained an ardent admirer of big dogs, fine horses and good yarns. An excellent revolver shot, he won a dramatic shootout with two escaped bandits in 1931. In Burnaby, he was known locally for his work in organizing charity and relief campaigns for the poor during the grimmest years of the Hungry Thirties. He was sixty-eight when he died in 1937.

Tommy "Towse" Anderson received eight dollars for his assistance in locating Ginger Goodwin, but it was a full year before the Dominion Police got around to paying him. Ruth Masters, writer and compiler of the important Ginger Goodwin album in Cumberland Museum from which much of the relevant oral history derives, heard from oldtimers that the trapper was so racked with guilt—fear, at least—that he never again ventured into Cumberland until the day he died, in St. Joseph's Hospital in Comox.

Ginger Goodwin, meanwhile, almost disappeared from history. Friends remembered, and told their friends, but such reminiscences all too often drift and dissipate like smoke on the wind.

Once he was buried little more was heard about him for many years, Peter Cameron said. "It was pretty well all gone by then. There was no talk about it then. There's more talk about Ginger Goodwin now than ever there was then."

Not everyone forgot. "Poor Ginger. I known him for a long time. I can still see him sometimes," Gert Somerville said. "Just walking around and giving everybody a little shake of his hand. You know, to lose a boy like that..." She shook her head, lost in her thoughts.

The government seemed to think he was dangerous, I suggested.

"Not any more than the government was dangerous to us at that time," Gert said. "Or now either. They're not honest at times.... We never know these things."

Then, in the mid-1930s, island coal miners stirred from a generation-long sleep and organized a union. For secrecy and self-protection they applied the Communist Party's cell system—only a few men knew the overall plan, and most knew only the activities of a few comrades—to form locals of the Mine Workers' Union of Canada, later becoming United Mine Workers of America locals. When Cumberland miners talked union again after the long intervening years they remembered their organizer Ginger Goodwin, nearly twenty years dead and buried in an unmarked grave.

Vincent Picketti, who had trained in Italy as a stonemason and cut much of the stone for Cumberland's post office, carved a headstone. He found a boulder of reddish stone and cut an irregular slice from one side; the rest of the boulder still sits behind the Cumberland Hotel, visible from the alley. He inscribed the headstone "Lest we forget, Ginger Goodwin, shot July 26th 1918, a workers friend." The date was one day early, an error that also crept into the courtroom testimony. The hammer and sickle symbol at the narrow top of the stone is a reflection of the 1930s miners' union affiliation, not Goodwin's. In the days before the term communism was in currency, Goodwin was a socialist.

Trail smelterworkers remembered their long-ago organizer, too, when they tried to bring back the union in the 1930s. Consolidated fired four union men for handing out pamphlets about their 1917 strike leader and his consequent pursuit and death. The union prevailed, and successfully organized the smelter. The last words of the *Trail News* on his shooting were, "He was a bright man, and could have made a name for himself." A bullet, it seems, didn't prevent him from doing so.

But what would Ginger Goodwin have gone on to do if he'd been able to wait out the remaining three and a half months of the war?

"I think he'd have kept on organizing as long as he was able, myself. But if they hadn't of caught him up there he probably would have succumbed up there. I don't know how good he was, living that rough life. He was pretty weak then. He could never have done hard work, I don't think," Karl Coe said. "Consumption, you see—they say he wouldn't have lived much longer anyway."

Tuberculosis probably would have killed him, since the lung lesions and debility cleared up in only a few cases. His prognosis would be little better if his ailment were "miner's TB", pneumoconiosis or another form of silicosis. But was either of these the lung disease that afflicted him? Given the absence of medical records and Dr. Millard's failure to perform a full autopsy, we cannot say.

Certainly he would have remained loyal—his loyalty never seemed to dim—to the Socialist Party of Canada, the United Mine Workers, maybe even to the International Union of Mine Mill and Smelter Workers which pulled the rug from under his feet in the 1917 smelter strike. Joe Naylor was bitter and disillusioned about that, judging by his statements at the 1918 British Columbia Federation of Labour convention, but nothing proves outright that Ginger Goodwin held a grudge. Eventually he might have fallen afoul of the righteous Socialist Party of Canada again, for the party's goals left little elbow room for personal ambition.

Ambition would have driven him onward, there seems little doubt. However kind and amiable he was among friends, he was clearly an ambitious and opportunistic man. The 1920s were not a favourable time for Canadian socialists, but the grim 1930s opened many doors in politics and the labour movement. Ginger Goodwin could well have shared a provincial legislature bench with socialists Ernest and Harold Winch, even eventually with another island coal miner's son, Dave Stupich. It's an intriguing thought. In British Columbia's traditionally explosive political forum, more than the usual rhetorical sparks would have flown.

But all this is pure speculation. It could be equally true that Ginger Goodwin's entire significance derives from the drama and injustice of his death. In 1906 Albert Goodwin was one of thousands of working-class people who arrived in Canada unremarked. Many of them were doubtless bright men and women who could have made names for themselves, and didn't for one reason or another. Probably most simply didn't need to, weren't driven to, didn't have as much to prove as the red-haired pit lad with a deep and abiding resentment of the master class.

Albert Goodwin has never yet gained mention in school history texts. He earns a few brief passages in chronically inaccurate publications from the political left and labour groups, where he's dubbed "a martyr of labour" or "a labour hero." In the general absence of fact, who can fault mainstream historians for uneasily relegating Goodwin to the realms of rose-tinted ideological iconography?

Some of the fallacies will circulate longer than the facts, sadly. Goodwin led the Big Strike in Cumberland. The Dunsmuirs had Goodwin killed. Goodwin was hounded to apply for military service exemption. Selwyn Blaylock had Goodwin killed out of personal enmity. Dan Campbell was a bounty hunter. Goodwin was shot in the back. Some of these contain a grain of truth; none is the whole truth.

"It all seems like a dream now," Josephine Bryden said.

But then Ginger Goodwin, like other men and women who somehow cast a shadow brighter and larger than their lives, is moving steadily out of obscurity and through history into myth. Songs, books of several kinds, poems, plays, paintings, sculptures, plaques, museum displays and on-site historical information are already in existence. We can reasonably look forward to musical theatre, films and other artistic interpretations. Vancouver Island has only a handful of myth-makers in recorded and remembered history. Maquinna, James Douglas, Emily Carr, Amor de Cosmos, Robert Dunsmuir, Tzouahalem, George Clutesi, Roderick Haig-Brown and Bruce Hutchison come to mind. These are not icons of official history but people like boulders in history's current, around whom events have had to flow and change direction. They make up the matter and spirit of Vancouver Island, the fact and essence, the stuff of legend. Among them belongs Ginger Goodwin.

"They tell me that someone goes to his grave and puts flowers on it," Doll Williams told an interviewer, and wondered who it could be. Whoever once left flowers, now many people do—florists' artful arrangements or wild daisies from the Minto meadows—when they pass by on the Cumberland Road. Myth needs no memorial, perhaps, but our habits die hard. Under the flowers and the uncommon headstone lies the material residue of a young man whose friends kept faith as long as they lived.

"Well, them things you know," Sam Robertson said at ninety-eight, "that was a part of my life."

Words after

> *I have therefore made a heap of all that I have found . . .*
>
> Nennius, c. 796 AD

Writing a book about Albert "Ginger" Goodwin with the intent of reaching beyond folklore and guesswork can only be an act of bravado, folly or ignorance. In my case it was mainly ignorance.

I grew up on stories of Cumberland and Bevan, Nanaimo and Wellington, the Vancouver Island coal towns where my grandfather Amos Mayse—a Yorkshire pit lad turned minister—worked, and my father Arthur Mayse grew up. As far back as I can remember, I knew that old-time coal miners could tie trout flies one-handed (the other hand served as the fly-vise they couldn't afford) and fished the mountain streams with nine- and ten-foot split cane rods. I knew that my grandfather's mostly Welsh congregation sang mournful hymns as they headed off shift to wash down the coal dust in the saloons. I knew the sweet smell of Cumberland in the rain was the smell of coal smoke, and that the fish and chips we always stopped for in Nanaimo on our way down-island were a coal miner's payday treat. I knew my grand-dad failed to blow the boulder in his Nanaimo yard with powder and fuse borrowed from the fireboss next door, though he did blow all the fireboss's windows. I knew Cumberland was a working coal town where the miners' hall had an impressive wooden turret, a nickel bought a Kik-Cola in Chinatown, and the streets and sidewalks flowed with traffic even between shift whistles. I knew—and forgot—that Cumberland had never forgiven a great injustice done long ago, when my own parents were children. Knowing all this, I thought everyone knew.

In 1979 I started researching for play on the Vancouver Island coal strike of 1912 to 1914. Lacking definitive books to read (though Lynne Bowen's fine history of island mining, *Boss Whistle*, came out as I worked) I talked with retired coal miners and their wives in Nanaimo and especially in Cumberland. Their generosity, honesty and encouragement from the start made possible an impossible project. I heard what coal miners ate and wore and drank, how to sprag a loaded car or shift a stubborn mule, what they feared most and liked best down pit, what their families did for fun, what killed them and how it felt. I drank enough beer and coffee with them to lay many tons of coal dust. Once I sat in a nursing home with an old, old woman who told me terrible things in a dry whisper. Once, in the dark, I heard half a mile of coal creaking over my head like an animal in pain as they pulled the pillars down near the face. I found the deep levels friendly and welcoming—not safe, mind you, any more than a hurt animal is safe—as my own legacy of coal dust in the blood.

Cumberland miners told me of the iridescent coal fossils they sometimes found far underground, strange sea creatures and insects and plants shimmering with all the sun's colours in a sunless world, until pick or shovel reduced them to another chunk of fuel. They told me of friendship, hardship, the unbelievably long struggle for fair wages and job security and safety. Through their adversity and endurance, shining like the fossils pressed in coal, ran one special seam of remembrance. In asides and offhand fragments they told me about "a worker's friend" who laboured to better their lot, and paid with his life. I found that I couldn't talk about coal mining in Cumberland without talking about Ginger Goodwin.

So I went to read the available books on Goodwin. The excellent Edmonton Public Library—I lived in Edmonton at the time—yielded nothing. The vast University of Alberta libraries yielded nothing. Perhaps that wasn't too surprising, since Goodwin was active in British Columbia and not Alberta. But it turned out that even the British Columbia provincial archives could offer little more than a few pages in BC Overtime's excellent *Sound Heritage* publication based on old-timers' recollections. More digging produced a page here, a paragraph there, of incomplete and contradictory information. Even Goodwin's true name, birthdate and birthplace were in question, and nothing else could be established without these.

Ginger Goodwin was a union organizer—his union papers went

up in smoke years ago. He was a political candidate—no party documents were available for public use. He was an immigrant—no indexed immigration papers could pinpoint his arrival in Canada. He was an employee—no company records survived. He was a draft evader—no military records were on file. Ginger Goodwin might as well not have existed. It began to seem as though somebody planned it that way. But why, after seventy years, would anyone go to the trouble? The Cumberland old-timers' view was that the government wanted to shut Ginger up, and that's just what it did by means of a policeman's soft-nosed bullet. It was tempting to agree.

I didn't agree. This story was too romantic, too maudlin, too absolutely paranoid. Such things could happen in banana republics, not in Canada. When RCMP officers questioned me under the War Measures Act in 1970, they were impeccably Canadian. They nodded politely at my belief that our university newspaper should print the FLQ Manifesto in the interests of understanding the FLQ's apparently half-baked theories. The RCMP then pulled copy, leaving us with a two-column half-page white hole which was infinitely more dramatic and significant to Vancouver Island students than the manifesto. Censorship! Oppression! Canadian style, mannerly and bloodless. By comparison, a tale of police murder on a wild hillside near Cumberland was too sensational to be true. Obviously there was more to the story.

I wrote the play *Deep Seams* for CBC radio in 1986. I decided against a novel—not enough information—and put island coal behind me. A publisher asked me to write a non-fiction biography of Ginger Goodwin. I declined. The Cumberland Museum wanted someone to undertake a similar project. I recommended half a dozen capable writers, who also declined. Who wanted to pursue nonexistent research across two continents? Who had the necessary time, energy and private fortune? Not a freelance writer like me, juggling creative and cashflow projects to make a living. Then the CBC commissioned *A Worker's Friend: The Shooting of Ginger Goodwin*.

Surprisingly, I found I had accreted more than enough information over a decade to put together a one-hour radio documentary. A creative producer and gifted actors made production an exhilarating experience. The program aired in May 1989. At this point I embraced folly, bravado, and a few more months of paying bills with cash advances on a credit card, and started work on *Ginger*.

That's how the book came to be written, but not why. Why is a harder question.

Almost everyone I told about Ginger Goodwin over the years wanted to know more. Whatever their personal backgrounds or interests or political leanings, people offered a startling response: *Why have I never heard this? Why didn't we learn this in school?* Many people insisted this book must be written. I agreed—by someone else. But no one else seemed to be writing it (two other books now in progress will be welcome contributions to a neglected topic). Certainly this was information that Canadians wanted, needed and deserved. It was a matter of public concern which had largely been kept from public knowledge. I was sitting on an untidy and incomplete heap of research which nonetheless seemed more complete than anything else available. I recognized, not entirely gracefully, my obligation to share it. And, truth to tell, I couldn't leave it alone. I had walked away from the Ginger Goodwin material several times and found myself drawn back in one way or another. Why?

Black Irish still after four Canadian generations, my father says that some voices speak beyond death and beyond time. I do appreciate the family ghost stories. To hear of the *bheann sidh* keening by an Ontario township road always gives me a winter chill, though I prefer the tale of granddad Amos on the way back from the privy in his billowing nightshirt, stumbling into a blackberry patch and howling and cursing loudly enough to put the fear of the afterlife into a passing church lady. But I look further for explanations.

"A labour martyr" and "a worker's friend" are favoured epithets for Ginger Goodwin among his admirers. Many of them are committed to labour and socialism, as he was, and they distrust words redolent of the cult of personality. One of these words is "hero."

Brushes with anthropology and psychology, rather than ideology, lead me likewise to distrust the very concept of a hero. Accidental heroes, as granddad Amos became an accidental ghost, I can understand. Incidental heroes, having pulled children from burning houses or drivers from submerged cars, earn well-deserved medals from the Governor General. But fire-bringers, light-shedders, great leaders who die to buy life for their people—these trouble me like a monk's hair shirt. I weigh deliberate action against retrospective canonization, and usually call it a draw.

In researching Ginger Goodwin's case, though, the distinction was important. I assumed I would find hidden vices, feet of clay, to tarnish the shining portrait. Instead I consistently heard of a kind and courageous man, light-hearted even in his losing fight against lung disease, who cared first and last about other people. His greatest flaw—I had to assemble fragments to grasp his failings, since his friends spoke only of his virtues—was probably hubris, arrogance, an overestimation of his own importance and immortality. I think he could also be calculatedly charming and manipulative, and narrow to the point of intolerance in his political views. These traits could make a churlish dinner guest but a formidable organizer. It's no accident that Goodwin's friends loved him and the authorities did not.

Did the government suppress information about Goodwin to cover its own abuse of power? My intermittent research over the last decade suggests that many people, not just government, have a vested interest in whether and how this information becomes public.

A dark side of the undying interest in Ginger Goodwin is its intensity. As a teller of his story I have encountered startling reactions. Some doors remained closed because the doorkeepers believed I held a particular bias or affiliation, and wanted to ensure that any such book echoed their own views. One man cursed me on the telephone when I asked for an interview, and told me, "Goodwin was a god-damned son of a bitch who didn't get the half of what he deserved." But we did talk, and he ultimately inscribed his own book for me, "To another searcher for the truth." Not everyone is gracious enough to set aside his or her own views and recognize that whatever we seek, we may not arrive at the same truth.

One thing is beyond dispute: people take a strong interest in this material, and they take their interest personally. This has made me extremely careful in my use of sources and resources—I have neither solicited nor accepted any help, from any quarter, other than information and advice—and it has made me fastidious in choosing a publisher. While I am deeply grateful for the insights and expertise many people have contributed, this book is wholly my own interpretation of the available information on Ginger Goodwin's story.

Available information is certainly an issue. On the surface, there is very little documentary evidence of Albert Goodwin's existence, let alone his activities. Now unknown information may come to light over the next few years, including political and employment records and documents pertaining to the Trail smelter strike. If this information exists, it has not been in its caretakers' interests to make it available. Even so, the material is unusually sparse.

Files on Goodwin, Joe Naylor, the One Big Union and other early labour and socialist topics have allegedly been removed from the Public Archives of Canada in Ottawa by police and government agents acting without warrant. This has occurred steadily and by stealth over three-quarters of a century, I heard from more than one archivist; because this—if it happened—would essentially be theft, no record exists of which files are missing. This I do know: one can regularly order a file box from public archives indexes only to find that it has not been used or seen for years, can't be located in cataloguing or photocopying or the reading room, and is untraceable.

In institutions as understaffed and underfunded as most public archives in Canada, no doubt some files are simply mislabelled or mislaid. They may eventually reappear. Stories of police theft sound apocryphal, best told in smoky back rooms in the small hours. The files' absence alone is not evidence of theft by police or anyone else.

Perils of research are generally less exotic. Simple lack of information is the main problem. My research in early medieval history and literature—calling for knowledge of three modern and two archaic languages, early technology, church politics, trade routes, and other arcana—has taught me to demand nothing, accept everything, try the unlikely source first, constantly examine motives, expect to spend many years and many miles without result. Labour history, by comparison, is a lark. Once I realized there was almost nothing to research formally, I broadened my focus to try any conceivable source for a name or a date or a trace of activity. Apart from personal interviews which yielded rich contextual material rather than detail, this approach proved most fruitful.

Yet my findings remain slight. Others with similar interests have asked where I found "all my material." There isn't as much as we'd all like to believe. Every researcher must sooner or later suffer from this wishful thinking. Unfortunately, the material is fragmentary and widely scattered, not gathered in one "magic file."

Also, oral history has its hazards. Over and over again, people told me what a pity it was that I hadn't started interviewing old-timers ten years ago. Of course they were right. One or two men and women who knew Ginger Goodwin are still alive, but they are now in their eighties or nineties. Seventy-five years is an extreme outer limit for "living memory." So much time has passed since the Big Strike and that most terrible war that it seems miraculous for people to remember any of the events surrounding Ginger Goodwin's life and death. Not only from office files and archives, but from daily recollection, most things are now lost forever.

Accuracy has been an ongoing concern because of this dwindling storehouse of sources. The best documentary materials available are surprisingly inaccurate and contradictory: theses, popular histories, contemporary newspapers, reams of government papers. Often this means making the likeliest choice among a handful of dubious claims, and hoping for the best. A researcher proceeds with caution, and an acute sense of irony. A few years ago, when English archaeologist David Hill queried my interest in history, I described myself as (among other things) a fiction writer. He laughed and said, "We write fiction, too. We call it history." Only a rare scholar has the honesty or impetuosity to admit the true relationship between these two pursuits.

Karl Coe was even more nonchalant about the role of fiction in serving history, in this case the history of his friend Ginger Goodwin.

"Anything you print now, nobody can prove anything, they're all gone. You can practically print what you want and nobody could deny it," Karl said, and waved aside my objections to this approach. "You could add a little thing just to spice it up a little bit, here and there, because nobody around here would deny it."

For the record, however, I remained too squeamish for Karl's advice. In writing any obscure and difficult history I believe we must bridge the chasms between known facts; we must not reshape the known facts for our own purposes and claim that we have written either history or historically accurate fiction. "Faction" or "docudrama" is in bad odour for good reason. Any speculation in this book, and you'll find plenty, is identified as such.

This book is not biography in the purest sense, since much of it is contextual rather than personal. We know so little about Ginger Goodwin that I had to piece together his travels and actions from random fragments: a newspaper notice, a work record, an aside in an oral history. Much of what we do know is distilled and diffracted from the lives of other men and women on whom he had a profound effect. Also, a sense of place (especially of Cumberland) seemed essential for an understanding of Goodwin's life.

Inevitably these glimpses of Ginger Goodwin and early British Columbia filter through 1990 understanding, but I sought to be true to their original nature. This may offend some readers. I have used the racist language of the day— *Coontown, Japtown, Chinaman, nigger*—because it conveys the climate of intolerance and ethnic stratification more succinctly than any amount of narrative description could do. People then were more keenly aware of their differences than their similarities, although most of them got along with each other most of the time. Many lacked or shunned the cultured veneer we customarily smooth over our own such awareness. Indeed, some people even today are unaware they give offence by calling someone a Jap or a darkie. To gloss over these slurs with politer language would serve neither reader nor historical accuracy.

Women's roles in all these events likewise seem less significant, and less respected, than we might hope. Women and girls worked tirelessly, but either in their homes or in occupations that lacked the romance of early coal mining, logging and fishing. Only recently have people officially recognized the comradeship, dedication and humour of women's work. Women took a less overt and active role in political and social reform, as in the workplace, than do their granddaughters. Those who did take part generally received less recognition than their male counterparts, though Helena Gutteridge and her sisters in the British Columbia labour movement were inspiring exceptions. The covert and discredited nature of early female activism makes it difficult to assess. Older women whom I've interviewed have deferred to their husbands if they were present, or referred to them constantly if they were not. Also, both men's and women's memories of long-ago events emphasized men's actions almost exclusively, though the Big Strike and the supply lines which fed Ginger and his friends on the run, for example, would have been impossible without the initiative and carry-through of many unnamed women. But it would be false, if fashionable, to claim pre-eminence in these events for women.

Much remains to learn about Ginger Goodwin and his times. I lacked the resources to thoroughly investigate the public archives and other collections in Ottawa, union archives in the United States, and any remaining traces in England. Documents such as British military intelligence files are still closed to the public—if they exist. Whenever possible I enlisted the help of residents and travellers (see acknowledgments) who turned up excellent information. A full study of contemporary newspapers is still needed, however, as is an exhaustive search of available government documents.

Labour history and other "unofficial" histories, as distinct from colonization and administrative and corporate history, rank low. Working people can choose to perpetuate the official history—by waiting for encouragement and funding and applause before write or broadcast—or to challenge it. This is our history as working people. If we want it on record—not just the patronizing and distorted views of the privileged—we must speak out.

What would Ginger Goodwin, I sometimes wonder, want a book to say about him? His first concern would be its propaganda value— by propaganda he meant simply the dissemination of ideas—for labour, socialism and somewhat conditional pacifism. He would appreciate a flattering personal portrait of both the suave organizer in his smart suit and the resolute workers' friend in his pit clothes. He would also enjoy occupying a niche in Canadian history, even if shocked to learn he was better known than his friend Joe Naylor. He would want a book to sound the alarm, awakening people to the dangers and inequities they accept until it's too late, reminding them that every one of our rights and freedoms was hard won and through complacency would be easily lost. He would want justice, denied him in the courts and the official accounts, now available only through books like this and their readers. One of his last letters was an appeal to help "a slave fighting for what liberty the system will permit. . ."

This pursuit ends where I began it, on a wet evening in Cumberland. No longer a child hearing stories of blood and coal dust, I sit out of the rain on the porch of my house away down camp.

Robert Dunsmuir's exploited workers built these minimal miners' houses alike as peas in a pod, but a hundred years later each has a different character. Mine has two striped grey cats, a bay window for stargazing on clear nights and a porch in hailing distance of good neighbours. Barbara's husband, a fisherman, distributes cod and salmon. Barbara comes to pick my apples; her kids visit the grey cats. Elsie lends a vacuum cleaner and her old lawn mower, which meets its fate among my weeds. Buck and Dot share a surplus of corn and sweet peas. None of us is wealthy, but none of us is exploited.

When I came to Cumberland I also came home. I didn't grow up here, and I now spend most of my time in Vancouver. All the same, Cumberland is home. The spirit that somehow keeps Cumberland alive is also the spirit that fiercely defended Ginger Goodwin a long lifetime ago and for all the years since. It embodies one small industrial town's resolve that this story is important and shall not be forgotten. This is Cumberland's voice, despite all the other voices that join in, and this is Cumberland's book.

Dusk is the best time on a camp house porch. Mist rolls down from Comox Lake, along the abandoned rail line to Number Four pit, below the lower range of camp houses, to fill the now-wooded crease of Coal Creek. Above it coal smoke drifts in a layer sweet with rain. Children go in to their supper, dogs fall quiet, kitchen lights glow on. In the growing dark it's easier to see women in long skirts treading the boardwalk, miners swinging their dinner pails, Ginger and Joe walking back from an off-shift fishing trip, all heading home.

Works Consulted

Articles

Bliss, J.M. "The Methodist Church and World War I." *Canadian Historical Review.* XLIX (3), September, 1968.

Bowen, Lynne. "The Great Vancouver Island Coal Miners' Strike 1912-14." *Journal of the West.* Vol. XXIII, No. 4 (1984).

"The Small Beginnings of Cominco's Big Zinc Plant." *Cominco Magazine.* February 1964.

Gallagher, Daniel T. "Unhealed Wound: Changing Views on British Columbia's Greatest Coal Strike." [unpublished paper?], n.d.

McKelvie, B.A. "Blaylock of Trail." *MacLean's Magazine.* May 15, 1928.

Robin, Martin. "Registration, Conscription, and Independent Labour Politics, 19916-1917." *Canadian Historical Review.* XLVII (2), June, 1966.

Books

A time to remember. Trail: The United Steelworkers of America, 1976.

Anderson, Aili. *History of Sointula.* Revised edition. Sointula: Sointula Centennial Committee, 1969.

Angus, Ian. *Canadian Bolsheviks.* Montreal: Vanguard, 1981.

Atkinson, Linda. *Mother Jones, the most dangerous woman in America.* New York: Crown, 1978.

Avery, Donald. *"Dangerous foreigners."* 1979. Toronto: McClelland and Stewart, 1988.

Bennett, William. *Builders of British Columbia.* Vancouver: n.p., [1937?].

Bercuson, David J. *Fools and Wise Men: The Rise and Fall of the One Big Union.* Toronto: McGraw-Hill Ryerson, 1978.

—, editor. *Alberta's Coal Industry 1919.* Vol. 2 of *Historical Society of Alberta.* Calgary: Historical Society of Alberta, 1978.

Bowen, Lynne. *Boss whistle.* Lantzville: Oolichan, 1982.

Canadian Encyclopedia. 4 vols., 2nd edition. Edmonton: Hurtig, 1988.

Caragata, Warren. *Alberta Labour.* Toronto: James Lorimer, 1979.

Chan, Anthony. *Gold Mountain.* Vancouver: New Star, 1983.

Clark, Cecil. *Tales of the British Columbia Provincial Police.* Sidney: Gray's, 1971.

Cousins, William James. *A History of the Crow's Nest Pass.* Lethbridge: The Historic Trails Society of Alberta, 1981.

Crisafio, Robert, editor. *Backtracking*. Fernie: Fernie and District Historical Society, 1977.

The Crowsnest and Its People. Coleman, Alberta: Crowsnest Pass Historical Society, 1979.

Fish, Gordon. *Dreams of Freedom, Bella Coola, Cape Scott, Sointula*. Sound Heritage Series Number 36. Victoria: Provincial Archives of British Columbia, 1982.

Forbes, Jamie. *Historical Portraits of Trail*. Trail: Trail City Archives, 1980.

Isenor, D.E., E.G. Stephens, and D.E. Watson. *One hundred spirited years: a history of Cumberland*. Campbell River: Ptarmigan, 1988.

Johnston, Hugh. *The Voyage of the Komagata Maru*. Delhi: Oxford University Press, 1979.

Johnstone, Bill. *Coal dust in my blood*. Heritage Record Number 9. Victoria: British Columbia Provincial Museum, 1980.

Knightley, Phillip. *The First Casualty*. New York and London: Harcourt Brace Jovanovich, 1975.

McEwen, Tom. *The Forge Glows Red*. Toronto: Progress, 1974.

Morton, Desmond. *A Military History of Canada*. Edmonton: Hurtig, 1985.

– Ormsby, Margaret A. *British Columbia: a History*. Student edition. [Toronto]: Macmillan of Canada, 1971.

Phillips, Paul. *No Power Greater: A Century of Labour in British Columbia*. Vancouver: B.C. Federation of Labour; Boag Foundation, 1967.

Reed, John. *Ten Days That Shook the World*. Harmondsworth, Middlesex: Penguin, 1982.

Schlesinger, Arthur M. Jr., gen. ed. *The Almanac of American History*. New York: G.P. Putnam's Sons, 1983.

Scott, Jack. *Canadian Workers, American Unions*. Vol. 2 of *Trade Unions and Imperialism in America*. Vancouver: New Star, 1978.

—, *Sweat and Struggle*. Vol. 1: 1789-1899 of *Working Class Struggles in Canada*. Vancouver: New Star, 1974.

Sheils, Jean Evans, and Ben Swankey. *"Work and Wages"!* Vancouver: Trade Union Research Bureau, 1977.

Solski, Mike, and John Smaller. *Mine Mill*. Ottawa: Steel Rail, 1985.

Songs of the Workers. 34th Edition. Chicago: Industrial Workers of the World, 1973.

Steeves, Dorothy G. *The Compassionate Rebel*. Vancouver: Boag Foundation, 1960. Vancouver: J.J. Douglas Ltd., 1977.

Trail, B.C.: A Half Century, 1901-1951. Trail: Trail Golden Jubilee Society, 1951.

Turnbull, Elsie. *Topping's Trail*. 1964. Reprinted as *Trail, a smelter city*. Langley: Sunfire, 1985.

Wejr, Patricia, and Howie Smith, B.C. Overtime, compilers and editors. *Fighting for Labour*. Vol. VII, Number 4 of *Sound Heritage*. Victoria: Province of British Columbia, 1978.

Whittaker, Lance H., editor. *Rossland, The Golden City*. Rossland: Miner Printing, 1949.

Government records
British Columbia Attorney General's papers. British Columbia Archives and
    Records Service.
British Columbia Public Accounts. Vancouver Public Library.
Coroner's inquest into the death of Albert Goodwin, Cumberland, July 31,
    1918.
McBride papers. Additional manuscripts 112, 347 and 996. British Colum-
    bia Archives and Records Service.
Preliminary investigation, Rex v. Daniel Campbell, Victoria, August 7 and
    8, 1918.
British Columbia Provincial Police papers. British Columbia Archives and
    Records Service.

Newspapers and periodicals
British Columbia Federationist
Cumberland Islander
Cumberland News
Daily Colonist (Victoria)
District Ledger (Fernie)
Edmonton Journal
Fernie Free Press
Financial Post
J.P.'s Weekly
Nanaimo Free Press
Rossland Miner
Sydney Record
Trail News
United Mine Workers Journal
Vancouver Province
Vancouver Sun
Vancouver World
Victoria Times
Western Clarion

Pamphlets
Jordan, Rosa. *The Struggle: A Brief History of Local Labour Movements
    and the Rossland Miners' Union Hall*. Trail: Local 480 USWA [United
    Steelworkers of America], 1985.

Personal correspondence
Louvain (Rushford) Brovenlow, 1989
A.J. Warrington, 1989

Theses, dissertations, manuscripts and other papers
Brown, H.H. *The Pass*. Unpublished manuscript, 1977. Additional Manu-
    script 736, British Columbia Archives and Records Service.

Devitt, William. Unpublished field notebook and personal correspondence. Personal collection of T. Dennis Devitt.

Diamond, R.W. *Stories of, or Relating in Some Way to the Early Days of Cominco.* Unpublished manuscript, n.d. Additional Manuscript 333, British Columbia Archives and Records Service.

Cominco papers. Additional Manuscript 15, British Columbia Archives and Records Service.

Crow's Nest Pass Coal Company papers. Glenbow Archives.

Lockead, Richard. "Labour History, Oral History and the Ginger Goodwin Case." Unpublished paper. 1973.

Masters, Ruth. *Ginger Goodwin.* Handmade display album. Cumberland: Cumberland Museum, 1982.

Scott, Stanley H. "A Profusion of Issues: Immigrant Labour, The World War, and The Cominco Strike of 1917." Paper presented to the Pacific Northwest Labour History Conference, 1976. Additional Manuscript 473, British Columbia Archives and Records Service.

Wargo, Alan. *The Great Coal Strike.* Unpublished thesis. Vancouver: UBC, 1962.

Transcripts from taped interviews

Interviewed by Ian Forbes, quoted in Ruth Masters' Ginger Goodwin album, Cumberland Museum
        Pansy (Jimmy) Ellis, 1968

Interviewed by Stephen Hume, notes and transcripts in interviewer's personal collection.

Joseph Brown, 1987	Newton Campbell, 1990
T. Dennis Devitt, 1990	Mrs. Eva Harris, 1990
Bromley Quinney, 1990	Ben Swindell, 1990

Interviewed by Ruth Masters, quoted in her Ginger Goodwin album, Cumberland Museum

Harold and Nellie Banks, 1982	Josephine Bryden, 1982
Karl Coe, 1981	Jack Horbury, 1982
Elsie Marocchi, 1982	Sam Robertson, 1981
Gertie Somerville, 1982	Ed and Doll Williams, 1981
Winnie Williamson, 1981	

Interviewed by David Millar, quoted in Richard Lockead, "Labour History, Oral History and the Ginger Goodwin Case," unpublished paper, 1973

William Pritchard, 1984	David Rees, 1984

Interviewed by Paul Phillips, transcript in the collection of the University of British Columbia Library, Special Collections
        Les Walker, 1964

Interviewed by Dale Reeves and John Stanton, transcript in Cumberland Museum
        Elsie Marocchi, 1987

Interviewed by Howie Smith and quoted in *Fighting For Labour*, 1978

Ben Horbury, c.1975	Andrew Waldie, 1975

Interviews

Many people allowed interviewers to record their recollections of Ginger Goodwin, the Big Strike, the 1917 Trail Strike, and other aspects of British Columbia labor history. Without their generosity this book, and others like it, would be impossible. A number of them have died since their interviews. Now they survive in the history they witnessed and faithfully remembered as landmarks of their own daily lives.

Interviewed by Buddy de Vito
Andrew Waldie, 1979

Interviewed by Susan Mayse
Torchy (H.H.C.) Anderson, 1980
Piggy (Jim) Brown, 1986
John and Win Buchanan, 1989
Harold Calnan, 1989
Peter Cameron, 1984, 1986, 1989
Cecil Clark, 1986
Karl Coe, 1986
Peter Corrigan, 1986
Tab Davis, 1986
Margaret Eggar, 1986, 1989
Wink English, 1984
Mary Fedichin, 1986
Joe Franceschini, 1989
Roy Genge, 1984
Robert Gisborne, 1984
Noble Harrigan, 1989
Mike Landucci, 1986
Teddy Littler, 1986
Mr. and Mrs. Charles Lowe, 1986
Barney McGuire, 1986

Jean McKinnon, 1986
Johnny Marocchi, 1986
Arthur Mayse, 1984, 1988
Bronco (William) Moncrief, 1986
Louis Pinotti, 1986
Mike Raines, 1984
Donetta Rallison, 1986
Gert Somerville, 1986
Barbara Stannard, 1984
Chuna (Charles) Tobacco, 1989
John Tonzetich, 1984
Dr. David Turner, 1986
Richard Weighill, 1984
Jim Weir, 1986

Interviewers unknown
(Cumberland Museum collection)
Ben Horbury, 1979
Bill Johnstone, 1975
Bill Marshall, 1975
Tom Mumford, 1975
Chuna (Charles) Tobacco, 1975
Jim Weir, 1975
Sid Williams, 1975

Index

227